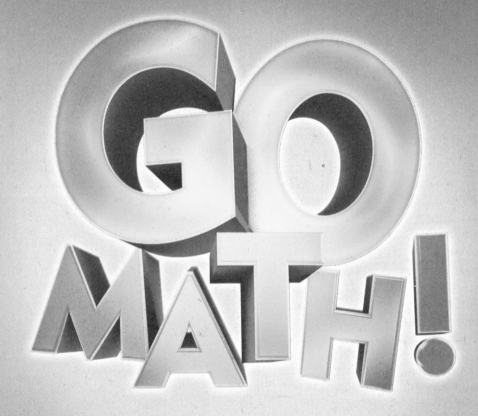

# GO MATH!

## Volume 1

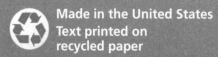

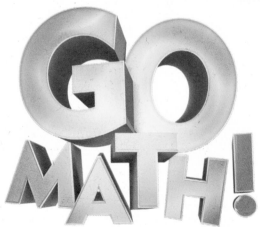

**Houghton Mifflin Harcourt**

ISBN 978-0-544-43269-7

20 21 22 23 24  0029  26 25 24 23 22 21

4500841544          C D E F G

Dear Students and Families,

Welcome to **Go Math!**, Kindergarten! In this exciting mathematics program, there are hands-on activities to do and real-world problems to solve. Best of all, you will write your ideas and answers right in your book. In **Go Math!**, writing and drawing on the pages helps you think deeply about what you are learning, and you will really understand math!

By the way, all of the pages in your **Go Math!** book are made using recycled paper. We wanted you to know that you can Go Green with **Go Math!**

Sincerely,

The Authors

Made in the United States
Text printed on recycled paper

# GO MATH!

## Authors

**Juli K. Dixon, Ph.D.**
Professor, Mathematics Education
University of Central Florida
Orlando, Florida

**Edward B. Burger, Ph.D.**
President, Southwestern University
Georgetown, Texas

**Steven J. Leinwand**
Principal Research Analyst
American Institutes for
    Research (AIR)
Washington, D.C.

## Contributor

**Rena Petrello**
Professor, Mathematics
Moorpark College
Moorpark, CA

**Matthew R. Larson, Ph.D.**
K-12 Curriculum Specialist for
    Mathematics
Lincoln Public Schools
Lincoln, Nebraska

**Martha E. Sandoval-Martinez**
Math Instructor
El Camino College
Torrance, California

## English Language Learners Consultant

**Elizabeth Jiménez**
CEO, GEMAS Consulting
Professional Expert on English
    Learner Education
Bilingual Education and
    Dual Language
Pomona, California

**Critical Area**

**GO DIGITAL**

Go online! Your math lessons are interactive. Use *i*Tools, Animated Math Models, the Multimedia *e*Glossary, and more.

**Chapter 1 Overview**

In this chapter, you will explore and discover answers to the following **Essential Questions**:

• How can you show, count, and write numbers?
• How can you show numbers 0 to 5?
• How can you count numbers 0 to 5?
• How can you write numbers 0 to 5?

**Chapter 2 Overview**

In this chapter, you will explore and discover answers to the following **Essential Questions**:

• How can building and comparing sets help you compare numbers?
• How does matching help you compare sets?
• How does counting help you compare sets?
• How do you know if the number of counters in one set is the same as, greater than, or less than the number of counters in another set?

Chapter 3 Overview

In this chapter, you will explore and discover answers to the following **Essential Questions**:

• How can you show, count, and write numbers 6 to 9?

• How can you show numbers 6 to 9?

• How can you count numbers 6 to 9?

• How can you write numbers 6 to 9?

**Practice and Homework**

Lesson Check and Spiral Review in every lesson

## 3 Represent, Count, and Write Numbers 6 to 9

115

**Domain** Counting and Cardinality
COMMON CORE STATE STANDARDS
K.CC.A.3, K.CC.B.5, K.CC.C.6, K.CC.C.7

## 4 Represent and Compare Numbers to 10     177

**Domains** Counting and Cardinality
Operations and Algebraic Thinking
COMMON CORE STATE STANDARDS
K.CC.A.2, K.CC.A.3, K.CC.B.5, K.CC.C.6, K.CC.C.7, K.OA.A.3, K.OA.A.4

**Chapter 4 Overview**

In this chapter, you will explore and discover answers to the following **Essential Questions**:

• How can you show and compare numbers to 10?
• How can you count forward to 10?
• How can you show numbers from 1 to 10?
• How can using models help you compare two numbers?

## 5 Addition     227

**Domain** Operations and Algebraic Thinking
COMMON CORE STATE STANDARDS
K.OA.A.1, K.OA.A.2, K.OA.A.3, K.OA.A.4, K.OA.A.5

**Chapter 5 Overview**

In this chapter, you will explore and discover answers to the following **Essential Questions**:

• How can you show addition?
• How can using objects or pictures help you show addition?
• How can you use numbers and symbols to show addition?

**Personal Math Trainer**
Online Assessment
and Intervention

In this chapter, you will explore and discover answers to the following **Essential Questions**:

- How can you show subtraction?
- How can you use numbers and symbols to show a subtraction sentence?
- How can using objects and drawings help you solve word problems?
- How can acting it out help you solve subtraction word problems?
- How can using addition help you solve subtraction word problems?

**Personal Math Trainer**
Online Assessment and Intervention

# 6 Subtraction 307

**Domain** Operations and Algebraic Thinking
COMMON CORE STATE STANDARDS
K.OA.A.1, K.OA.A.2, K.OA.A.5

Sheep and Ducks

# 7 Represent, Count, and Write 11 to 19    357

**Domains** Counting and Cardinality
Number and Operations in Base Ten

COMMON CORE STATE STANDARDS
K.CC.A.3, K.NBT.A.1

**Chapter 7 Overview**

In this chapter, you will explore and discover answers to the following **Essential Questions**:

• How can you show, count, and write numbers 11 to 19?

• How can you show numbers 11 to 19?

• How can you read and write numbers 11 to 19?

• How can you show the teen numbers as 10 and some more?

# 8 Represent, Count, and Write 20 and Beyond    425

**Domain** Counting and Cardinality

COMMON CORE STATE STANDARDS
K.CC.A.1, K.CC.A.2, K.CC.A.3, K.CC.B.5, K.CC.C.6, K.CC.C.7

**Chapter 8 Overview**

In this chapter, you will explore and discover answers to the following **Essential Questions**:

• How can you show, count, and write numbers to 20 and beyond?

• How can you show and write numbers to 20?

• How can you count numbers to 50 by ones?

• How can you count numbers to 100 by tens?

## Critical Area

### GO DIGITAL

Go online! Your math lessons are interactive. Use *i*Tools, Animated Math Models, the Multimedia *e*Glossary, and more.

**Essential Question**
How can you identify and name circles?
Start

### Chapter 9 Overview

In this chapter, you will explore and discover answers to the following **Essential Questions**:

- How can you identify, name, and describe two-dimensional shapes?

- How can knowing the parts of two-dimensional shapes help you join shapes?

- How can knowing the number of sides and vertices of two-dimensional shapes help you identify shapes?

**Personal Math Trainer**
Online Assessment and Intervention

**VOLUME 2**

# Geometry and Positions

**Common Core** **Critical Area** Describing shapes and space

# 10 Identify and Describe Three-Dimensional Shapes 569

**Domain** Geometry

COMMON CORE STATE STANDARDS
K.G.A.1, K.G.A.2, K.G.A.3, K.G.B.4, K.G.B.5

## Chapter 10 Overview

In this chapter, you will explore and discover answers to the following **Essential Questions**:

• How can identifying and describing shapes help you sort them?

• How can you describe three-dimensional shapes?

• How can you sort three-dimensional shapes?

## Practice and Homework

Lesson Check and Spiral Review in every lesson

### Chapter 11 Overview

In this chapter, you will explore and discover answers to the following **Essential Questions**:

• How can comparing objects help you measure them?

• How can you compare the length of objects?

• How can you compare the height of objects?

• How can you compare the weight of objects?

### Chapter 12 Overview

In this chapter, you will explore and discover answers to the following **Essential Questions**:

• How does sorting help you display information?

• How can you sort and classify objects by color?

• How can you sort and classify objects by shape?

• How can you sort and classify objects by size?

• How do you display information on a graph?

# Measurement and Data

 **Common Core** **Critical Area** Representing, relating, and operating on whole numbers, initially with sets of objects

## 11 Measurement 645

**Domain** Measurement and Data

COMMON CORE STATE STANDARDS
K.MD.A.1, K.MD.A.2

## 12 Classify and Sort Data 683

**Domain** Measurement and Data

COMMON CORE STATE STANDARDS
K.MD.B.3

# Fall Festival!

written by Alison Juliano

**Common Core**

**CRITICAL AREA** Representing, relating, and operating on whole numbers, initially with sets of objects

Fall is here! What do you see?

One big apple tree.

Science

What season is this?

Fall is here!  What do you see?

Two pumpkins for you and me.

Science

What do you know about fall?

Fall is here! What do you see?

Bales of hay—1, 2, 3!

Science

What do people wear in fall?

Fall is here! What do you see?

Four leaves falling from a tree.

Science

What changes in fall?

Fall is here! What do you see?

Five stalks of corn. Do you see me?

### Science

How is fall different from
the other seasons?

Name _____

# Write About the Story

**DIRECTIONS** Look at the picture of the fall scene. Using the numbers you have learned, draw a story about fall. Invite a friend to count the objects in your story.

# Count How Many

1 2 3 4 5

1 2 3 4 5

1 2 3 4 5

1 2 3 4 5

1 2 3 4 5

**DIRECTIONS** 1–5. Look at the picture. Count how many.
Circle the number.

**8** eight

# Represent, Count, and Write Numbers 0 to 5

Chapter **1**

Navel oranges have no seeds.

- How many seeds do you see?

Name _____

## Explore Numbers

Match Numbers to Sets

| 1 | 2 | 3 | 4 | 5 |

This page checks understanding of important skills needed for success in Chapter 1.

**DIRECTIONS** 1. Circle all of the sets of three oranges.
2. Draw a line to match the number to the set.

Name _____

## Vocabulary Builder

match

set

**DIRECTIONS** Draw a line to match a set of chicks to a set of flowers.

• **Interactive Student Edition**
• **Multimedia eGlossary**

# Game Bus Stop

START
0

1

3

2

FIRE STATION

4

POST OFFICE

5

END

SCHOOL

**DIRECTIONS** Each player rolls the number cube. The first player to roll a 1 moves to the bus stop marked 1. Continue playing until each player has rolled the numbers in sequence and stopped at each bus stop. The first player to reach 5 wins the game.

**MATERIALS** game marker for each player, number cube (0–5)

# Chapter 1 Vocabulary

**and**

y

4

**fewer**

menos

23

**five**

cinco

26

**four**

cuatro

**larger**

más grande

37

**match**

emparejar

41

**more**

más

43

**one**

uno

47

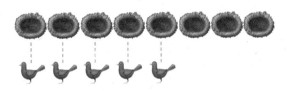

3 **fewer** birds

 **and**

$2 + 2$

4

5

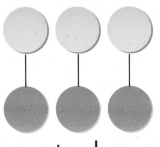

Each counter has a **match**.

A quantity of 3 is **larger** than a quantity of 2.

1

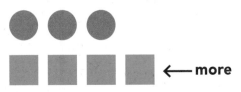 ← **more**

**pairs**

pares

50

**three**

tres

77

**two**

dos

82

**zero**

cero, ninguno

86

3

3

3     0
2     1
1     2
0     3

**pairs** for 3

↑        ↑

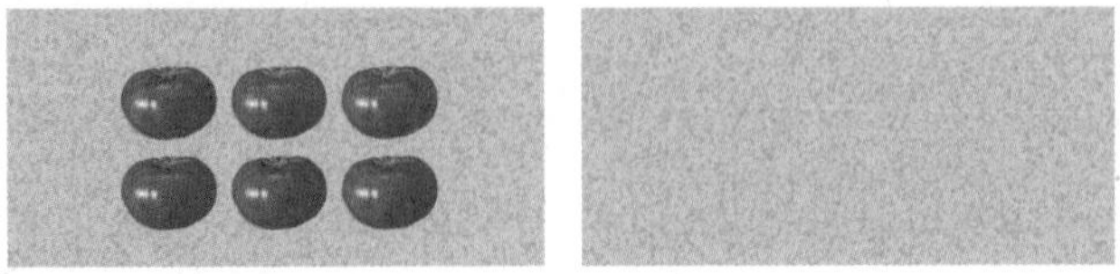

six tomatoes      zero tomatoes

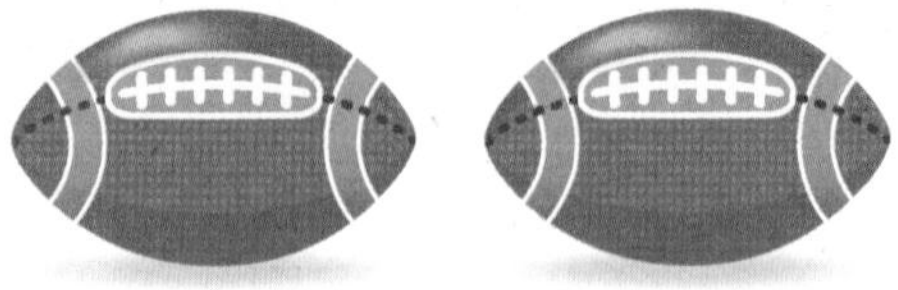

2

# Number Words

**one**

**two**

**three**

**four**

**five**

**zero**

**match**

**and**  **and**  **3**

**DIRECTIONS** Say each word. Tell something you know about the word.

**Game**

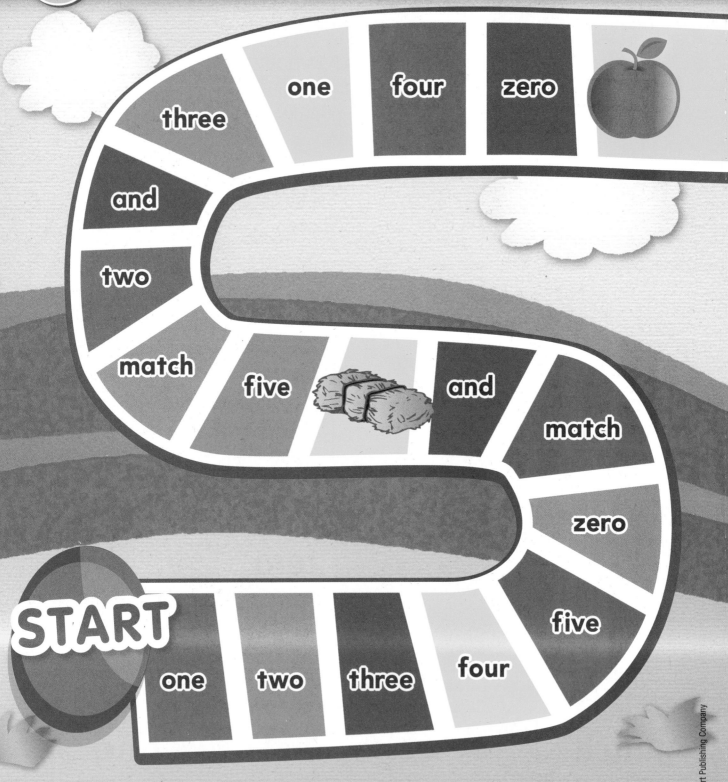

**START**

three · one · four · zero

and

two

match · five · and · match

zero

five

one · two · three · four

**DIRECTIONS** Shuffle all the cards and place them facedown in a pile. Play with a partner. Place game pieces on START. Take turns choosing a card and moving game pieces to the first space with that word or picture. If a player can tell about the word or picture, the player moves ahead I space. Return the card to the bottom of the pile. The first player to reach FINISH wins.

**MATERIALS** I connecting cube per player • 3 sets of Vocabulary Cards • I set of Picture Cards

**I2B** twelve

one

three

zero

five

two

four

and

match

three

and

two

five

one

match

four

zero

**FINISH**

# The Write Way

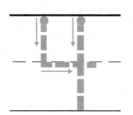

**DIRECTIONS** Trace the 4. Draw to show what you know about 4.
**Reflect** Be ready to tell about your drawing.

Name _____

# Model and Count 1 and 2

**Essential Question** How can you show and count
1 and 2 with objects?

Common Core **Counting and Cardinality—K.CC.B.4a**
*Also K.CC.B.4b, K.CC.B.4c, K.CC.B.5*
**MATHEMATICAL PRACTICES**
MP2

**DIRECTIONS** Place a counter on each object in the set as you count
them. Move the counters to the five frame. Draw the counters.

**Chapter 1 • Lesson 1**

thirteen **13**

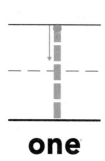

**one**

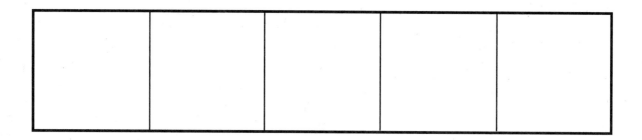

**two**

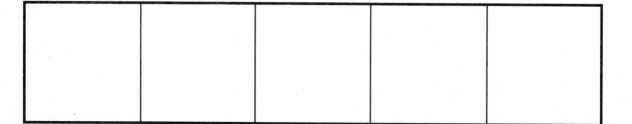

**DIRECTIONS** 1–2. Place a counter on each object in the set as you count them. Tell how many counters. Trace the number. Move the counters to the five frame. Draw the counters.

14 fourteen

Name ______________________________

3

1

one

4

2

two

5

1

one

6

2

two

**DIRECTIONS** **3–6.** Say the number. Count out that many counters in the five frame. Draw the counters.

## Problem Solving · Applications Real World

**7**

**8**

**9**

**DIRECTIONS** **7.** Jen has 2 matching lunch boxes. Max has 1 lunch box. Circle to show Jen's lunch boxes. **8.** Draw to show what you know about the number 1. **9.** Draw to show what you know about the number 2. Tell a friend about your drawings.

**HOME ACTIVITY** • Ask your child to show a set that has one or two objects, such as books or buttons. Have him or her point to each object as he or she counts it to tell how many objects are in the set.

**16** sixteen

# Model and Count I and 2

Common Core

**COMMON CORE STANDARD—K.CC.B.4a**
*Count to tell the number of objects.*

**1**

2
**two**

**2**

1
**one**

**3**

2
**two**

**4**

1
**one**

**DIRECTIONS** I–4. Say the number. Count out that many counters in the five frame. Draw the counters.

Chapter I

seventeen **17**

## Lesson Check (K.CC.B.4a)

 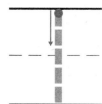 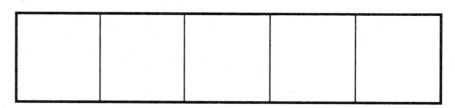

## Spiral Review (K.CC.B.4a)

 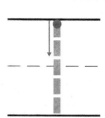 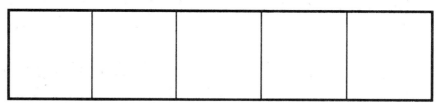

**DIRECTIONS** 1–3. Trace the number. How many counters would you place in the five frame to show the number? Draw the counters.

FOR MORE PRACTICE
GO TO THE
**Personal Math Trainer**

# Count and Write 1 and 2

**Essential Question** How can you count and write 1 and 2 with words and numbers?

Common Core **Counting and Cardinality—K.CC.A.3**
*Also K.CC.B.4b, K.CC.B.5*
**MATHEMATICAL PRACTICES**
MP2

## Listen and Draw (Real World)

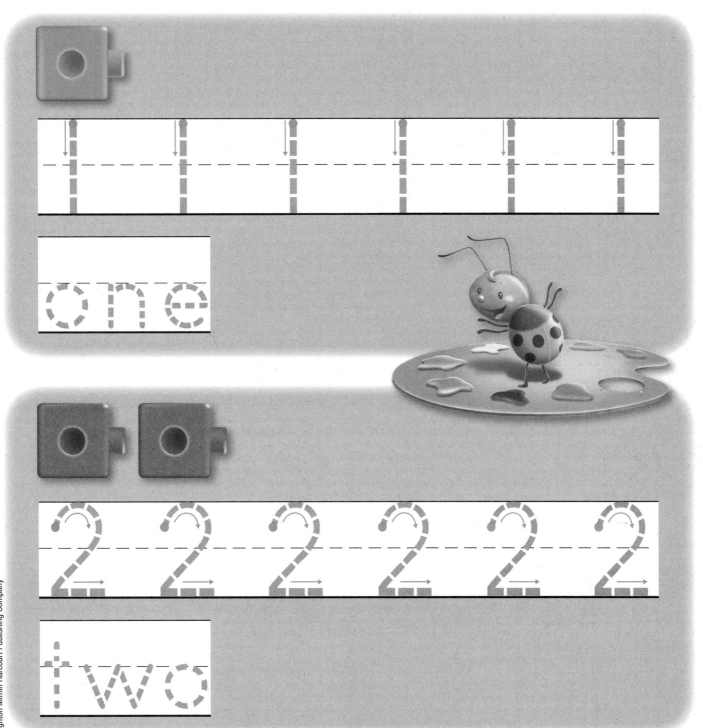

one

two

**DIRECTIONS** Count the cubes. Tell how many. Trace the numbers and words.

1

2

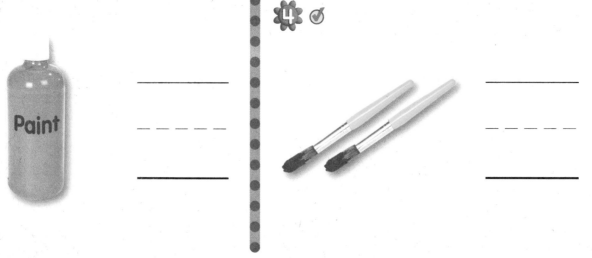

3 ✓

Paint

4 ✓

**DIRECTIONS** 1–2. Count the cubes. Say the number. Trace the numbers. 3–4. Count and tell how many. Write the number.

Name _____

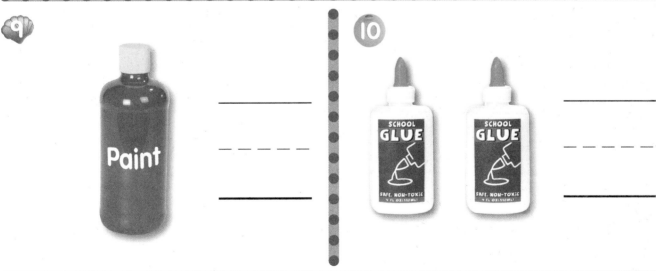

**5**

**6**
Glue Stick Glue Stick

**7**

**8**

**9**
Paint

**10**
SCHOOL GLUE  SCHOOL GLUE
SAFE, NON-TOXIC  SAFE, NON-TOXIC

**DIRECTIONS** 5–10. Count and tell how many. Write the number.

## Problem Solving • Applications

11.

WRITE Math

_____

- - - - - - -

_____

_____

- - - - - - -

_____

**DIRECTIONS** 11. Draw to show what you know about the numbers 1 and 2. Write the number beside each drawing. Tell a friend about your drawings.

**HOME ACTIVITY** • Ask your child to write the number 1 on a sheet of paper. Then have him or her find an object that represents that number. Repeat with objects for the number 2.

# Count and Write 1 and 2

Common Core

**COMMON CORE STANDARD—K.CC.A.3**
*Know number names and the count sequence.*

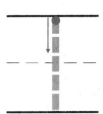

**DIRECTIONS** 1–4. Count and tell how many. Write the number.

----
- - - - - -
----

## Spiral Review (K.CC.B.4a)

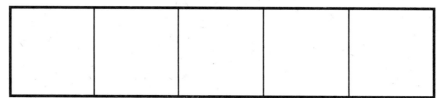

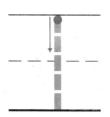

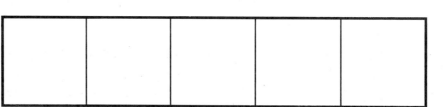

**DIRECTIONS** 1. Count and tell how many cubes. Write the number.
2–3. Trace the number. How many counters would you place in the five frame to show the number? Draw the counters.

FOR MORE PRACTICE
GO TO THE
**Personal Math Trainer**

Name _____

# Model and Count 3 and 4

**Essential Question** How can you show and count 3 and 4 with objects?

Common Core **Counting and Cardinality—K.CC.B.4a**
*Also K.CC.B.4b, K.CC.B.4c, K.CC.B.5*
**MATHEMATICAL PRACTICES**
**MP1, MP2**

**Listen and Draw** Real World

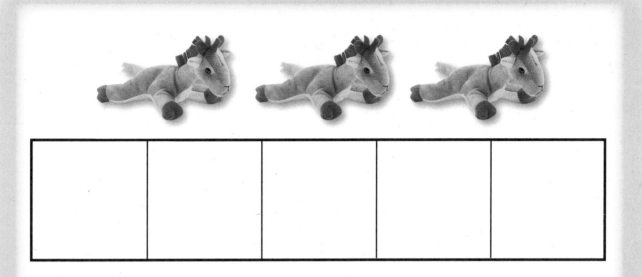

**DIRECTIONS** Place a counter on each object in the set as you count them. Move the counters to the five frame. Draw the counters.

**Chapter 1 • Lesson 3**

twenty-five **25**

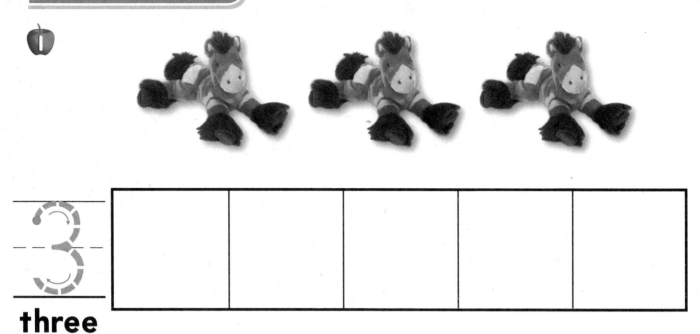

3
**three**

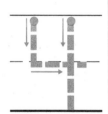
**four**

**DIRECTIONS** 1–2. Place a counter on each object in the set as you count them. Tell how many counters. Trace the number. Move the counters to the five frame. Draw the counters.

Name ______________________________

3 ✓

3

three

4 ✓

4

four

5

4

four

6

3

three

**DIRECTIONS** 3–6. Say the number as you trace it. Count out that many counters in the five frame. Draw the counters.

# Problem Solving • Applications  Real World

WRITE Math

**7**

**8**

**9**

**DIRECTIONS**   **7.** Lukas has 3 matching toys. Jon has a number of matching toys greater than Lukas. Circle to show Jon's toys.   **8.** Draw to show what you know about the number 3.   **9.** Draw to show what you know about the number 4. Tell a friend about your drawings.

**HOME ACTIVITY** • Draw a five frame or cut an egg carton to have just five sections. Have your child show a set of up to four objects and place the objects in the five frame.

# Model and Count 3 and 4

Common Core

**COMMON CORE STANDARD—K.CC.B.4a**
*Count to tell the number of objects.*

**1**

3

**three**

**2**

4

**four**

**3**

3

**three**

**4**

4

**four**

**DIRECTIONS** 1–4. Say the number as you trace it. Count out that many counters in the five frame. Draw the counters.

## Spiral Review (K.CC.A.3, K.CC.B.4a)

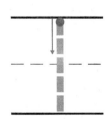 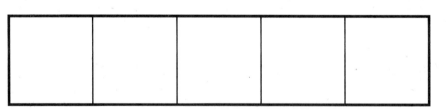

---

**DIRECTIONS** I. Trace the number. How many counters would you place in the five frame to show the number? Draw the counters. **2.** Count and tell how many umbrellas. Write the number. **3.** Trace the number. How many counters would you place in the five frame to show the number? Draw the counters.

**FOR MORE PRACTICE
GO TO THE
Personal Math Trainer**

Name _____

# Count and Write 3 and 4

**Essential Question** How can you count and write 3 and 4 with words and numbers?

Common Core
**Counting and Cardinality—K.CC.A.3**
*Also K.CC.B.4b, K.CC.B.4c, K.CC.B.5*
**MATHEMATICAL PRACTICES**
**MP2**

**Listen and Draw** Real World

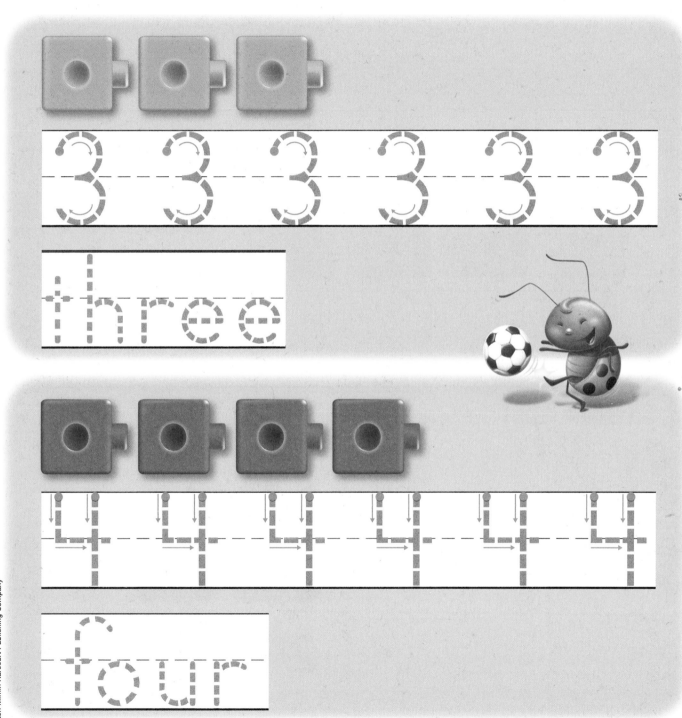

3 3 3 3 3 3

three

4 4 4 4 4 4

four

**DIRECTIONS** Count the cubes. Tell how many. Trace the numbers and the words.

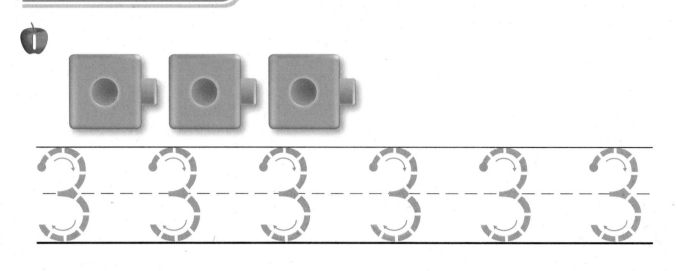

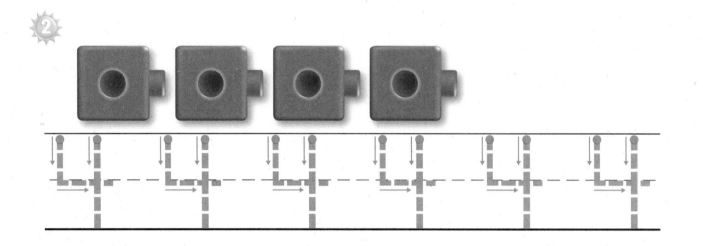

**DIRECTIONS** 1–2. Count the cubes. Say the number. Trace the numbers. 3–4. Count and tell how many. Write the number.

Name _____

 **5**

 _____

- - - - - - - -

_____

 **6**

  _____

- - - - - - - -

_____

**7**

 _____

 - - - - - - - -

_____

**8**

 _____

- - - - - - - -

_____

 _____

**9**

 _____

- - - - - - - -

_____

**10**

 _____

- - - - - - - -

_____

 _____

**DIRECTIONS** 5–10. Count and tell how many. Write the number.

 **HOME ACTIVITY •** Ask your child to show a set of three or four objects. Have him or her write the number on paper to show how many objects.

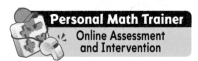

## Concepts and Skills

| | | | | |
|---|---|---|---|---|

_____

      _____

      _____

**DIRECTIONS** **I.** Place counters in the five frame to show the number 3. Draw the counters. Write the number. (K.CC.B.4a)  **2–3.** Count and tell how many. Write the number. (K.CC.A.3)  **4.** Count each set of bags. Circle all the sets that show 3 bags. (K.CC.B.4b)

# Count and Write 3 and 4

Common Core

**COMMON CORE STANDARD—K.CC.A.3**
*Know number names and the count sequence.*

**1**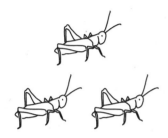

3

**2**

**3**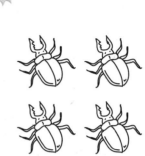

**4**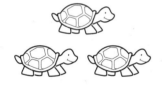

**5**

**6**

**DIRECTIONS** 1–6. Count and tell how many. Write the number.

# Lesson Check (K.CC.A.3)

_____

- - - - - - - -

_____

# Spiral Review (K.CC.A.3, K.CC.B.4a)

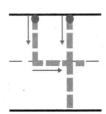

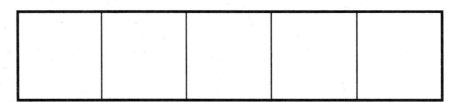

_____

- - - - - - - -

_____

**DIRECTIONS** **I.** Count and tell how many butterflies. Write the number. **2.** Trace the number. How many counters would you place in the five frame to show the number? Draw the counters. **3.** Count and tell how many flowers. Write the number.

FOR MORE PRACTICE
GO TO THE
**Personal Math Trainer**

Name _____

# Model and Count to 5

**Essential Question** How can you show and count up to 5 objects?

**Listen and Draw** Real World   Hands On

Common Core **Counting and Cardinality—K.CC.B.4a**
*Also K.CC.B.4b, K.CC.B.5*
**MATHEMATICAL PRACTICES**
MP1, MP2

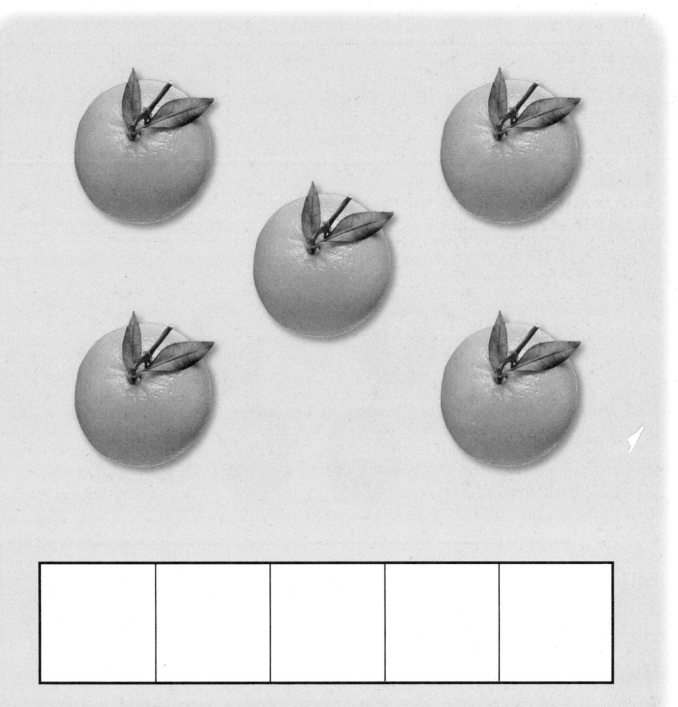

**DIRECTIONS** Place a counter on each orange as you count them. Move the counters to the five frame. Draw the counters.

**Chapter 1 • Lesson 5**

thirty-seven **37**

**1**

5
**five**

**2**

5
**five**

**DIRECTIONS** 1–2. Place a counter on each object in the set as you count them. Tell how many counters. Trace the number. Move the counters to the five frame. Draw the counters.

Name _____

**3** ✓

```
┌──────┬──────┬──────┬──────┬──────┐        _____
│      │      │      │      │      │        - - - - -
│      │      │      │      │      │        _____
└──────┴──────┴──────┴──────┴──────┘
```

**4**

```
┌──────┬──────┬──────┬──────┬──────┐        _____
│      │      │      │      │      │        - - - - -
│      │      │      │      │      │        _____
└──────┴──────┴──────┴──────┴──────┘
```

**5**

```
┌──────┬──────┬──────┬──────┬──────┐        _____
│      │      │      │      │      │        - - - - -
│      │      │      │      │      │        _____
└──────┴──────┴──────┴──────┴──────┘
```

**6**

```
┌──────┬──────┬──────┬──────┬──────┐        _____
│      │      │      │      │      │        - - - - -
│      │      │      │      │      │        _____
└──────┴──────┴──────┴──────┴──────┘
```

**DIRECTIONS** 3. Place counters to show five. Draw the counters. Write the number. 4. Place counters to show four. Draw the counters. Write the number. 5. Place counters to show five. Draw the counters. Write the number. 6. Place counters to show three. Draw the counters. Write the number.

## Problem Solving • Applications  *Real World*

WRITE Math

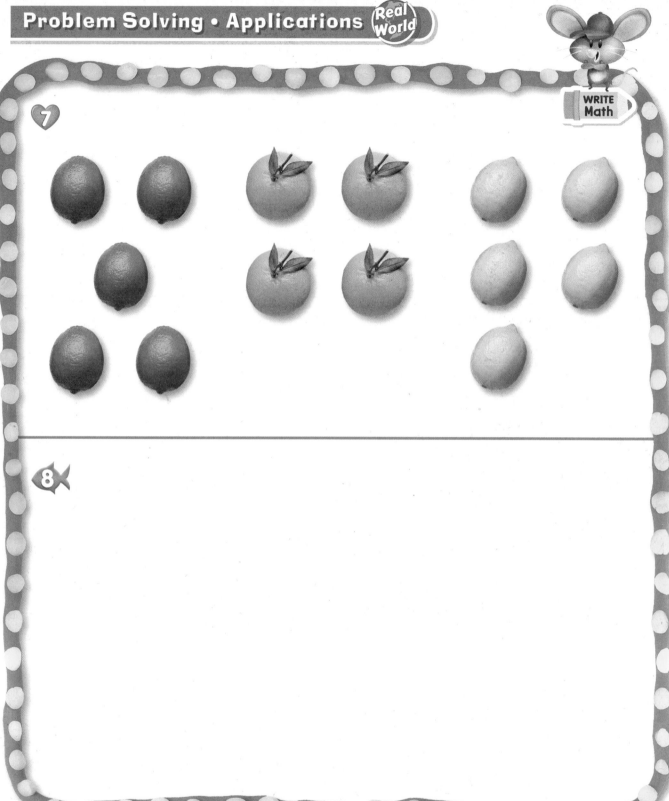

**7**

**8**

**DIRECTIONS 7.** Carl needs 5 pieces of each kind of fruit. Circle to show all the sets Carl could use. **8.** Draw to show what you know about the number 5. Tell a friend about your drawing.

**HOME ACTIVITY •** Draw a five frame or use an egg carton with just five sections. Have your child show a set of five objects and place the objects in the five frame.

# Model and Count to 5

**Common Core** COMMON CORE STANDARD—K.CC.B.4a
*Count to tell the number of objects.*

**1**

**2**

**3**

**4**

**DIRECTIONS** **1.** Place counters to show five. Draw the counters. Write the number. **2.** Place counters to show three. Draw the counters. Write the number. **3.** Place counters to show four. Draw the counters. Write the number. **4.** Place counters to show five. Draw the counters. Write the number.

## Lesson Check (K.CC.B.4a)

 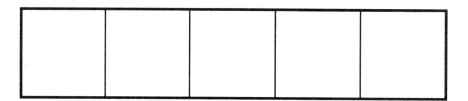

---

## Spiral Review (K.CC.A.3)

_____

- - - - - - - - - -

_____

_____

- - - - - - - - - -

_____

**DIRECTIONS** 1. Trace the number. How many counters would you place in the five frame to show the number? Draw the counters.
2-3. Count and tell how many. Write the number.

**42** forty-two

FOR MORE PRACTICE
GO TO THE
**Personal Math Trainer**

Name _____

# Count and Write to 5

**Essential Question** How can you count and write up to 5 with words and numbers?

Common Core **Counting and Cardinality—K.CC.A.3** *Also K.CC.B.4b, K.CC.B.5* **MATHEMATICAL PRACTICES** **MP2**

**Listen and Draw** *Real World*

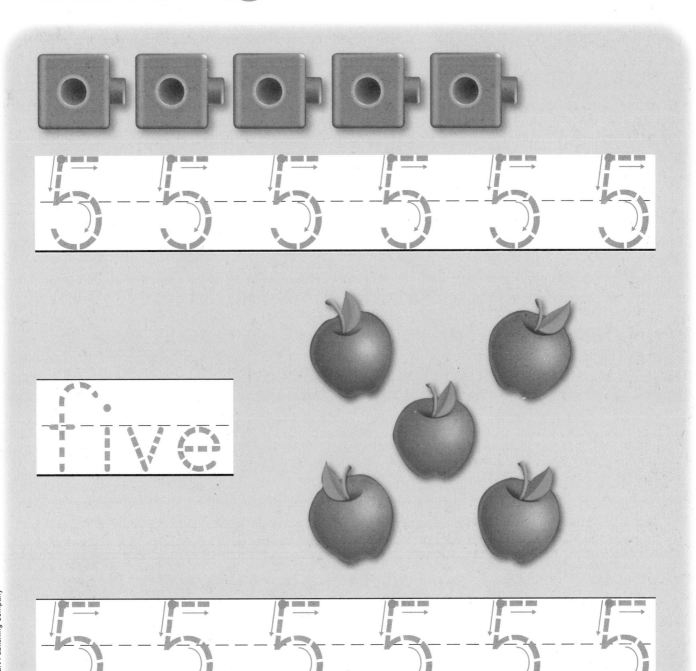

**DIRECTIONS** Count the cubes. Tell how many. Trace the numbers and the word. Count the apples. Tell how many. Trace the numbers.

**Chapter 1 • Lesson 6**

**①**

5 5 5 5

**five**

**②**

**DIRECTIONS** 1. Count and tell how many apples. Trace the numbers.
2. Circle all the sets of five apples.

Name _____

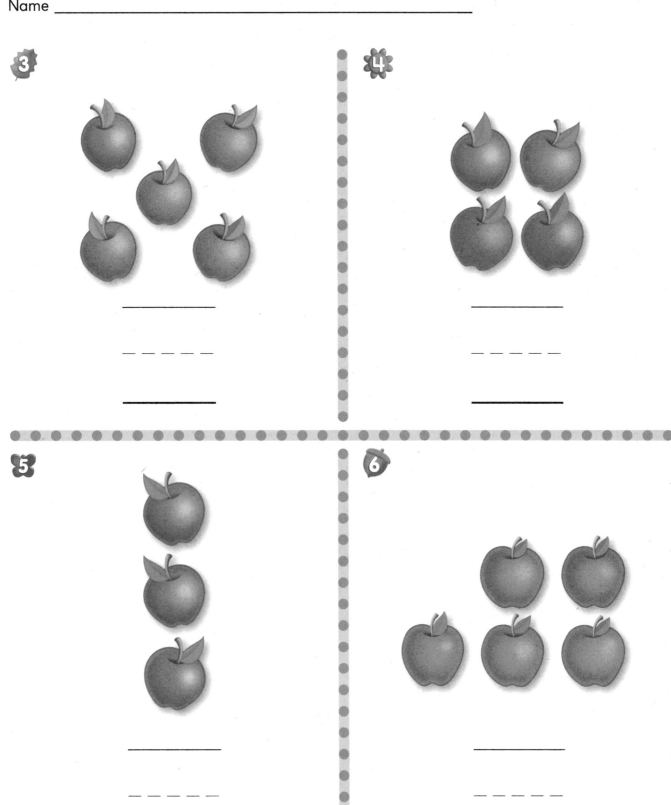

© Houghton Mifflin Harcourt Publishing Company

**DIRECTIONS** 3–6. Count and tell how many apples.
Write the number.

**Chapter I • Lesson 6**

## Problem Solving • Applications

**7**

_____

- - - - - - - - - -

_____

**DIRECTIONS  7.** Draw to show what you know about the number 5. Write the number. Tell a friend about your drawing.

**HOME ACTIVITY •** Ask your child to write the number 5 on a sheet of paper. Then have him or her find objects to show that number.

# Count and Write to 5

Common Core **COMMON CORE STANDARD—K.CC.B.4b**
*Count to tell the number of objects.*

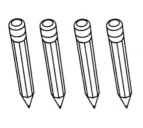

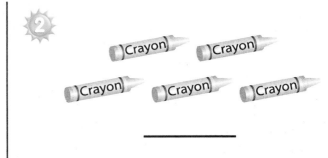

_____

- - - - -

_____

_____

- - - - -

_____

_____

- - - - -

_____

_____

- - - - -

_____

_____

- - - - -

_____

_____

- - - - -

_____

**DIRECTIONS** 1–6. Count and tell how many. Write the number.

# Lesson Check (K.CC.B.4b)

_____
- - - - -
_____

# Spiral Review (K.CC.A.3, K.CC.B.4a)

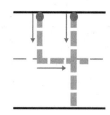

_____
- - - - -
_____

DIRECTIONS **1.** Count and tell how many animals. Write the number. **2.** Trace the number. How many counters would you place in the five frame to show the number? Draw the counters. **3.** Count and tell how many cubes. Write the number.

FOR MORE PRACTICE
GO TO THE
**Personal Math Trainer**

Name _____

# Algebra • Ways to Make 5

**Essential Question** How can you use two sets of objects to show 5 in more than one way?

Counting and Cardinality—
**K.CC.B.4b, K.OA.A.3**
MATHEMATICAL PRACTICES
MP4, MP7

**DIRECTIONS** Jessica has 5 marbles in the bag. The marbles can be red or yellow. Describe the marbles that might be in Jessica's bag. Use counters to show one pair of marbles. Trace and color the counters.

**Chapter 1 • Lesson 7**

forty-nine **49**

1

4 ⬤ **and** 1 ◯

・・・・・・・・・・・・・・・・・・・・・・・・・・・・・・・・・・

2 ✓

_ _ _ ⬤ **and** _ _ _ ◯

**DIRECTIONS** 1. Look at the counters in the five frame. Trace the numbers to show the pair that makes 5. 2. Use two colors of counters to show a different way to make 5. Write the numbers to show the pair that makes 5.

Name _____

**3**

| | | | | |
|---|---|---|---|---|

_ _ _ _ _     ●     **and**     _ _ _ _ _     ○
_ _ _ _ _           _ _ _ _ _

**4**

| | | | | |
|---|---|---|---|---|

_ _ _ _ _     ●     **and**     _ _ _ _ _     ○
_ _ _ _ _           _ _ _ _ _

**DIRECTIONS**  3–4. Use *i*Tools or two colors of counters to show a different way to make 5. Write the numbers to show the pair that makes 5.

Chapter 1 • Lesson 7

## Problem Solving • Applications (Real World)

**WRITE Math**

**5**

○ ○ ○ ○ ○

I ⬤ and _____ ⬤

**6**

[ ◌ | ◌ | ◌ | ◌ | ◌ ]

_____ ⬛ and _____ ⬛

**DIRECTIONS** **5.** Austin has 5 counters. One counter is red. How many yellow counters does he have? Color the counters. **6.** Madison has 5 red and blue cubes. Color to show the cubes. Write the pair of numbers that makes up Madison's cubes.

**HOME ACTIVITY •** Have your child use two colors of buttons to show all the different ways to make 5. Then have him or her write the number of each color used in the pairs to make 5.

Name _____

# Algebra • Ways to Make 5

COMMON CORE STANDARD—K.CC.B.4b, K.OA.A.3
Understand addition as putting together and adding to, and understand subtraction as taking apart and taking from.

**1**

_____ ◯ **and** _____ ◯

**2**

_____ ◯ **and** _____ ◯

**DIRECTIONS** 1–2. Use two colors of counters to show a way to make 5. Color to show the counters. Write the numbers to show the pair that makes 5.

fifty-three **53**

## Lesson Check (K.OA.A.3)

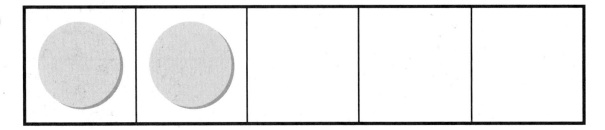

2  and _____ more

## Spiral Review (K.CC.A.3, K.CC.B.4b)

2

_____

3

_____

**DIRECTIONS** 1. How many more counters would you place in the five frame to show a way to make 5? Draw the counters. Write the number. **2–3.** Count and tell how many. Write the number.

FOR MORE PRACTICE
GO TO THE
**Personal Math Trainer**

Name _____

# Count and Order to 5

**Essential Question** How do you know that the order of numbers is the same as a set of objects that is one larger?

Common Core **Counting and Cardinality—K.CC.B.4c**
*Also K.CC.B.4a, K.CC.B.5*
**MATHEMATICAL PRACTICES**
**MP2, MP5, MP7**

|  1  |  2  |  3  |  4  |  5  |

**DIRECTIONS** Use cubes to make cube towers that have 1 to 5 cubes. Place the cube towers in order to match the numbers 1 to 5. Draw the cube towers in order.

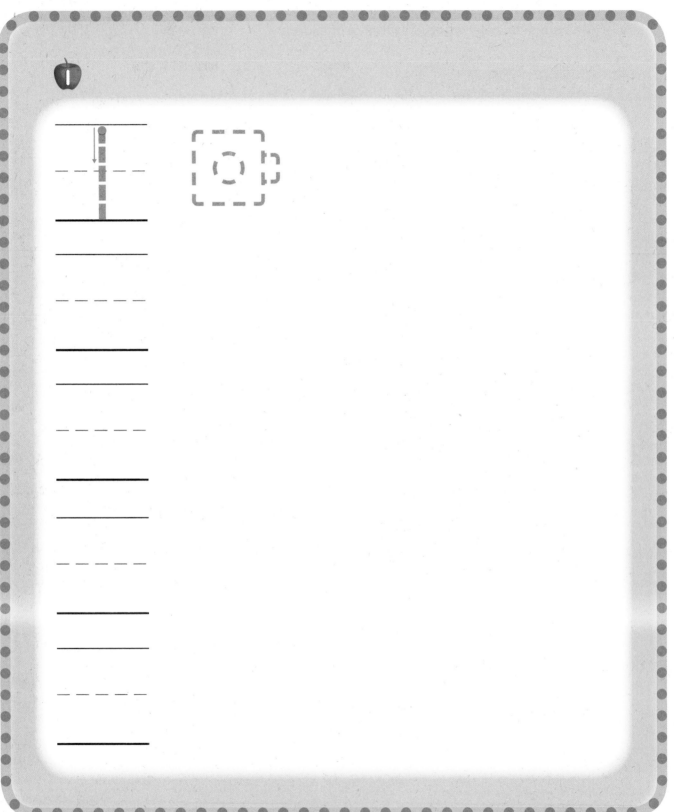

**DIRECTIONS** I. Use cubes to make cube trains that have I to 5 cubes. Place the cube trains in order beginning with I. Draw the cube trains and trace or write the numbers in order. Tell a friend what you know about the numbers and the cube trains.

Name _____

⭐2 ☑️

_____
- - - - - - - - -
_____

- - - - - - - - -

_____
_____

- - - - - - - - -

_____

- - - - - - - - -

_____

- - - - - - - - -

_____

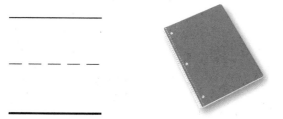

_____  _____  _____  _____
- - - -  - - - -  - - - -  - - - -
_____  _____  _____  _____

**DIRECTIONS** **2.** Count the objects in each set. Write the
number beside the set of objects. Write those numbers in order
beginning with the number 1.

**Chapter 1 • Lesson 8**                                    fifty-seven **57**

# Problem Solving • Applications Real World

WRITE Math

**3**

**4**

**DIRECTIONS** 3. Paul has a set of blocks that is one larger than a set of 3 blocks. Circle Paul's blocks. Check to make sure your answer makes sense. 4. Draw to show what you know about the order of sets I to 5. Tell a friend about your drawing.

**HOME ACTIVITY** • Show your child sets of objects from I to 5. Have him or her place the sets in order from I to 5.

**58** fifty-eight

# Count and Order to 5

Common
Core

**COMMON CORE STANDARD—K.CC.B.4c**
*Count to tell the number of objects.*

**1**

© Houghton Mifflin Harcourt Publishing Company

**DIRECTIONS** **1.** Count the objects in each set. Write the number beside the set of objects. Write those numbers in order beginning with the number 1.

## Lesson Check (K.CC.B.4c)

1, 2, 3, ___, 5

## Spiral Review (K.CC.A.3c, K.CC.B.4a)

★ ★ ★ ★

_____

- - - - - -

_____

| | | | | |
|---|---|---|---|---|

**DIRECTIONS** 1. Trace or write the numbers in order. 2. Count and tell how many stars. Write the number. 3. Trace the number. How many counters would you place in the five frame to show the number? Draw the counters.

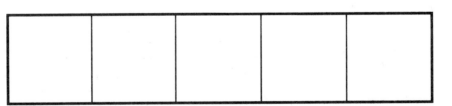

FOR MORE PRACTICE
GO TO THE
**Personal Math Trainer**

Name _____

# Problem Solving • Understand 0

**Essential Question** How can you solve problems using the strategy *make a model*?

Common Core  Counting and Cardinality—K.CC.A.3

MATHEMATICAL PRACTICES
MP1, MP2, MP4

 Unlock the Problem  Real World     Hands On

**zero**

**DIRECTIONS** Use counters to model this problem. There are two horses in the pen. The horses leave the pen and go to the field. How many horses are in the pen now? Trace the number. Tell a friend what you know about that number.

© Houghton Mifflin Harcourt Publishing Company

_____
- - - - - - -
_____

_____
- - - - - - -
_____

**DIRECTIONS** I. Use counters to model this problem. Three children each have one backpack on a peg. Draw counters to show the backpacks. How many backpacks are there? Write the number. **2.** Use counters to model a backpack on each peg. Three children each take one backpack. How many backpacks are there now? Write the number.

Name _____

**3** ✓

_____

- - - - - - - - -

_____

**4**

_____

- - - - - - - - -

_____

**DIRECTIONS** Use counters to model these problems. **3.** Drew has one book. Adam has one fewer book than Drew. How many books does Adam have? Write the number. **4.** Bradley has no pencils. Matt has one more pencil than Bradley. How many pencils does Matt have? Write the number.

**Chapter I • Lesson 9**

## On Your Own

5

_____

— — — — —

_____

6

_____

— — — — —

_____

**DIRECTIONS** **5.** Vera has 2 apples. She eats 1 apple and gives 1 apple to her friend. How many apples does Vera have now? Write the number. **6.** Amy has 3 crayons. She gives some away. Now she has no crayons. How many crayons did she give away? Write the number.

**HOME ACTIVITY •** Have your child place a set of up to five coins in a cup. Remove some or all of the coins and have him or her tell how many coins are in the cup and write the number.

# Problem Solving • Understand 0

Common Core

**COMMON CORE STANDARD—K.CC.A.3**
*Know number names and the count sequence.*

**1**

_____

- - - - - - -

_____

— ▪ — ▪ — ▪ — ▪ — ▪ — ▪ — ▪ — ▪ — ▪ — ▪ — ▪ — ▪ — ▪ — ▪ —

**2**

_____

- - - - - - -

_____

**DIRECTIONS** Use counters to model these problems. **1.** Oliver has one juice box. Lucy has one fewer juice box than Oliver. How many juice boxes does Lucy have? Write the number. **2.** Jessica has no books. Wesley has 2 more books than Jessica. How many books does Wesley have? Write the number.

# Lesson Check

 1

_____

_ _ _ _ _ _ _ _

_____

# Spiral Review (K.CC.A.3)

 2

_____

_ _ _ _ _ _ _ _

_____

 3

_____

_ _ _ _ _ _ _ _

_____

**DIRECTIONS** **1.** Use counters to model this problem. Eva has 2 apples in her basket. She eats 1 apple and gives 1 apple to her friend. How many apples does Eva have now? Write the number. **2–3.** Count and tell how many. Write the number.

FOR MORE PRACTICE
GO TO THE
**Personal Math Trainer**

Name _____

# Identify and Write 0

**Essential Question** How can you identify and write 0 with words and numbers?

Common Core **Counting and Cardinality—K.CC.A.3**

**MATHEMATICAL PRACTICES**
MP2

## Listen and Draw *Real World*

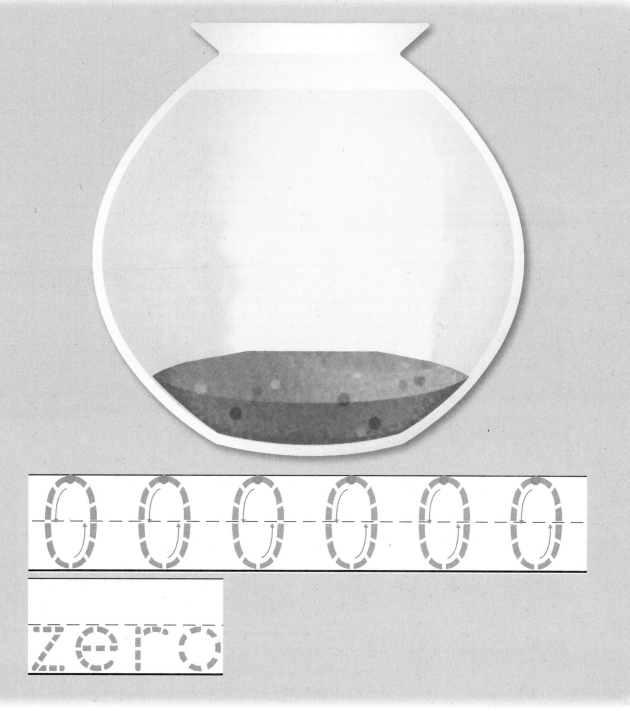

0 0 0 0 0 0

zero

**DIRECTIONS** How many fish are in the bowl? Trace the numbers and the word. Tell a friend what you know about that number.

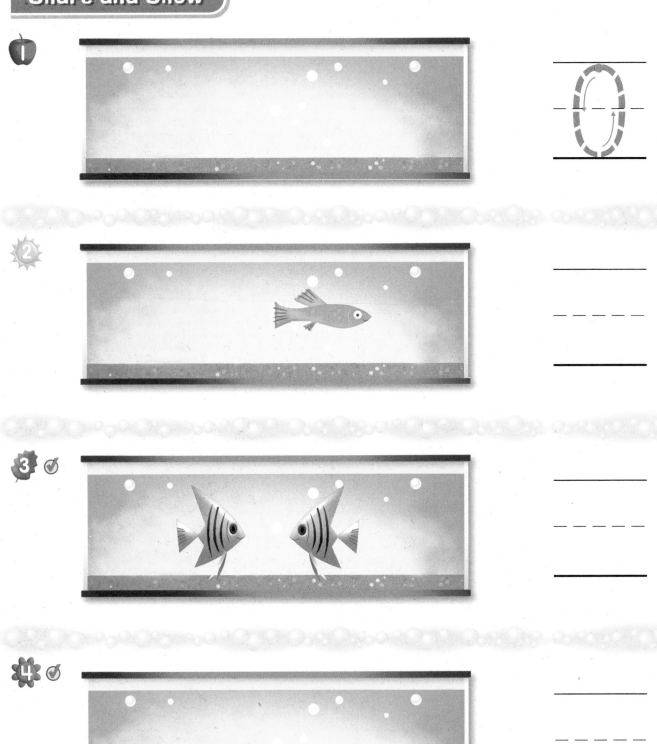

**1** 0

**DIRECTIONS** 1. How many fish are in the tank? Trace the number.
**2–4.** How many fish are in the tank? Write the number. Circle the tanks that have 0 fish.

Name _____

**5** 

_____
- - - - - - -
_____

**6**

_____
- - - - - - -
_____

**7**

_____
- - - - - - -
_____

**8**

_____
- - - - - - -
_____

**DIRECTIONS** 5–8. How many fish are in the tank?
Write the number. Circle the tanks that have 0 fish.

**Chapter 1 • Lesson 10**

# Problem Solving • Applications Real World

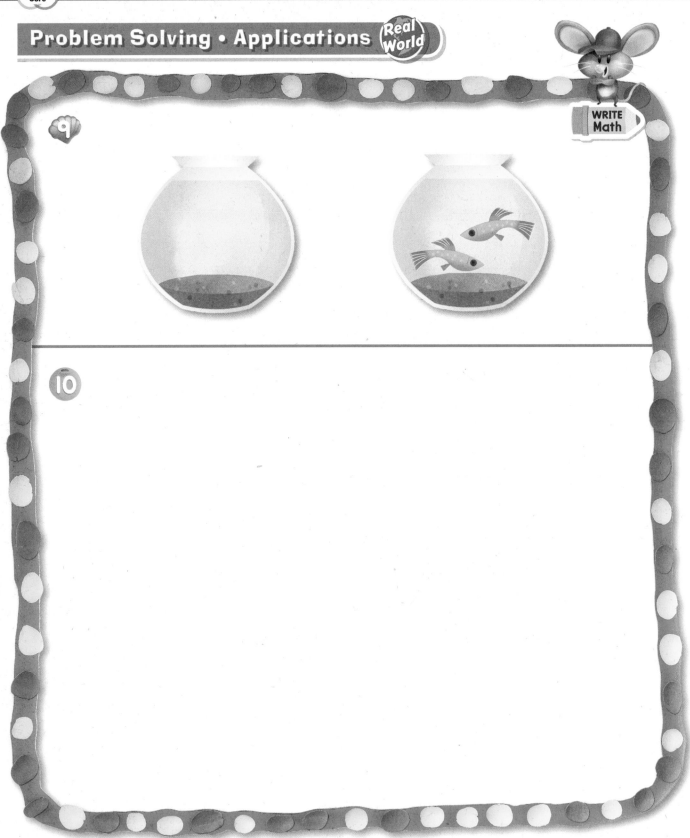

**9**

**WRITE Math**

**10**

**DIRECTIONS  9.** Bryce has two fish. Chris has no fish. Circle to show which fish bowl belongs to Chris.   **10.** Draw to show what you know about the number 0. Tell a friend about your drawing.

**HOME ACTIVITY •** Draw a five frame or use an egg carton that has just five sections. Have your child show a set of up to 3 or 4 objects and place the objects in the five frame. Then have him or her remove the objects and tell how many are in the five frame.

# Identify and Write 0

**COMMON CORE STANDARD—K.CC.A.3**
*Know number names and the count sequence.*

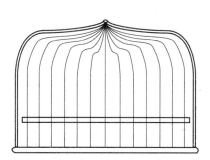

_____

– – – – – – –

_____

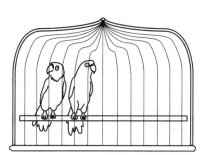

_____

– – – – – – –

_____

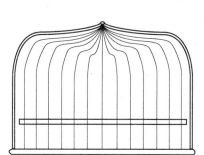

_____

– – – – – – –

_____

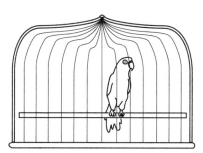

_____

– – – – – – –

_____

**DIRECTIONS** 1–4. How many birds are in the cage? Write the
number. Circle the cages that have 0 birds.

_____

- - - - -

_____

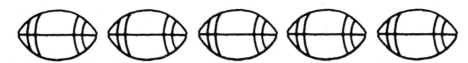

_____

- - - - -

_____

_____

- - - - -

_____

**DIRECTIONS** 1. How many fish are in the bowl? Write the number. 2. Count and tell how many. Write the number. 3. Draw a set of 5 marbles. Write the number.

FOR MORE PRACTICE
GO TO THE
**Personal Math Trainer**

Name _____

○ I
○ 2
○ one

○ four
○ five
○ 5

_____
_ _ _ _ _
_____

_____
_ _ _ _ _
_____

_____
_ _ _ _ _
_____

**DIRECTIONS** 1–2. Choose all the answers that tell how many. 3. How many eggs are in the nest? Write the number. 4–5. Count how many. Write the number.

**6**

**7**

_____   _____   _____   _____   _____

- - - - - -   - - - - - -   - - - - - -   - - - - - -   - - - - - -

_____   _____   _____   _____   _____

**8**

_____   _____   _____   _____   _____

- - - - - -   - - - - - -   - - - - - -   - - - - - -   - - - - - -

_____   _____   _____   _____   _____

**DIRECTIONS** **6.** Circle all sets that show 4. **7.** Count the cubes in each tower. Write the number. **8.** Write the numbers 1 to 5 in counting order.

**74** seventy-four

Name _____

 THINK SMARTER +

| | | |
|---|---|---|
| 4 2 1 | ○ Yes | ○ No |
| 3 4 5 | ○ Yes | ○ No |
| 1 2 3 | ○ Yes | ○ No |

_____

_ _ _ _ _

_____

_____

_ _ _ _ _

_____

_____

_ _ _ _ _

_____

**DIRECTIONS** **9.** Are the numbers in counting order? Choose Yes or No.
**10.** Three children each bring one book to school. Draw counters to show
the books. Write the number. **11.** Sam has no apples in a basket. How many
apples does Sam have? Write the number. **12.** There are two apples on the
table. Kia takes the two apples to a friend. How many apples are on the table
now? Write the number.

**Chapter 1** seventy-five **75**

**13** THINK SMARTER +

◯ ◯ ◯ ◯ ◯

___ and ___

◯ ◯ ◯ ◯ ◯

___ and ___

**14**

___

**DIRECTIONS** 13. Show 2 ways to make 5. Color some counters red. Color some counters yellow. Write the numbers. 14. Write the number that comes after 3 in counting order. Draw counters to show the number.

# Chapter 2

# Compare Numbers to 5

Curious About Math with Curious George

Butterflies have taste buds in their feet so they stand on their food to taste it!

- Are there more butterflies or more flowers in this picture?

Name _____

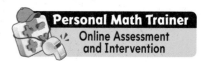

## One-to-One Correspondence

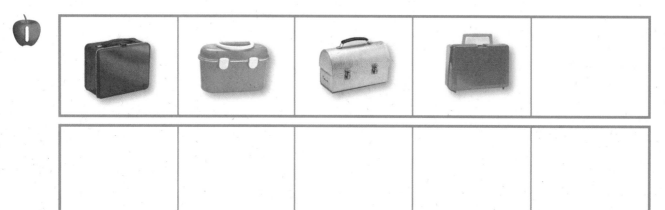

## Model Numbers 0 to 5

## Write Numbers 0 to 5

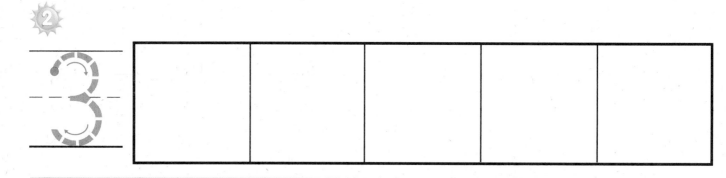

This page checks understanding of important skills needed for success in Chapter 2.

**DIRECTIONS** I. Draw one apple for each lunch box. **2.** Place counters in the five frame to model the number. Draw the counters. Trace the number. **3–4.** Count and tell how many. Write the number.

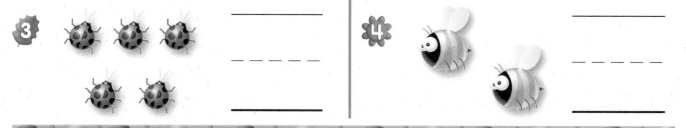

© Houghton Mifflin Harcourt Publishing Company

Name _____

## Vocabulary Builder

four

three

three

one

two

five

**DIRECTIONS** Circle the sets with the same number of animals. Count and tell how many trees. Draw a line below the word for the number of trees.

• **Interactive Student Edition**
• **Multimedia eGlossary**

# Game

# Counting to Blastoff

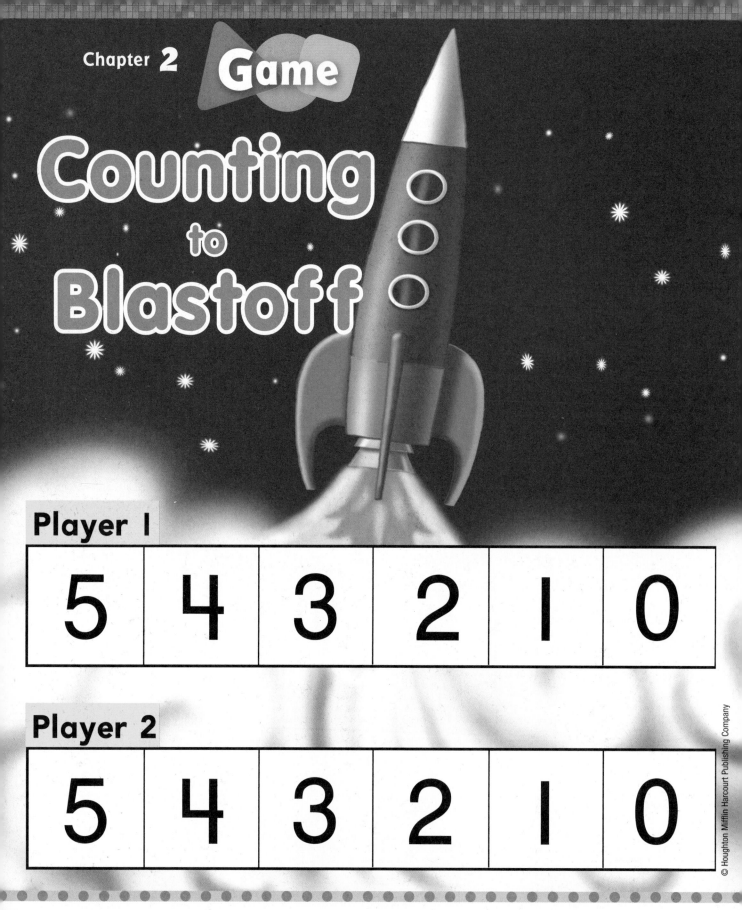

**Player 1**

| 5 | 4 | 3 | 2 | 1 | 0 |
|---|---|---|---|---|---|

**Player 2**

| 5 | 4 | 3 | 2 | 1 | 0 |
|---|---|---|---|---|---|

**DIRECTIONS** Each player tosses the number cube and finds that number on his or her board. The player covers the number with a counter. Players take turns in this way until they have covered all of the numbers on the board. Then they are ready for blastoff.

**MATERIALS** 6 counters for each player, number cube (0–5)

# Chapter 2 Vocabulary

**compare**

comparar

13

**fewer**

menos

23

**greater**

mayor

31

**less**

menor, menos

38

**match**

emparejar

41

**more**

más

43

**one**

uno

47

**same number**

el mismo número

57

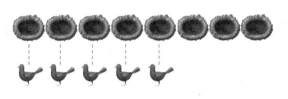

## 3 **fewer** birds

The number of blue counters **compares** equally to the number of red counters.

← less

## 3 is **less** than 4

6

9

## 9 is **greater** than 6

## 2 **more** leaves

Each counter has a **match**.

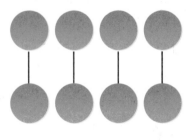

**same number** of red counters in each row

1

# Bingo

**Word Box**

compare
fewer
greater
less
match
more
one
same number

## Player 1

| fewer | same number | match | more | greater | less |
|-------|-------------|-------|------|---------|------|

## Player 2

| greater | more | one | fewer | compare | same number |
|---------|------|-----|-------|---------|-------------|

**DIRECTIONS** Shuffle the Vocabulary Cards and place them in a pile. A player takes the top card and tells what he or she knows about the word. The player puts a counter on that word on the board. Players take turns. The first player to cover all the words on his or her board says "Bingo."

**MATERIALS** 2 sets of Vocabulary Cards, 6 two-color counters for each player

# The Write Way

**DIRECTIONS** Draw to show how to compare sets.
**Reflect** Be ready to tell about your drawing.

Name _____

# Same Number

**Essential Question** How can you use matching and counting to compare sets with the same number of objects?

Common Core
**Counting and Cardinality—K.CC.C.6**
*Also K.CC.B.4b, K.CC.C.7*
**MATHEMATICAL PRACTICES**
**MP3, MP5**

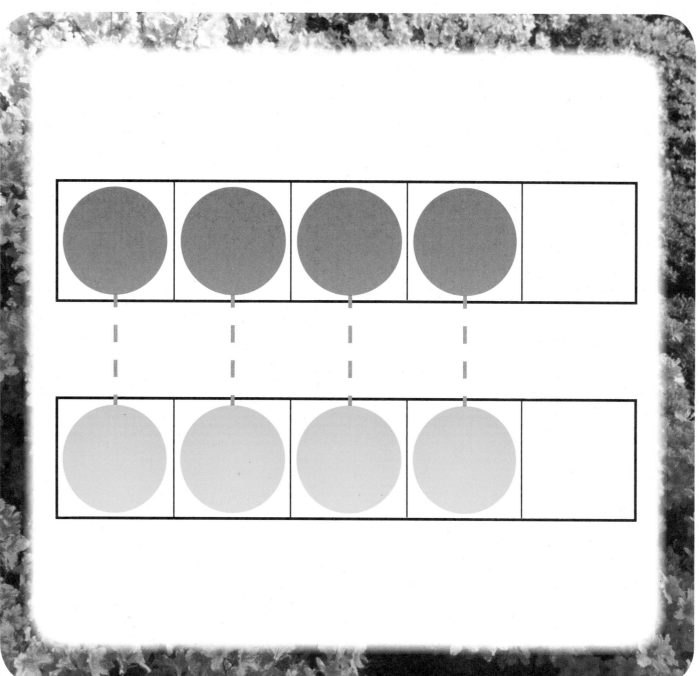

**DIRECTIONS** Place counters as shown. Trace the lines to match each counter in the top five frame to a counter below it in the bottom five frame. Count how many in each set. Tell a friend about the number of counters in each set.

**Chapter 2 • Lesson 1**

eighty-one **81**

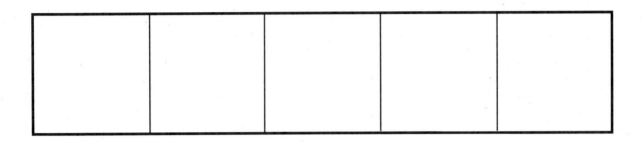

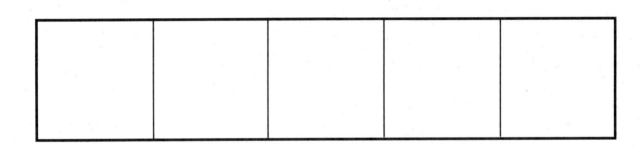

**DIRECTIONS** 1. Place a counter on each car in the set as you count them. Move the counters to the five frame below the cars. Draw the counters. Place a counter on each finger puppet in the set as you count them. Move the counters to the five frame above the puppets. Draw those counters. Is the number of objects in one set greater than, less than, or the same as the number of objects in the other set? Draw a line to match a counter in each set.

Name _____

_____

- - - - - - -

_____

_____

- - - - - - -

_____

●●●●●●●●●●●●●●●●●●●●●●●●●●●●●●●●●●●●●●●●●●●●●●●●●

**DIRECTIONS** **2.** Compare the sets of objects. Is the number of hats greater than, less than, or the same as the number of juice boxes? Count how many hats. Write the number. Count how many juice boxes. Write the number. Tell a friend what you know about the number of objects in each set.

**Chapter 2 • Lesson 1**

# Problem Solving • Applications Real World

WRITE Math

**3**

_____

- - - - - - - - -

_____

- - - - - - - - -

_____

**4**

---

**DIRECTIONS** **3.** Count how many buses. Write the number. Draw to show a set of counters that has the same number as the set of buses. Write the number. Draw a line to match the objects in each set. **4.** Draw two sets that have the same number of objects shown in different ways. Tell a friend about your drawing.

**HOME ACTIVITY •** Show your child two sets that have the same number of up to five objects. Have him or her identify whether the number of objects in one set is greater than, less than, or has the same number of objects as the other set.

# Same Number

Common Core

**COMMON CORE STANDARD—K.CC.C.6**
*Compare numbers.*

**1**

_____

- - - - - - -

_____

_____

- - - - - - -

_____

**DIRECTIONS** 1. Compare the sets of objects. Is the number of dolphins greater than, less than, or the same as the number of turtles? Count how many dolphins. Write the number. Count how many turtles. Write the number. Tell a friend what you know about the number of objects in each set.

**Chapter 2**

eighty-five **85**

# Lesson Check (K.CC.C.6)

_____

- - - -

_____

- - - -

_____

# Spiral Review (K.CC.A.3, K.CC.B.4a)

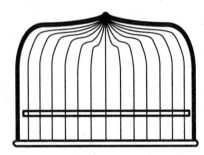

_____

- - - -

_____

**DIRECTIONS** 1. Count how many cars. Write the number. Draw to show a set of counters that has the same number as the set of cars. Write the number. Draw lines to match the objects in each set. **2.** Count and tell how many birds are in the cage. Write the number. **3.** Trace the number. How many counters would you place in the five frame to show the number? Draw the counters.

**86** eighty-six

FOR MORE PRACTICE
GO TO THE
**Personal Math Trainer**

Name _____

# Greater Than

**Essential Question** How can you compare sets when the number of objects in one set is greater than the number of objects in the other set?

Common Core **Counting and Cardinality—K.CC.C.6**
*Also K.CC.C.7*
**MATHEMATICAL PRACTICES**
**MP2, MP3, MP5**

**Listen and Draw**

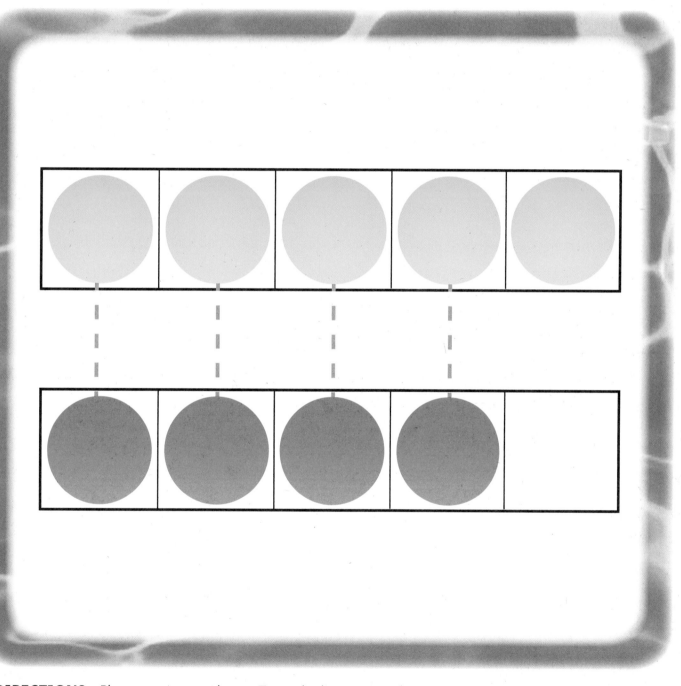

**DIRECTIONS** Place counters as shown. Trace the lines to match a counter in the top five frame to a counter below it in the bottom five frame. Count how many in each set. Tell a friend which set has a number of objects greater than the other set.

**Chapter 2 • Lesson 2**

## Share and Show

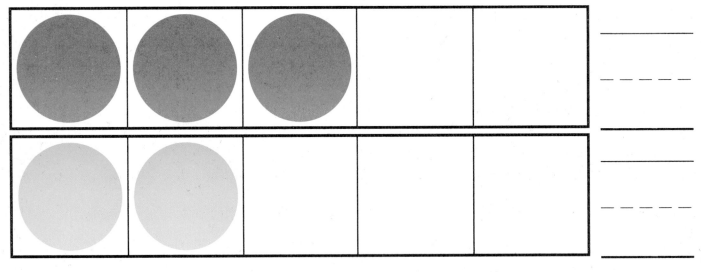

**DIRECTIONS** 1. Place counters as shown. Count and tell how many in each set. Trace the numbers. Compare the sets by matching. Circle the number that is greater. 2. Place counters as shown. Count and tell how many in each set. Write the numbers. Compare the sets by matching. Circle the number that is greater.

**3**

_____
- - - - -
_____

_____
- - - - -
_____

**4**

_____
- - - - -
_____

_____
- - - - -
_____

**DIRECTIONS 3–4.** Place counters as shown. Count and tell how many in each set. Write the numbers. Compare the numbers. Circle the number that is greater.

## Problem Solving • Applications

**DIRECTIONS  5.** Brianna has a bag with three apples in it. Her friend has a bag with a number of apples that is one greater. Draw the bags. Write the numbers on the bags to show how many apples. Tell a friend what you know about the numbers.

**HOME ACTIVITY** • Show your child a set of up to four objects. Have him or her show a set with a number of objects greater than your set.

# Greater Than

Common Core    **COMMON CORE STANDARD—K.CC.C.6**
*Compare numbers.*

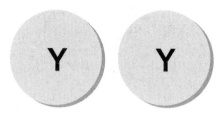

_____

– – – – –

_____

- - - - - - - - - - - - - - - - - - - - - - - - - - - -

_____

– – – – –

_____

_____

– – – – –

_____

**DIRECTIONS   1–2.** Place counters as shown. Y is for yellow, and
R is for red. Count and tell how many are in each set. Write the
numbers. Compare the numbers. Circle the number that is greater.

## Lesson Check (K.CC.C.6)

_____

– – – – – –

_____

## Spiral Review (K.CC.B.4a)

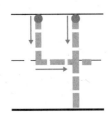

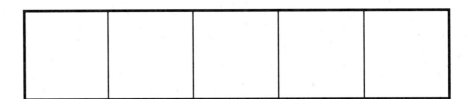

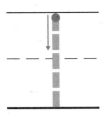

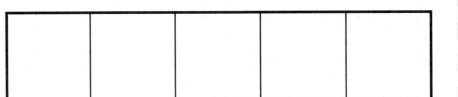

**DIRECTIONS** 1. Place counters as shown. Y is for yellow, and R is for red. Count and tell how many are in each set. Write the numbers. Compare the numbers. Circle the number that is greater. **2–3.** Trace the number. How many counters would you place in the five frame to show the number? Draw the counters.

**FOR MORE PRACTICE GO TO THE Personal Math Trainer**

Name _____

# Less Than

**Essential Question** How can you compare sets when the number of objects in one set is less than the number of objects in the other set?

Common Core **Counting and Cardinality—K.CC.C.6**
*Also K.CC.C.7*
**MATHEMATICAL PRACTICES**
**MP2, MP3, MP5**

**Listen and Draw**

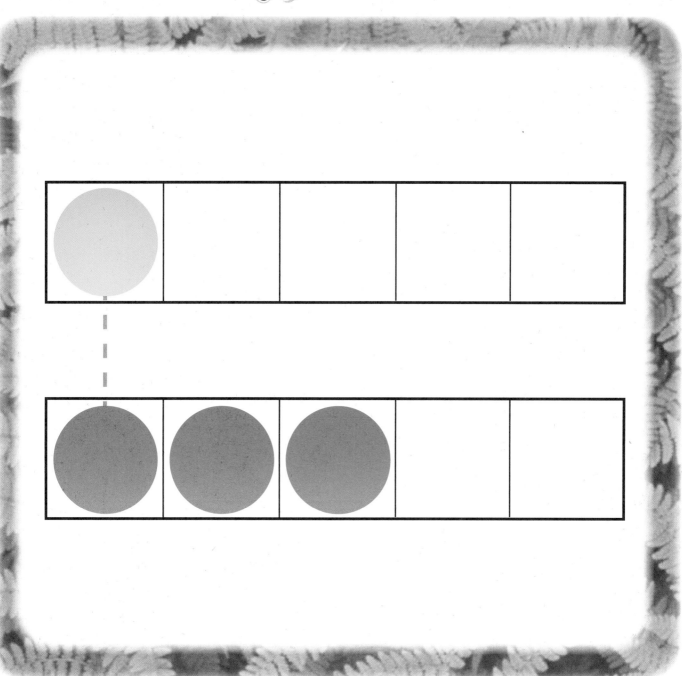

**DIRECTIONS** Place counters as shown. Trace the line to match a counter in the top five frame to a counter below it in the bottom five frame. Count how many in each set. Tell a friend which set has a number of objects less than the other set.

**Chapter 2 • Lesson 3**

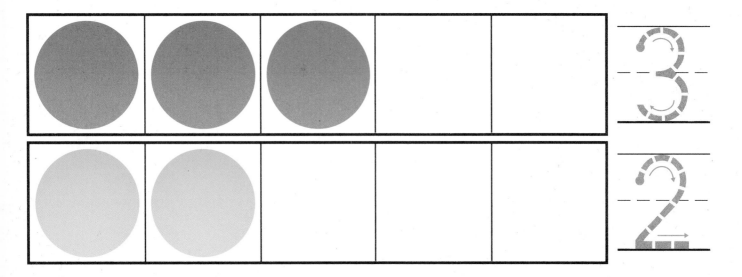

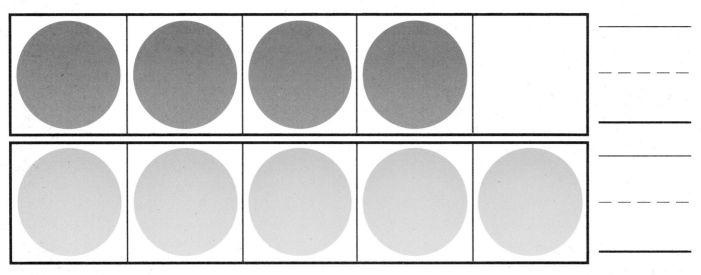

**DIRECTIONS**  **1.** Place counters as shown. Count and tell how many in each set. Trace the numbers. Compare the sets by matching. Circle the number that is less.  **2.** Count and tell how many in each set. Write the numbers. Compare the sets by matching. Circle the number that is less.

**94** ninety-four

Name _____

_____     _____

‒ ‒ ‒ ‒ ‒           ‒ ‒ ‒ ‒ ‒

_____     _____

_____     _____

‒ ‒ ‒ ‒ ‒           ‒ ‒ ‒ ‒ ‒

_____     _____

**DIRECTIONS**  3–4.  Count and tell how many in each set. Write the numbers. Compare the numbers. Circle the number that is less.

 **HOME ACTIVITY** • Show your child a set of two to five objects. Have him or her show a set of objects that has a number of objects less than you have.

**Chapter 2 • Lesson 3**                    ninety-five **95**

**Personal Math Trainer**
Online Assessment
and Intervention

## Concepts and Skills

_____

- - - - - - - - - - -

_____

- - - - - - - - - - -

_____

- - - - - - - - - - -

_____

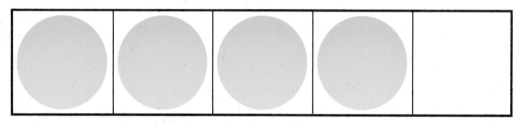

- - - - - - - - - - -

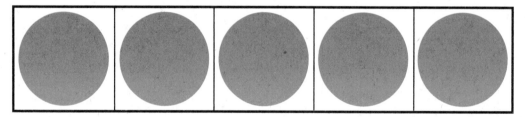

- - - - - - - - - - -

_____

**THINK SMARTER**

**DIRECTIONS** 1. Place a counter below each object to show the same number of objects. Draw and color each counter. Write how many objects in each row. (K.CC.C.6) 2. Place counters as shown. Count and tell how many in each set. Write the numbers. Compare the sets by matching. Circle the number that is greater. (K.CC.C.6) 3. Count the fish in the bowl at the beginning of the row. Circle all the bowls that have a number of fish less than the bowl at the beginning of the row. (K.CC.C.6)

# Less Than

**COMMON CORE STANDARD—K.CC.C.6**
*Compare numbers.*

_____          _____

_ _ _ _ _               _ _ _ _ _

_____          _____

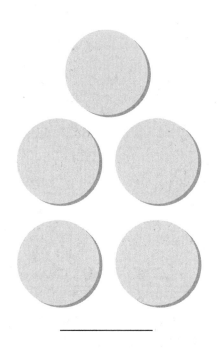

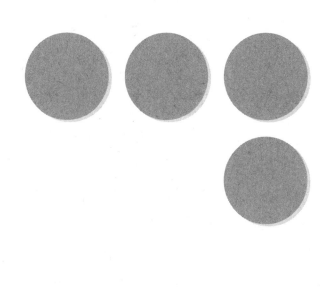

_____          _____

_ _ _ _ _               _ _ _ _ _

_____          _____

**DIRECTIONS** 1–2. Count and tell how many are in each set. Write
the numbers. Compare the numbers. Circle the number that is less.

# Lesson Check (K.CC.C.6)

_____

_ _ _ _ _ _ _

_____

_____

_ _ _ _ _ _ _

_____

# Spiral Review (K.CC.B.4a, K.CC.B.4b)

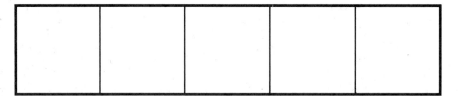

_____

_ _ _ _ _ _ _

_____

**DIRECTIONS** **1.** Count and tell how many are in each set. Write the numbers. Compare the numbers. Circle the number that is less. **2.** Trace the number. How many counters would you place in the five frame to show the number? Draw the counters. **3.** Count how many birds. Write the number.

FOR MORE PRACTICE
GO TO THE
**Personal Math Trainer**

Name _____

# Problem Solving • Compare by Matching Sets to 5

**Essential Question** How can you make a model to solve problems using a matching strategy?

Common Core · **Counting and Cardinality—K.CC.C.6**
*Also K.CC.C.7*
MATHEMATICAL PRACTICES
**MP3, MP4, MP5**

 **Unlock the Problem**

**DIRECTIONS** These are Brandon's toy cars. How many toy cars does Brandon have? Jay has a number of toy cars that is less than the number of toy cars Brandon has. Use cubes to show how many toy cars Jay might have. Draw the cubes. Use matching to compare the sets.

**Chapter 2 • Lesson 4**

# Try Another Problem

**1**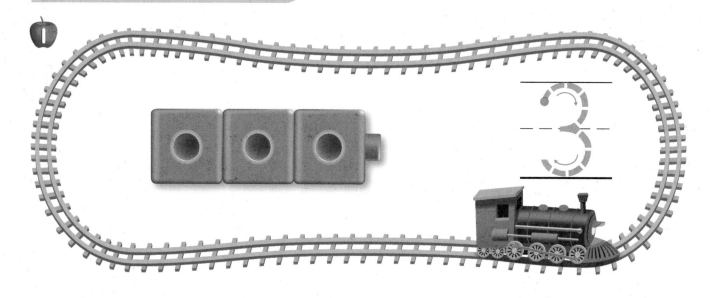

**2**

**3** ✓

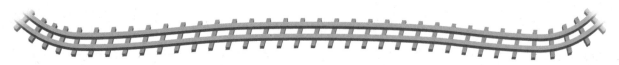

**DIRECTIONS** I. How many cubes? Trace the number. **2–3.** Model a cube train that has a number of cubes greater than 3. Draw the cube train. Write how many. Use matching to compare the cube trains you drew. Tell a friend about the cube trains.

**4** _____

_ _ _ _ _ _

_____

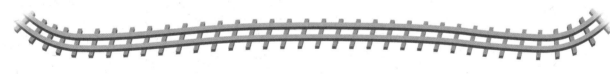

**5** _____

_ _ _ _ _ _

_____

**6** _____

_ _ _ _ _ _

_____

**DIRECTIONS** **4.** How many cubes? Write the number. **5–6.** Model a cube train that has a number of cubes less than 5. Draw the cube train. Write how many. Use matching to compare the cube trains you drew. Tell a friend about the cube trains.

## On Your Own (Real World)

**7**

_____

— — — — —

_____

_____

— — — —

_____

**8**

_____

— — — — —

_____

_____

— — — —

_____

**DIRECTIONS** **7.** Kendall has a set of three pencils. Her friend has a set with the same number of pencils. Draw to show the sets of pencils. Compare the sets by matching. Write how many in each set.    **8.** Draw to show what you know about matching to compare two sets of objects. Write how many in each set.

**HOME ACTIVITY** • Show your child two sets with a different number of objects in each set. Have him or her use matching to compare the sets.

## Problem Solving • Compare by Matching Sets to 5

Common Core
**COMMON CORE STANDARD—K.CC.C.6**
*Compare numbers.*

_____
- - - - - - - - - -
_____
- - - - - - - - - -
_____

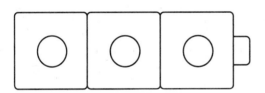

_____
- - - - - - - - - -
_____
- - - - - - - - - -
_____

**DIRECTIONS** **I.** How many cubes are there? Write the number. Model a cube train that has a number of cubes greater than 4. Draw the cube train. Write how many. Compare the cube trains by matching. Tell a friend about the cube trains. **2.** How many cubes are there? Write the number. Model a cube train that has a number of cubes less than 3. Draw the cube train. Write how many. Compare the cube trains by matching. Tell a friend about the cube trains.

# Lesson Check

_____

- - - - - - - - - -

_____

- - - - - - - - - -

_____

## Spiral Review (K.CC.B.4a)

  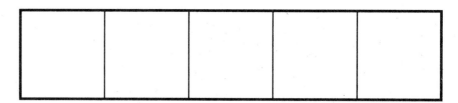

  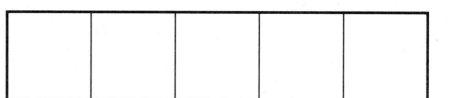

**DIRECTIONS** 1. How many cubes are there? Write the number. Model a cube train that has a number of cubes greater than 3. Draw the cube train. Write how many. Compare the cube trains by matching. Tell a friend about the cube trains. **2–3.** Trace the number. How many counters would you place in the five frame to show the number? Draw the counters.

FOR MORE PRACTICE
GO TO THE
**Personal Math Trainer**

Name _____

# Compare by Counting Sets to 5

**Essential Question** How can you use a counting strategy to compare sets of objects?

Common Core **Counting and Cardinality—K.CC.C.6** *Also K.CC.C.7*
**MATHEMATICAL PRACTICES**
**MP2, MP3, MP6**

## Listen and Draw (Real World)

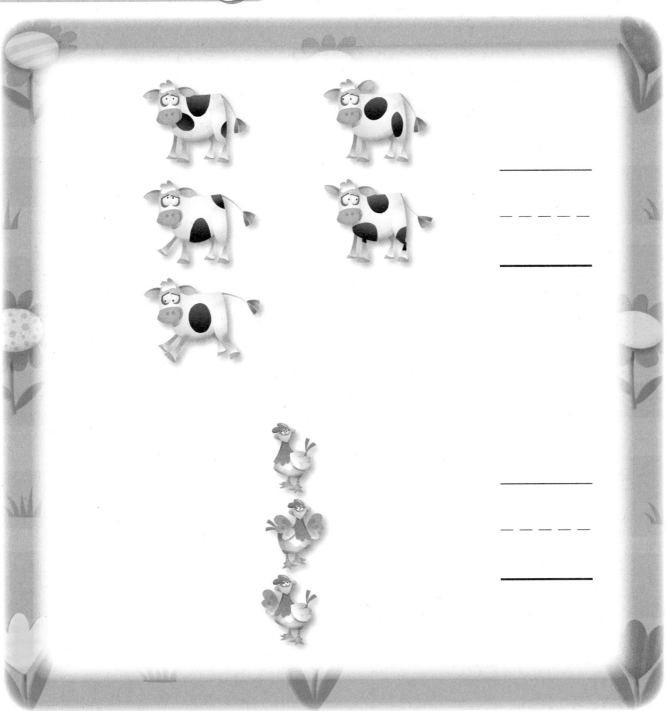

**DIRECTIONS** Look at the sets of objects. Count how many objects in each set. Write the numbers. Compare the numbers and tell a friend which number is greater and which number is less.

**Chapter 2 • Lesson 5**

one hundred five **105**

## Share and Show

**1**

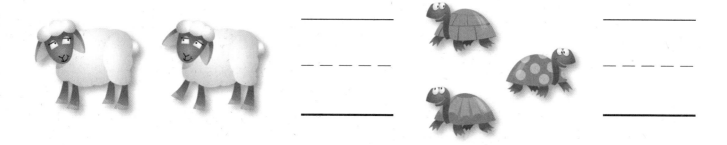

_____

_____

_____

**2**

_____

_____

_____

 **3** ✓

_____

_____

_____

_____

_____

_____

**DIRECTIONS** 1–3. Count how many objects in each set. Write the numbers. Compare the numbers. Circle the number that is greater.

Name _____

_____

- - - - - - - -

_____

_____

- - - - - - - -

_____

**5**

_____

- - - - - - - -

_____

_____

- - - - - - - -

_____

**6**

_____

- - - - - - - -

_____

_____

- - - - - - - -

_____

**DIRECTIONS   4–6.** Count how many objects in each set.
Write the numbers. Compare the numbers. Circle the number
that is less.

## Problem Solving • Applications *Real World*

**WRITE Math**

**7**

**8**

**DIRECTIONS 7.** Tony has stuffed toy frogs. His friend has stuffed toy turkeys. Count how many objects in each set. Write the numbers. Compare the numbers. Tell a friend what you know about the sets. **8.** Draw to show what you know about counting to compare two sets of objects. Write how many in each set.

**HOME ACTIVITY •** Draw a domino block with up to three dots on one end. Ask your child to draw on the other end a number of dots greater than the set you drew.

Name _____

# Compare by Counting Sets to 5

COMMON CORE STANDARD—K.CC.C.6
Compare numbers.

_____

- - - - - - -

_____                                          _____

_____

- - - - - - -

_____                                          _____

_____

- - - - - - -

_____                                          _____

**DIRECTIONS** **1–2.** Count how many objects are in each set. Write the numbers. Compare the numbers. Circle the number that is greater. **3.** Count how many objects are in each set. Write the numbers. Compare the numbers. Circle the number that is less.

**Chapter 2**

# Lesson Check (K.CC.C.6)

_____   _____

- - - -   - - - -

_____   _____

## Spiral Review (K.CC.A.3, K.CC.B.4c)

_____

- - - -

_____

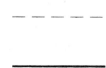

**DIRECTIONS** **I.** Count how many objects are in each set. Write the numbers. Compare the numbers. Circle the number that is less. **2.** Count and tell how many cats. Write the number. **3.** Trace or write the numbers in order.

**110** one hundred ten

© Houghton Mifflin Harcourt Publishing Company

**Chapter 2 Review/Test**

_____

- - - - - - - - -

_____

_____

- - - - - - - - -

_____

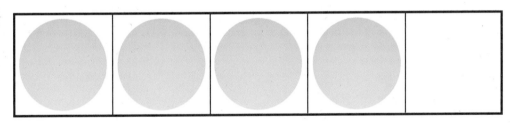

- - - - - - - - -

_____

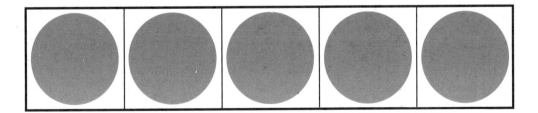

- - - - - - - - -

_____

**DIRECTIONS** 1. Draw a counter below each finger puppet to show the same number of counters as puppets. Write how many puppets. Write how many counters. 2. How many counters are there in each row? Write the numbers. Compare the sets by matching. Circle the number that is greater.

Chapter 2

 **Assessment Options**
**Chapter Test**

one hundred eleven **111**

© Houghton Mifflin Harcourt Publishing Company

**3**

○         ○         ○

**4**

○         ○         ○

**5**

○         ○         ○

**6**

○ **1**      ○ **2**      ○ **3**

**DIRECTIONS** **3.** Mark under all the sets that have the same number of counters as the number of cars. **4.** Mark under all the sets that have a number of counters greater than the number of turtles. **5.** Mark under all the sets that have a number of counters less than the number of vans. **6.** Mark all the numbers less than 3.

Name _____

_____
- - - - - - -
_____

_____
- - - - - - -
_____

**Personal Math Trainer**

**8** THINK SMARTER +

_____
- - - - - - -
_____

_____
- - - - - - -
_____

**DIRECTIONS** **7.** Maria has these apples. Draw a set of oranges below the apples that has the same number. Compare the sets by matching. Write how many pieces of fruit in each set. **8.** Amy has two crayons. Draw Amy's crayons. Brad has 1 more crayon than Amy. How many crayons does Brad have? Draw Brad's crayons. Write how many in each set.

**9** THINK SMARTER +

• same number

• greater than

• less than

**10**

_____
_ _ _ _ _
_____

_____
_ _ _ _ _
_____

---

**DIRECTIONS** **9.** Compare the number of red counters in each set to the number of blue counters. Draw lines from the sets of counters to the words that show *same number*, *greater than*, or *less than*. **10.** Draw four counters. Now draw a set that has a greater number of counters. How many are in each set? Write the numbers. Use green to color the set with a greater number of counters. Use blue to color the set with a number of counters that is less than the green set.

# Represent, Count, and Write Numbers 6 to 9

Curious About Math with
**Curious George**

Rides are popular at fairs.

• What can you tell me about this ride?

Name _____

 **Show What You Know**

 **Personal Math Trainer**
Online Assessment and Intervention

## Explore Numbers to 5

## Compare Numbers to 5

## Write Numbers to 5

This page checks understanding of important skills needed for success in Chapter 3.

**DIRECTIONS** 1. Circle the dot cards that show 3. 2. Circle the dot cards that show 5. 3. Write the number of cubes in each set. Circle the greater number. 4. Write the numbers 1 to 5 in order.

 116 one hundred sixteen

## Vocabulary Builder

same number

more

fewer

**DIRECTIONS** Point to sets of objects as you count. Circle two sets that have the same number of objects. Tell what you know about sets that have more objects or fewer objects than other sets on this page.

**GO DIGITAL**  • **Interactive Student Edition**
• **Multimedia eGlossary**

Chapter 3

one hundred seventeen **117**

# Game

# Number Line Up

**DIRECTIONS** Play with a partner. Place numeral cards as shown on the board. Shuffle the remaining cards and place them face down in a stack. Players take turns picking one card from the stack. They place the card to the right to form a number sequence without skipping any numbers. The number sequence can be forward from 0 or backward from 5. If a player picks a card that is not next in either number sequence, the card is returned to the bottom of the stack. The first player to complete a number sequence wins the game.

**MATERIALS** 2 sets of numeral cards 0–5

# Chapter 3 Vocabulary

**eight**

ocho

20

**fewer**

menos

23

**five**

cinco

26

**more**

más

43

**nine**

nueve

45

**same number**

el mismo número

57

**seven**

siete

59

**six**

seis

64

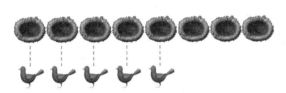

3 **fewer** birds

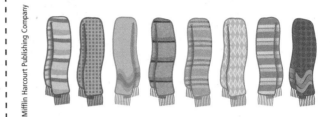

8

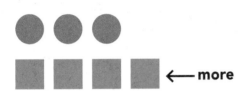

← **more**

5

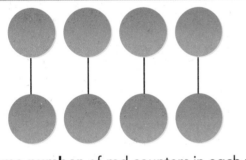

**same number** of red counters in each row

9

6

7

Game

# Picture It

© Houghton Mifflin Harcourt Publishing Company • Image Credits: (bg) ©Sean Gladwell 41/Alamy; (t) ©Dynamic Graphics Group/Jupiterimages/Getty Images

**Word Box**

six

seven

eight

nine

same number

more

fewer

five

## Secret Words

| Player 1 | | | | | |
|---|---|---|---|---|---|
| Player 2 | | | | | |

**DIRECTIONS** Players take turns. A player chooses a secret word from the Word Box and then sets the timer. The player draws pictures to give hints about the secret word. If the other player guesses the secret word before time runs out, he or she puts a counter in the chart. The first player who has counters in all his or her boxes wins.

**MATERIALS** timer, drawing paper, two-color counters for each player

# The Write Way

**DIRECTIONS** Trace the 8. Draw to show what you know about 8.
**Reflect** Be ready to tell about your drawing.

Name _____

# Model and Count 6

**Essential Question** How can you show and count 6 objects?

Common Core **Counting and Cardinality—K.CC.B.5**
*Also K.CC.B.4a, K.CC.B.4b*
MATHEMATICAL PRACTICES
MP4, MP5, MP7

**Listen and Draw** *Real World*

**DIRECTIONS** Place a counter on each ticket in the set as you count them. Move the counters to the ten frame. Draw the counters.

six

**DIRECTIONS** 1. Place a counter on each car in the set as you count them. Move the counters to the parking lot. Draw the counters. Say the number as you trace it.

**120** one hundred twenty

②

six

____ ⬤ and ____ ⬤

____ ⬤ and ____ ⬤

____ ⬤ and ____ ⬤

____ ⬤ and ____ ⬤

**DIRECTIONS** 2. Trace the number 6. Use two-color counters to model the different ways to make 6. Write to show some pairs of numbers that make 6.

Chapter 3 • Lesson 1

one hundred twenty-one **121**

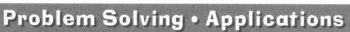 
## Problem Solving • Applications Real World

WRITE
Math

**3**

**4**

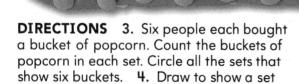 

**DIRECTIONS  3.** Six people each bought a bucket of popcorn. Count the buckets of popcorn in each set. Circle all the sets that show six buckets.  **4.** Draw to show a set of six objects. Tell about your drawing.

**HOME ACTIVITY •** Ask your child to show a set of five objects. Have him or her show one more object and tell how many objects are in the set.

**122** one hundred twenty-two

# Model and Count 6

Common Core  **COMMON CORE STANDARD—K.CC.B.5**
*Count to tell the number of objects.*

six

 **and**

**and**

 **and**

**and**

---

**DIRECTIONS** I. Trace the number 6. Use two-color counters to model the different ways to make 6. Color to show the counters below. Write to show some pairs of numbers that make 6.

**Chapter 3**

one hundred twenty-three **123**

# Lesson Check (K.CC.B.5)

**six**

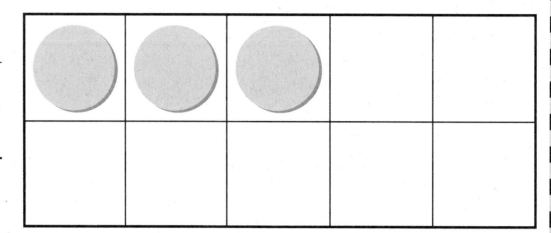

# Spiral Review (K.CC.A.3, K.CC.C.6)

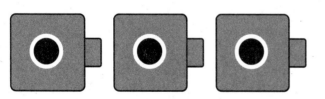

**DIRECTIONS** **I.** Trace the number. How many more counters would you place in the ten frame to model a way to make 6? Draw the counters. **2.** Count and tell how many are in each set. Write the numbers. Compare the numbers. Circle the number that is less. **3.** Count and tell how many. Write the number.

FOR MORE PRACTICE
GO TO THE
**Personal Math Trainer**

# Count and Write to 6

**Essential Question** How can you count and write up to 6 with words and numbers?

Common Core
**Counting and Cardinality—K.CC.A.3**
*Also K.CC.B.4b, K.CC.B.5*
**MATHEMATICAL PRACTICES**
**MP2**

**Listen and Draw** *Real World*

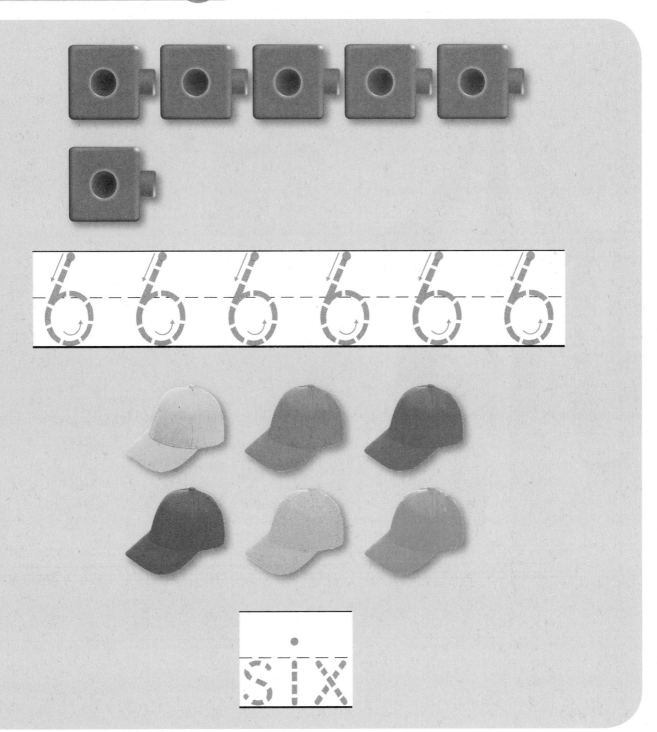

**DIRECTIONS** Count and tell how many cubes. Trace the numbers. Count and tell how many hats. Trace the word.

**DIRECTIONS** 1. Look at the picture. Circle all the sets of six objects. Circle the group of six people.

Name _____

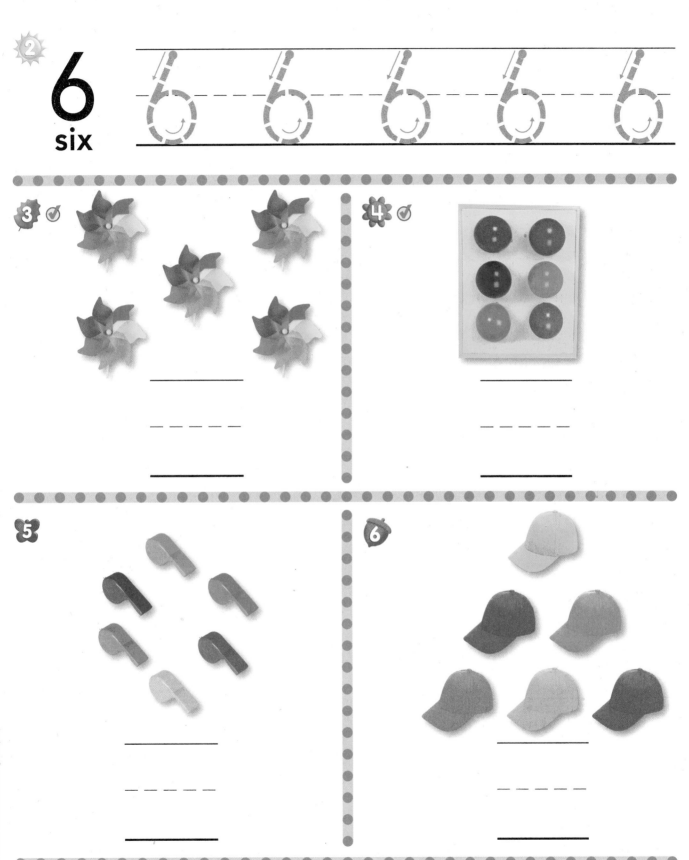

**6**
**six**

**DIRECTIONS** 2. Say the number. Trace the numbers.
3–6. Count and tell how many. Write the number.

**Chapter 3 • Lesson 2**                    one hundred twenty-seven **127**

## Problem Solving • Applications Real World

WRITE Math

**7**

**8**

_____

_ _ _ _ _

_____

**DIRECTIONS 7.** Marta has a number of whistles that is two less than 6. Count the whistles in each set. Circle the set that shows a number of whistles two less than 6. **8.** Draw a set of objects that has a number of objects one greater than 5. Tell about your drawing. Write how many objects.

**HOME ACTIVITY •** Show six objects. Have your child point to each object as he or she counts it. Then have him or her write the number on paper to show how many.

# Count and Write to 6

Common Core

**COMMON CORE STANDARD—K.CC.A.3**
*Know number names and the count sequence.*

**1**

# 6
## six

6 6 6 6 6 6 6

---

**2**

_____

– – – – – – –

_____

**3**

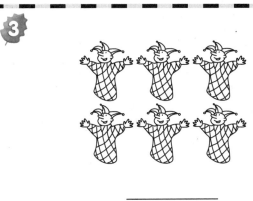

_____

– – – – – – –

_____

---

**4**

_____

– – – – – – –

_____

**5**

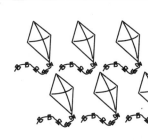

_____

– – – – – – –

_____

---

**DIRECTIONS** 1. Say the number. Trace the numbers.
**2–5.** Count and tell how many. Write the number.

## Lesson Check (K.CC.A.3)

_____

- - - - - - - - - - - -

_____

## Spiral Review (K.CC.B.4a, K.CC.C.6)

_____

- - - - - - - - - - - -

_____

_____

- - - - - - - - - - - -

_____

2

| | | | | |
|---|---|---|---|---|
| | | | | |

**DIRECTIONS** 1. How many school buses are there? Write the number.
2. Count and tell how many are in each set. Write the numbers. Compare the numbers. Circle the number that is greater. 3. How many counters would you place in the five frame to show the number? Draw the counters.

130 one hundred thirty

FOR MORE PRACTICE
GO TO THE
**Personal Math Trainer**

Name _____

# Model and Count 7

**Essential Question** How can you show
and count 7 objects?

Listen and Draw

Common Core  **Counting and Cardinality—K.CC.B.5**
*Also K.CC.B.4a, K.CC.B.4b, K.CC.B.4c*
MATHEMATICAL PRACTICES
MP5, MP7, MP8

**DIRECTIONS** Model 6 objects. Show one more object. How many
are there now? Tell a friend how you know. Draw the objects.

**Chapter 3 • Lesson 3**

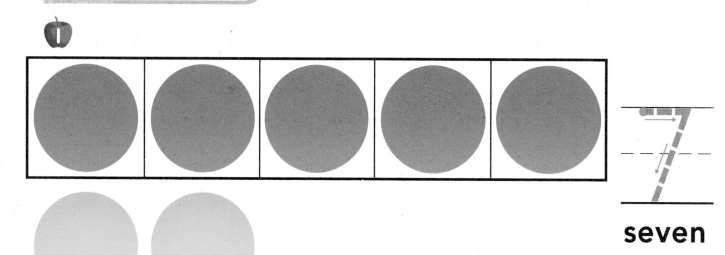

seven

5 and ___ more

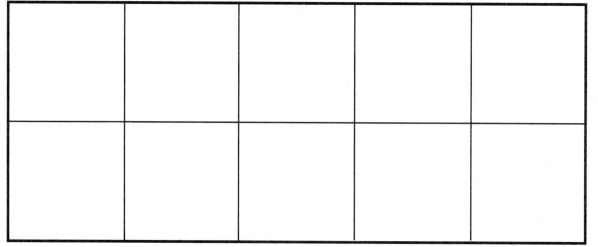

**DIRECTIONS** 1. Place counters as shown. Count and tell how many counters. Trace the number. **2.** How many more than 5 is 7? Write the number. **3.** Place counters in the ten frame to model seven. Tell a friend what you know about the number 7.

132 one hundred thirty-two

Name _____

✿ 4

<table>
<tr><td></td><td></td><td></td><td></td><td></td></tr>
<tr><td></td><td></td><td></td><td></td><td></td></tr>
</table>

7
seven

_____ ⚪ **and** _____ ⚫

_____ ⚪ **and** _____ ⚫

_____ ⚪ **and** _____ ⚫

_____ ⚪ **and** _____ ⚫

**DIRECTIONS** **4.** Trace the number 7. Use two-color counters to model the different ways to make 7. Write to show some pairs of numbers that make 7.

## Problem Solving • Applications  Real World

WRITE Math

**5**

**6**

**DIRECTIONS** **5.** A carousel needs seven horses. Count the horses in each set. Which sets show seven horses? Circle those sets. **6.** Draw to show what you know about the number 7. Tell a friend about your drawing.

**HOME ACTIVITY** • Ask your child to show a set of six objects. Have him or her show one more object and tell how many objects are in the set.

**Practice and Homework**
**Lesson 3.3**

# Model and Count 7

Common Core
**COMMON CORE STANDARD—K.CC.B.5**
*Count to tell the number of objects.*

7
**seven**

and

and

and

and

---

**DIRECTIONS** 1. Trace the number 7. Use two-color counters to model the different ways to make 7. Color to show the counters below. Write to show some pairs of numbers that make 7.

**Chapter 3**

one hundred thirty-five 135

## Lesson Check

**❶**

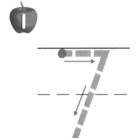

**seven**

---

## Spiral Review

**❷**

_____

- - - - - - - - - -

_____

_____

- - - - - - - - - -

_____

**❸**

_____

- - - - - - - - - -

_____

---

**DIRECTIONS** **I.** Trace the number. How many more counters would you place in the ten frame to model a way to make 7? Draw the counters. **2.** Count and tell how many are in each set. Write the numbers. Compare the numbers. Circle the number that is less. **3.** Count and tell how many. Write the number.

**FOR MORE PRACTICE
GO TO THE
Personal Math Trainer**

Name _____

# Count and Write to 7

**Essential Question** How can you count
and write up to 7 with words and numbers?

Common Core **Counting and Cardinality—K.CC.A.3**
*Also K.CC.B.4b, K.CC.B.5*
MATHEMATICAL PRACTICES
MP2

## Listen and Draw (Real World)

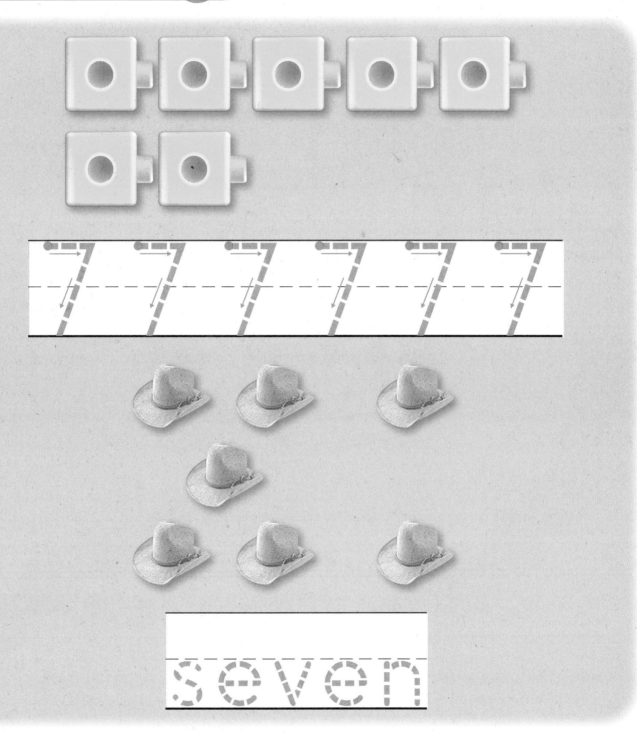

**DIRECTIONS** Count and tell how many cubes. Trace the
numbers. Count and tell how many hats. Trace the word.

**Chapter 3 • Lesson 4**

**I**

**DIRECTIONS** I. Look at the picture. Circle all the sets of seven objects.

Name _____

# 7
## seven

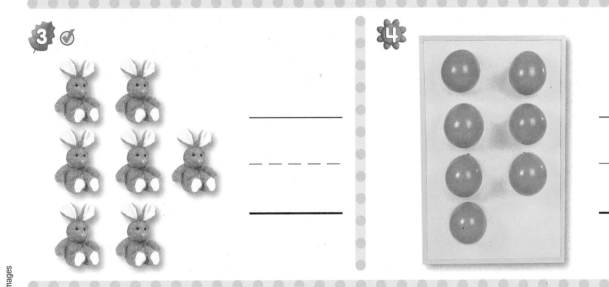

3 ✓

_____

- - - - - - -

_____

4

_____

- - - - - - -

_____

5

_____

- - - - - - -

_____

6

_____

- - - - - - -

_____

**DIRECTIONS** 2. Say the number. Trace the numbers. **3–6.** Count and tell how many. Write the number.

**HOME ACTIVITY** • Show your child seven objects. Have him or her point to each object as he or she counts it. Then have him or her write the number on paper to show how many objects.

© Houghton Mifflin Harcourt Publishing Company • Image Credits: (bl) ©Stockbyte/Getty Images (br) ©PhotoDisc/Getty Images

**Chapter 3 • Lesson 4**

**Concepts and Skills**

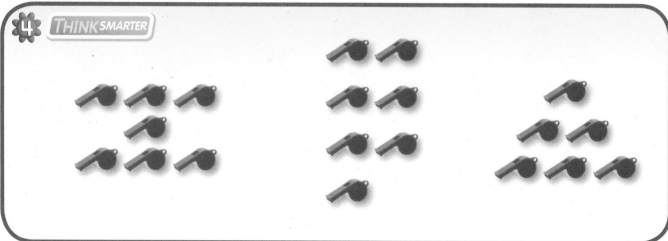

**DIRECTIONS** 1. Use counters to model the number 7. Draw the counters. Write the number. (K.CC.B.5) **2–3.** Count and tell how many. Write the number. (K.CC.A.3) **4.** Circle all the sets of 7 whistles. (K.CC.A.3)

**140** one hundred forty

## Count and Write to 7

Common Core
**COMMON CORE STANDARD—K.CC.A.3**
*Know number names and the count sequence.*

**1**

# 7
## seven

**2**

**3**

**4**

**5**

**DIRECTIONS** 1. Say the number. Trace the numbers.
**2–5.** Count and tell how many. Write the number.

**1**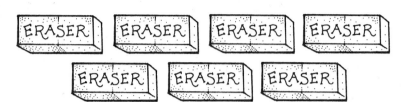

_____

- - - - - - -

_____

## Spiral Review (K.CC.A.3, K.CC.B.4a)

**2**

# 3

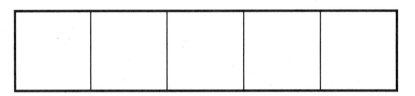

**3**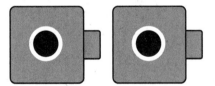

_____

- - - - - - -

_____

**DIRECTIONS** **I.** Count and tell how many erasers. Write the number.
**2.** How many counters would you place in the five frame to show the number?
Draw the counters. **3.** Count and tell how many cubes. Write the number.

**FOR MORE PRACTICE
GO TO THE
Personal Math Trainer**

Name _____

# Model and Count 8

**Essential Question** How can you show and count 8 objects?

 **Listen and Draw**

**Common Core** **Counting and Cardinality—K.CC.B.5**
*Also K.CC.B.4a, K.CC.B.4b, K.CC.B.4c*
**MATHEMATICAL PRACTICES**
**MP5, MP7, MP8**

**DIRECTIONS** Model 7 objects. Show one more object. How many are there now? Tell a friend how you know. Draw the objects.

**Share and Show**

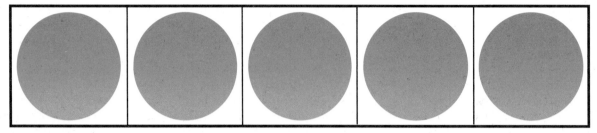

eight

5 and _____ more

**DIRECTIONS** 1. Place counters as shown. Count and tell how many counters. Trace the number.   2. How many more than 5 is 8? Write the number.   3. Place counters in the ten frame to model eight. Tell a friend what you know about the number 8.

❁ 4

8

eight

_____ _____ and _____ _____

_____ _____ and _____ _____

_____ _____ and _____ _____

_____ _____ and _____ _____

**DIRECTIONS** 4. Trace the number 8. Use two-color counters to model the different ways to make 8. Write to show some pairs of numbers that make 8.

## Problem Solving • Applications Real World

**5**

**6**

---

**DIRECTIONS** **5.** Dave sorted sets of balls by color. Count the balls in each set. Which sets show eight balls? Circle those sets. **6.** Draw to show what you know about the number 8. Tell a friend about your drawing.

 **HOME ACTIVITY** • Ask your child to show a set of seven objects. Have him or her show one more object and tell how many.

## Model and Count 8

COMMON CORE STANDARD—K.CC.B.5
*Count to tell the number of objects.*

8
**eight**

___ ___

___ and ___

___ and ___

___ and ___

___ and ___

**DIRECTIONS** I. Trace the number 8. Use two-color counters to model the different ways to make 8. Color to show the counters below. Write to show some pairs of numbers that make 8.

**Chapter 3**

## Lesson Check (K.CC.B.5)

**eight**

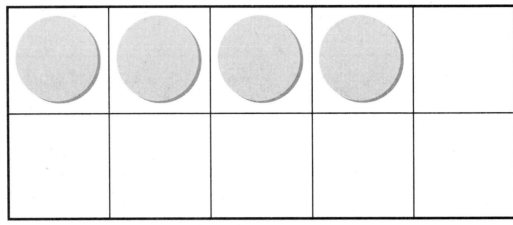

## Spiral Review (K.CC.A.3, K.CC.C.6)

**DIRECTIONS** 1. Trace the number. How many more counters would you place in the ten frame to model a way to make 8? Draw the counters. 2. Count and tell how many are in each set. Write the numbers. Compare the numbers. Circle the number that is greater. 3. Count and tell how many. Write the number.

FOR MORE PRACTICE
GO TO THE
**Personal Math Trainer**

Name _____

# Count and Write to 8

**Essential Question** How can you count and write up to 8 with words and numbers?

Common Core **Counting and Cardinality—K.CC.A.3** Also K.CC.B.4b, K.CC.B.5
MATHEMATICAL PRACTICES
MP2

## Listen and Draw Real World

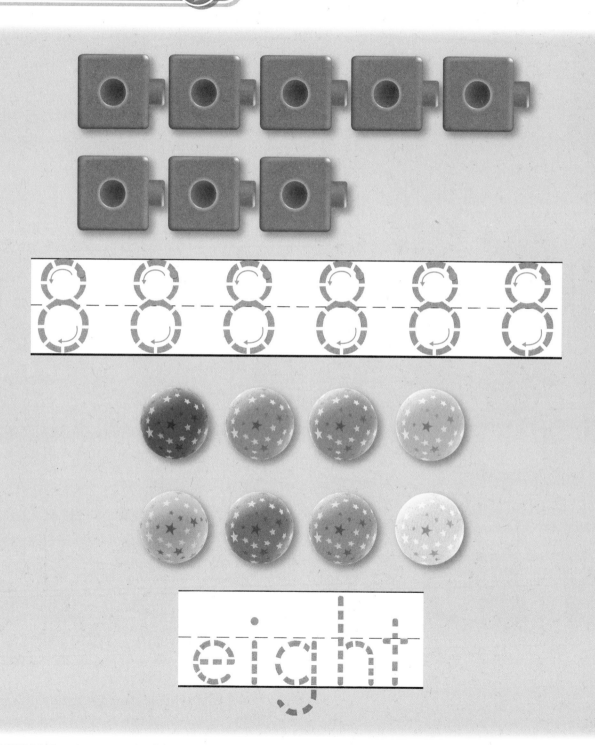

**DIRECTIONS** Count and tell how many cubes. Trace the numbers. Count and tell how many balls. Trace the word.

**Chapter 3 • Lesson 6**

**DIRECTIONS** 1. Look at the picture. Circle all the sets of eight objects.

**2**

# 8
eight

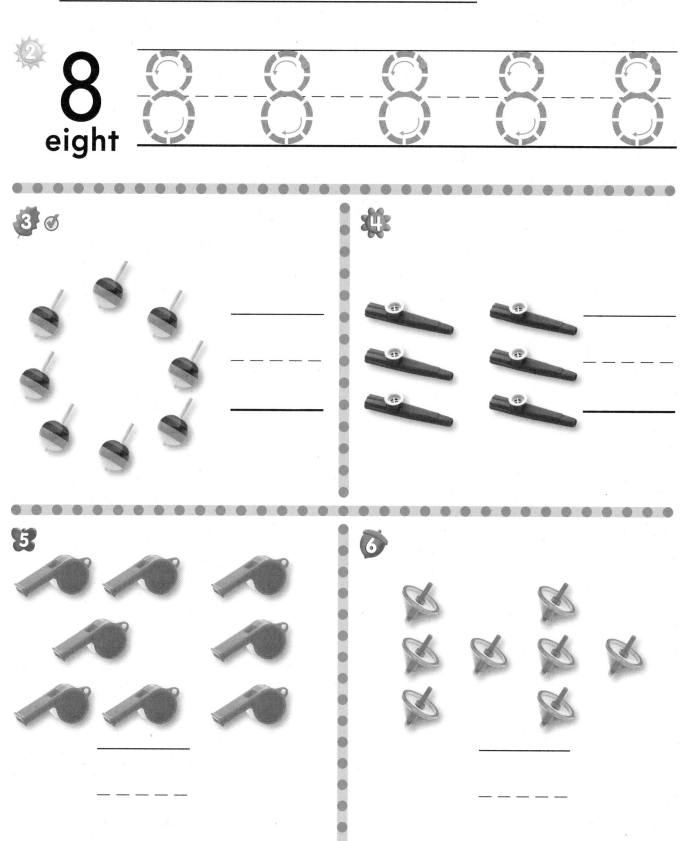

**3** ✓

**4**

**5**

**6**

**DIRECTIONS** **2.** Say the number. Trace the numbers.
**3–6.** Count and tell how many. Write the number.

**Chapter 3 • Lesson 6**

## Problem Solving • Applications (Real World)

WRITE Math

7

8

**DIRECTIONS** **7.** Ed has a number of toy frogs two greater than 6. Count the frogs in each set. Circle the set of frogs that belongs to Ed. **8.** Robbie won ten prizes at the fair. Marissa won a number of prizes two less than Robbie. Draw to show Marissa's prizes. Write how many.

**HOME ACTIVITY** • Show eight objects. Have your child point to each object as he or she counts it. Then have him or her write the number on paper to show how many objects.

# Count and Write to 8

Common Core **COMMON CORE STANDARD—K.CC.A.3**
*Know number names and the count sequence.*

**1** 

# 8
## eight

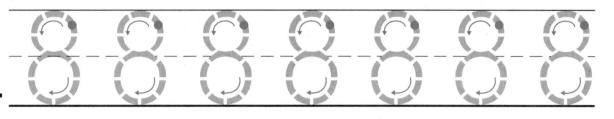

**2**

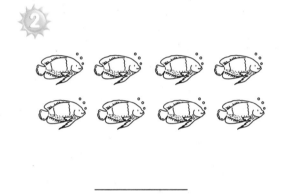

_____

- - - - - - -

_____

**3**

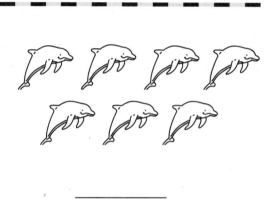

_____

- - - - - - -

_____

**4**

_____

- - - - - - -

_____

**5**

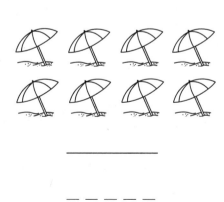

_____

- - - - - - -

_____

**DIRECTIONS** 1. Say the number. Trace the numbers.
**2–5.** Count and tell how many. Write the number.

# Lesson Check (K.CC.A.3)

_____

_ _ _ _ _

_____

---

# Spiral Review (K.CC.B.4b, K.CC.C.6)

_____          _____

_ _ _ _ _        _ _ _ _ _

_____          _____

---

_____

_ _ _ _ _

_____

---

**DIRECTIONS** **1.** Count and tell how many bees. Write the number. **2.** Count and tell how many are in each set. Write the numbers. Compare the numbers. Circle the number that is greater. **3.** Count and tell how many beetles. Write the number.

FOR MORE PRACTICE
GO TO THE
**Personal Math Trainer**

Name _____

# Model and Count 9

**Essential Question** How can you show and count 9 objects?

 **Listen and Draw**

Common Core **Counting and Cardinality—K.CC.B.5**
*Also K.CC.B.4a, K.CC.B.4b, K.CC.B.4c*
**MATHEMATICAL PRACTICES**
**MP5, MP7, MP8**

**DIRECTIONS** Model 8 objects. Show one more object. How many are there now? Tell a friend how you know. Draw the objects.

**Chapter 3 • Lesson 7**

one hundred fifty-five **155**

**1**

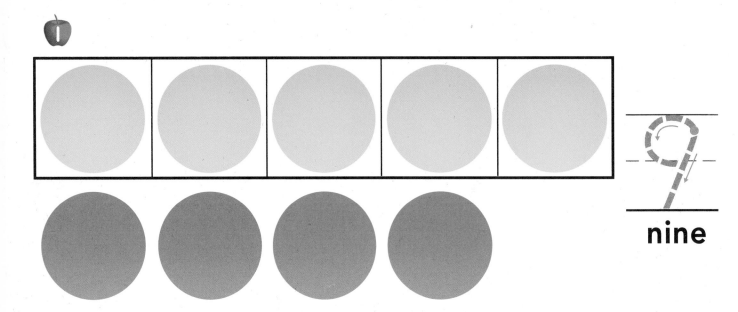

9

nine

**2**

# 5 and ____ more

**3**

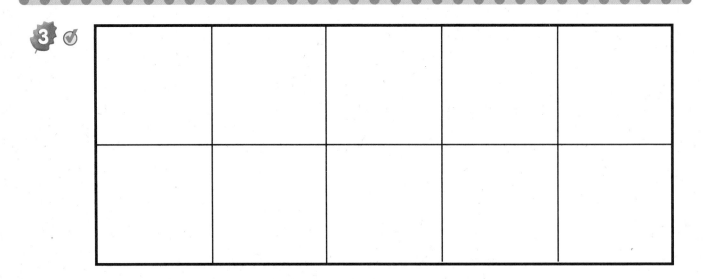

**DIRECTIONS** 1. Place counters as shown. Count and tell how many counters. Trace the number. **2.** How many more than 5 is 9? Write the number. **3.** Place counters in the ten frame to model nine. Tell a friend what you know about the number 9.

**4**

nine

and

and

and

and

**DIRECTIONS** **4.** Trace the number 9. Use two-color counters to model the different ways to make 9. Write to show some pairs of numbers that make 9.

## Problem Solving • Applications Real World

**WRITE Math**

**5**

**6**

**DIRECTIONS** 5. Mr. Lopez is making displays using sets of nine flags. Count the flags in each set. Which sets show nine flags? Circle those sets. **6.** Draw to show what you know about the number 9. Tell a friend about your drawing.

**HOME ACTIVITY** • Ask your child to show a set of eight objects. Have him or her show one more object and tell how many.

**158** one hundred fifty-eight

# Model and Count 9

Common Core

**COMMON CORE STANDARD—K.CC.B.5**
*Count to tell the number of objects.*

**1**

nine

and

and

and

and

**DIRECTIONS** 1. Trace the number 9. Use two-color counters to model the different ways to make 9. Color to show the counters below. Write to show some pairs of numbers that make 9.

## Lesson Check (K.CC.B.5)

nine

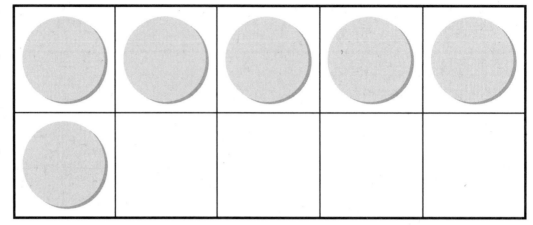

## Spiral Review (K.CC.A.3, K.CC.C.6)

_____

_ _ _ _ _ _ _

_____

_____

_ _ _ _ _ _ _

_____

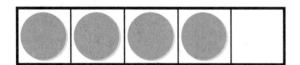

_____

_ _ _ _ _ _ _

_____

**DIRECTIONS** **1.** Trace the number 9. How many more counters would you place in the ten frame to model a way to make 9? Draw the counters. **2.** Count and tell how many are in each set. Write the numbers. Compare the numbers. Circle the number that is greater. **3.** Count and tell how many. Write the number.

FOR MORE PRACTICE
GO TO THE
**Personal Math Trainer**

Name _____

# Count and Write to 9

**Essential Question** How can you count and write up to 9 with words and numbers?

**Common Core** Counting and Cardinality—K.CC.A.3
*Also K.CC.B.4b, K.CC.B.5*
MATHEMATICAL PRACTICES
MP2

**Listen and Draw** *Real World*

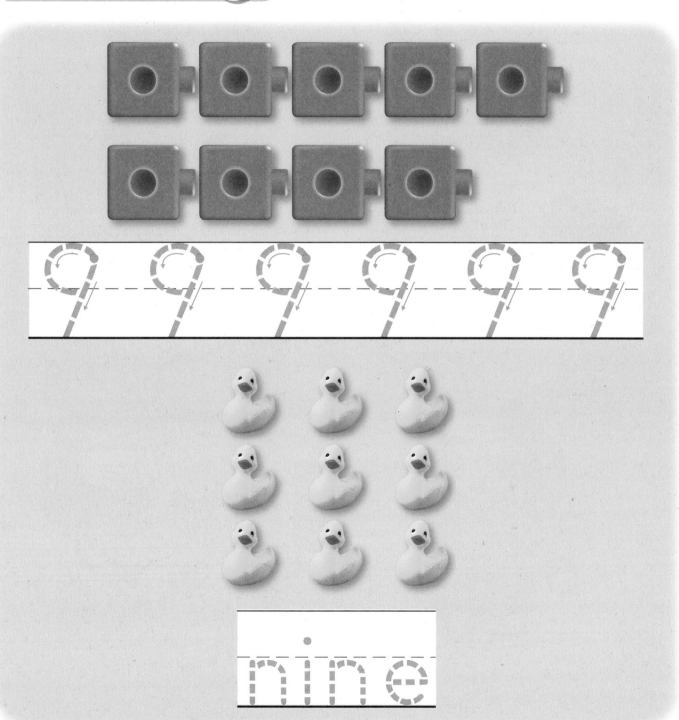

**DIRECTIONS** Count and tell how many cubes. Trace the numbers. Count and tell how many ducks. Trace the word.

**Chapter 3 • Lesson 8**

**DIRECTIONS** I. Look at the picture. Circle all the sets of nine objects.

Name _____

**2**

# 9
## nine

9 9 9 9 9

**3** ✓

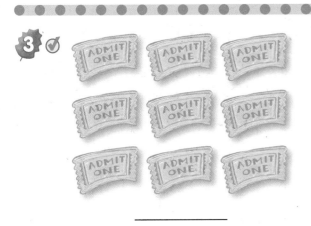

_____

- - - - - -

_____

**4**

_____

- - - - - -

_____

**5**

_____

- - - - - -

_____

**6**

_____

- - - - - -

_____

**DIRECTIONS** **2.** Say the number. Trace the numbers.
**3–6.** Count and tell how many. Write the number.

Chapter 3 • Lesson 8

## Problem Solving • Applications

**7**

**8**

_____

_ _ _ _ _ _

_____

**DIRECTIONS 7.** Eva wants to find the set that has a number of bears one less than 10. Circle that set. **8.** Draw a set that has a number of objects two greater than 7. Write how many.

 **HOME ACTIVITY •** Ask your child to find something in your home that has the number 9 on it, such as a clock or a phone.

© Houghton Mifflin Harcourt Publishing Company • Image Credits: (bear) ©Shutterstock

# Count and Write to 9

COMMON CORE STANDARD—K.CC.A.3
*Know number names and the count sequence.*

**1**

**9**
**nine** _____

9 9 9 9 9 9 9

---

**2**

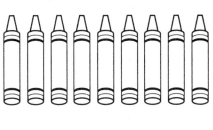

_____
- - - - - - -
_____

**3**

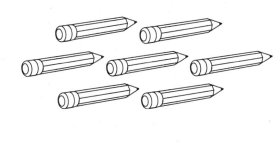

_____
- - - - - - -
_____

---

**4**

_____
- - - - - - -
_____

**5**

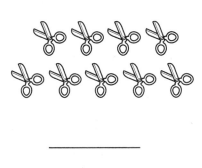

_____
- - - - - - -
_____

---

**DIRECTIONS** 1. Say the number. Trace the numbers.
**2–5.** Count and tell how many. Write the number.

# Lesson Check (K.CC.A.3)

_____

- - - - - - - - - - -

_____

# Spiral Review (K.CC.A.3, K.CC.B.4b)

_____

- - - - - - - - - - -

_____

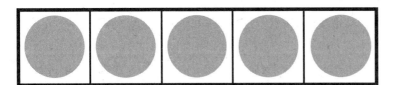

_____

- - - - - - - - - - -

_____

**DIRECTIONS** **1.** Count and tell how many squirrels. Write the number. **2.** How many birds are in the cage? Write the number. **3.** How many counters are there? Write the number.

FOR MORE PRACTICE
GO TO THE
Personal Math Trainer

Name _____

# Problem Solving • Numbers to 9

**Essential Question** How can you solve problems using the strategy *draw a picture*?

Common Core **Counting and Cardinality—K.CC.C.6, K.CC.C.7**
**MATHEMATICAL PRACTICES**
**MP1, MP3, MP4**

## ¡Unlock the Problem Real World

**DIRECTIONS** There are seven flags on the red tent. Trace the flags. The blue tent has a number of flags one greater than the red tent. How many flags are on the blue tent? Draw the flags. Tell a friend about your drawing.

**Chapter 3 • Lesson 9**                    one hundred sixty-seven **167**

**DIRECTIONS** **1.** Bianca buys five hats. Leigh buys a number of hats two greater than 5. Draw the hats. Write the numbers. **2.** Donna wins nine tokens. Jackie wins a number of tokens two less than 9. Draw the tokens. Write the numbers.

Name _____

**DIRECTIONS** 3. Gary has eight tickets. Four of the tickets are red. The rest are blue. How many are blue? Draw the tickets. Write the number beside each set of tickets. 4. Ann has seven balloons. Molly has a set of balloons less than seven. How many balloons does Molly have? Draw the balloons. Write the number beside each set of balloons.

## On Your Own

**5**

_____

_ _ _ _ _ _

_____

**6**

**DIRECTIONS** **5.** There are six seats on a teacup ride. The number of seats on a train ride is two less than 8. How many seats are on the train ride? Draw the seats. Write the number. **6.** Pick two numbers between 0 and 9. Draw to show what you know about those numbers.

**HOME ACTIVITY •** Have your child say two different numbers from 0–9 and tell what he or she knows about them.

# Problem Solving • Numbers to 9

Common Core

**COMMON CORE STANDARD—K.CC.C.6,
K.CC.C.7**
*Compare numbers.*

**1**

_____

– – – – – –

_____

_____

– – – – – –

_____

**2**

_____

– – – – – –

_____

_____

– – – – – –

_____

**DIRECTIONS  1.** Sally has six flowers. Three of the flowers are yellow. The rest are red. How many are red? Draw the flowers. Write the number beside each set of flowers.  **2.** Tim has seven acorns. Don has a number of acorns that is two less than 7. How many acorns does Don have? Draw the acorns. Write the numbers.

# Lesson Check (K.CC.C.6)

_____

- - - - - - - - - - -

_____

_____

- - - - - - - - - - -

_____

## Spiral Review (K.CC.B.4b, K.CC.C.6)

_____

- - - - - - - - - - -

_____

_____          _____

- - - - - - - -          - - - - - - - -

_____          _____

**DIRECTIONS** **1.** Pete has 5 marbles. Jay has a number of marbles that is two more than 5. How many marbles does Jay have? Draw the marbles. Write the numbers. **2.** Count and tell how many books. **3.** Count and tell how many are in each set. Write the numbers. Compare the numbers. Circle the number that is greater.

**172** one hundred seventy-two

FOR MORE PRACTICE
GO TO THE
**Personal Math Trainer**

# ✓ Chapter 3 Review/Test

**Personal Math Trainer**
Online Assessment
and Intervention

_____

_ _ _ _ _ _ _ _

_____

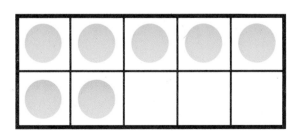

_____

_ _ _ _ _ _ _ _

_____

**DIRECTIONS** 1. Circle all the sets that show 6. 2. Circle all the sets that show 7. 3–4. Count and tell how many. Write the number.

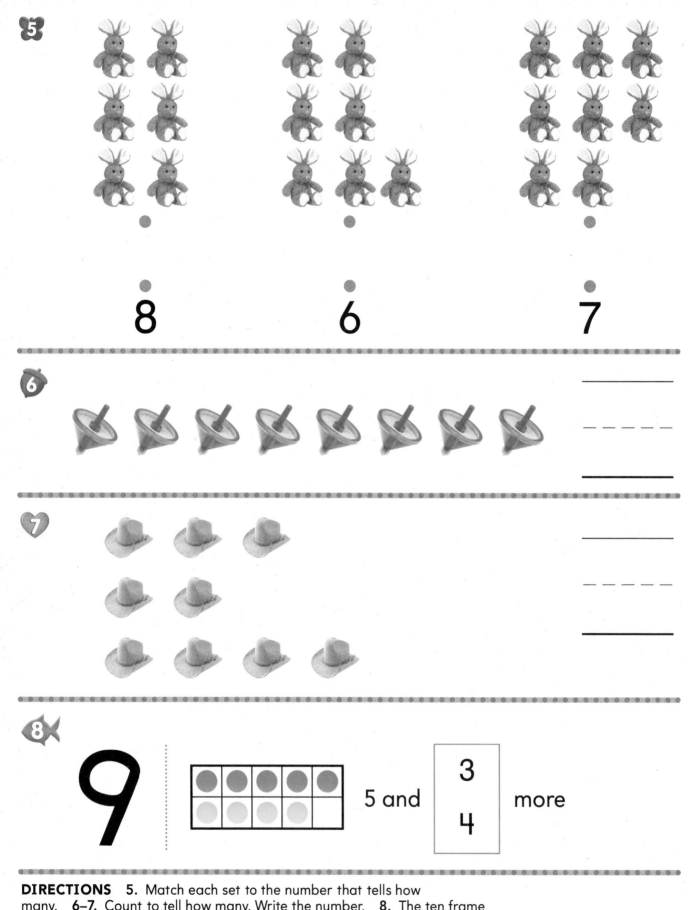

**5** 8

6

7

**6**

_____

- - - - - - - -

_____

**7**

_____

- - - - - - - -

_____

**8** 9 | 5 and | 3
4 | more

**DIRECTIONS** **5.** Match each set to the number that tells how many. **6–7.** Count to tell how many. Write the number. **8.** The ten frame shows 5 red counters and some yellow counters. Five and how many more make 9? Choose the number.

**174** one hundred seventy-four

Personal Math Trainer

**9** THINK SMARTER +

_____

- - - - - - -

_____

_____

- - - - - - -

_____

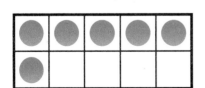        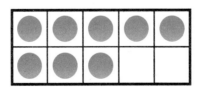        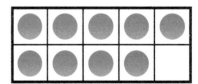

○                    ○                    ○

**DIRECTIONS** **9.** Jeffrey has 8 marbles. Sarah has a number of marbles that is one greater than 8. Draw the marbles. Write the number for each set of marbles. **10.** Choose all the ten frames that have a number of counters greater than 6.

**Chapter 3**                                             one hundred seventy-five **175**

11 | THINK SMARTER +

12

_____

_ _ _ _ _

_____

- - - - - - - - - - - - - - - - - - - - - - - - - - - - - - - - - - - - - - -

**DIRECTIONS** 11. The number of turtles in a pond is 2 less than 9. Draw counters to show the turtles. Write the number. 12. Draw a set that has a number of objects that is 2 more than 6. Write the number.

# Represent and Compare Numbers to 10

**Curious About Math with Curious George**

Apple trees grow from a small seed.

• About how many seeds are in an apple?

Name _____

## Draw Objects to 9

 **1**

# 9

**2**

# 7

## Write Numbers to 9

 **3**

_____

- - - - - - - - -

_____

**4**

_____

- - - - - - - - -

_____

 **5**

_____

- - - - - - - - -

_____

**6**

_____

- - - - - - - - -

_____

This page checks understanding of important skills needed for success in Chapter 4.

**DIRECTIONS**  1. Draw 9 flowers.  2. Draw 7 flowers.
3–6. Count and tell how many. Write the number.

## Vocabulary Builder

greater

less

same number

**DIRECTIONS** Circle the words that describe the number of carrots and the number of celery sticks. Use *greater* and *less* to describe the number of trees and the number of bushes.

 • **Interactive Student Edition**
• **Multimedia eGlossary**

# Game

# Spin and Count!

**START**

**END**

**DIRECTIONS** Play with a partner. Place game markers on START. Use a pencil and a paper clip to spin for a number. Take turns spinning. Each player moves his or her marker to the next space that has the same number of objects as the number on the spinner. The first player to reach END wins.

**MATERIALS** two game markers, pencil, paper clip

# Chapter 4 Vocabulary

**and**

y

4

**compare**

comparar

13

**greater**

mayor

31

**less**

menor, menos

38

**match**

emparejar

41

**pairs**

pares

50

**same number**

el mismo número

57

**ten**

diez

74

**Compare** the cubes.

 **and**

2 + 2

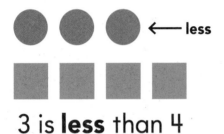 ← **less**

3 is **less** than 4

 6

9

9 is **greater** than 6

3

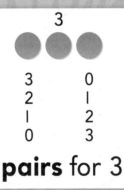

3  0
2  1
1  2
0  3

**pairs** for 3

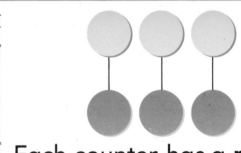

Each counter has a **match**.

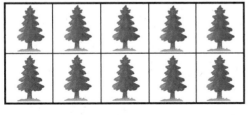

10

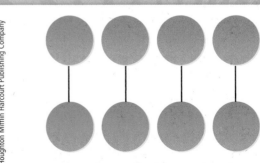

**same number** of red counters in each row

# Memory

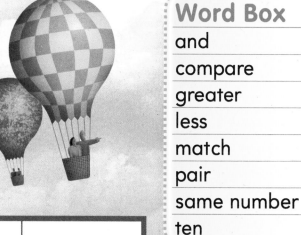

### Word Box

and
compare
greater
less
match
pair
same number
ten

**DIRECTIONS** Shuffle the Word Cards. Place each card facedown on a different square above. A player turns over two cards. If they match, the player tells what they know about the word and keeps the cards. If they do not match, the player turns the cards facedown again. Players take turns. The player with more pairs wins.

**MATERIALS** I set of Word Cards

# The Write Way

**DIRECTIONS** Draw to show how to compare two sets of objects.
**Reflect** Be ready to tell about your drawing.

© Houghton Mifflin Harcourt Publishing Company • Image Credits: (t) ©Dynamic Graphics Group/Getty Images

Name _____

# Model and Count 10

**Essential Question** How can you show and count 10 objects?

Common Core   **Counting and Cardinality—K.CC.B.5, K.OA.A.3** *Also K.CC.B.4a, K.CC.B.4b, K.CC.B.4c*

**MATHEMATICAL PRACTICES**
**MP4, MP5**

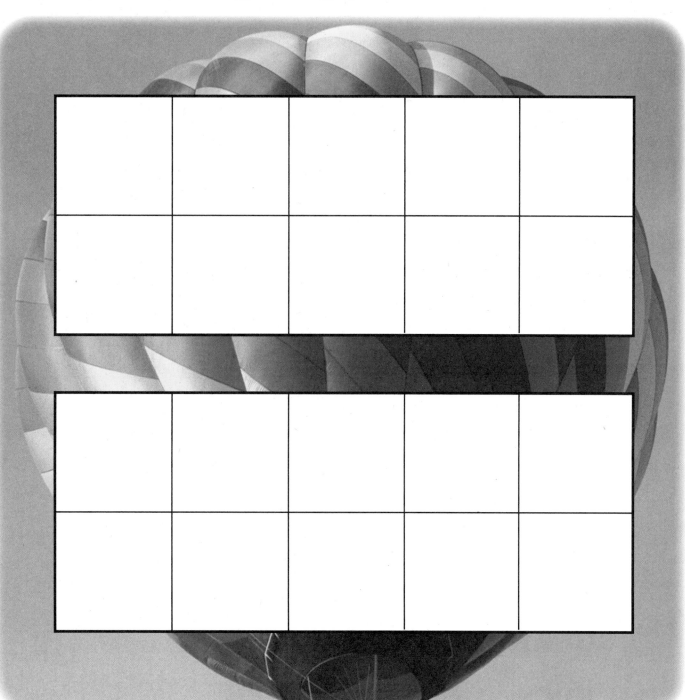

**DIRECTIONS** Use counters to model 9 in the top ten frame. Use counters to model 10 in the bottom ten frame. Draw the counters. Tell about the ten frames.

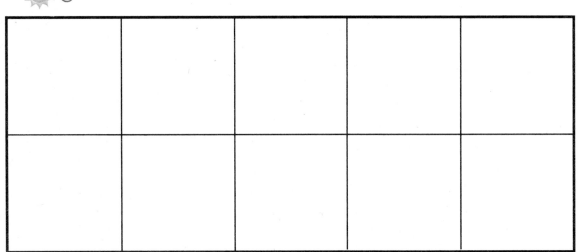

ten

**DIRECTIONS** 1. Place a counter on each balloon. 2. Move the counters to the ten frame. Draw the counters. Point to each counter as you count it. Trace the number.

**3**

**10**

**ten**

___ ⬤ **and** ___ ⬤

___ ⬤ **and** ___ ⬤

___ ⬤ **and** ___ ⬤

___ ⬤ **and** ___ ⬤

**DIRECTIONS** **3.** Trace the number. Use counters to model the different ways to make 10. Write to show some pairs of numbers that make 10.

Chapter 4 • Lesson 1

# Problem Solving • Applications (Real World)

WRITE Math

**4.**

**5.**

© Houghton Mifflin Harcourt Publishing Company

**DIRECTIONS  4.** Michelle puts her star stickers in sets of 10. Circle all the sets of star stickers that belong to Michelle.  **5.** Draw to show what you know about the number 10. Tell a friend about your drawing.

**HOME ACTIVITY •** Ask your child to show a set of nine objects. Then have him or her show one more object and tell how many objects are in the set.

# Model and Count 10

**Common Core** **COMMON CORE STANDARD—K.CC.B.5,**
**K.OA.A.3**
*Count to tell the number of objects.*

**ten**

_____ _____

_____ **and** _____

_____ _____

_____ **and** _____

_____ _____

_____ **and** _____

_____ _____

_____ **and** _____

---

**DIRECTIONS** Trace the number. Use counters to model the different ways to make 10.
Color to show the counters below. Write to show some pairs of numbers that make 10.

**Chapter 4**

one hundred eighty-five **185**

## Lesson Check <sub>(K.CC.B.5)</sub>

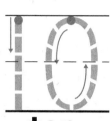

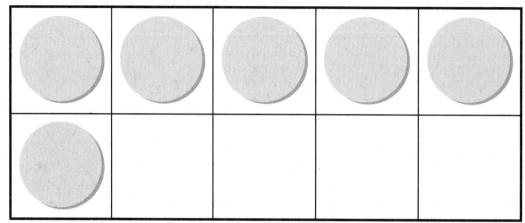

## Spiral Review <sub>(K.CC.C.6, K.CC.A.3)</sub>

**DIRECTIONS** **1.** Trace the number. How many more counters would you place in the ten frame to model a way to make 10? Draw the counters. **2.** Count how many kites. Write the number. Draw to show a set of counters that has the same number as the set of kites. Write the number. **3.** Count and tell how many. Write the number.

**186** one hundred eighty-six

FOR MORE PRACTICE GO TO THE Personal Math Trainer

Name _____

# Count and Write to 10

**Essential Question** How can you count and write up to 10 with words and numbers?

Common Core **Counting and Cardinality—K.CC.A.3**
*Also K.CC.B.4b, K.CC.B.5*
MATHEMATICAL PRACTICES
MP2

Listen and Draw (Real World)

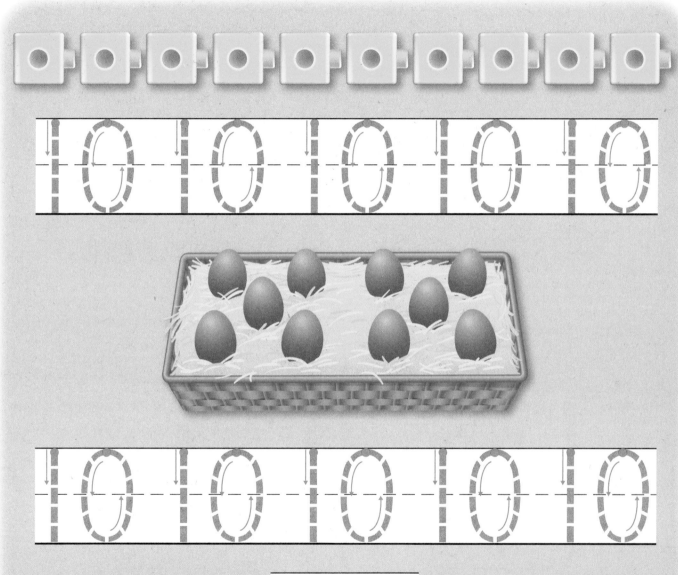

**DIRECTIONS** Count and tell how many cubes. Trace the numbers. Count and tell how many eggs. Trace the numbers and the word.

**Chapter 4 • Lesson 2**

one hundred eighty-seven **187**

**10**

**ten**

❷

_____

- - - - - - - -

_____

❸

_____

- - - - - - - -

_____

❹ ✓

_____

- - - - - - - -

_____

❺ ✓

_____

- - - - - - - -

_____

**DIRECTIONS** 1. Count and tell how many eggs. Trace the number. **2–5.** Count and tell how many eggs. Write the number.

**6**

# 10
**ten**

10  10  10  10  10

**7**

_____

- - - - - - - - - -

_____

**8**

_____

- - - - - - - - - -

_____

**9**

_____

- - - - - - - - - -

_____

**DIRECTIONS   6.** Say the number. Trace the numbers.
**7–9.** Count and tell how many. Write the number.

## Problem Solving • Applications

**WRITE Math**

10

_____

_ _ _ _ _ _ _ _

_____

**DIRECTIONS** 10. Draw to show a set that has a number of objects one greater than 9. Write how many objects. Tell a friend about your drawing.

**HOME ACTIVITY** • Show ten objects. Have your child point to each object in the set as he or she counts them. Then have him or her write the number on paper to show how many objects.

Name _____

# Count and Write to 10

Common Core

**COMMON CORE STANDARD—K.CC.A.3**
*Know number names and the count sequence.*

**1**

## 10
ten

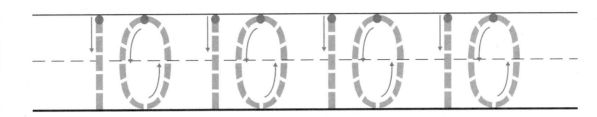

---

**2**

_____

- - - - - - - - -

_____

---

**3**

_____

- - - - - - - - -

_____

---

**4**

_____

- - - - - - - - -

_____

---

**DIRECTIONS**  1. Say the number. Trace the numbers.
**2–4.** Count and tell how many. Write the number.

## Lesson Check (K.CC.A.3)

_____

- - - - - - - - - - -

_____

## Spiral Review (K.CC.C.6, K.CC.B.4a)

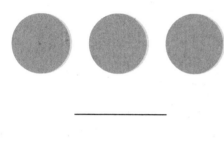          

_____          _____

- - - - - - -          - - - - - - -

_____          _____

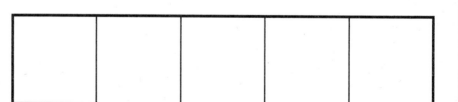

**DIRECTIONS** I. Count and tell how many ears of corn. Write the number.  **2.** Count and tell how many are in each set. Write the numbers. Compare the numbers. Circle the number that is less.  **3.** How many counters would you place in the five frame? Trace the number.

FOR MORE PRACTICE
GO TO THE
**Personal Math Trainer**

Name _____

# Algebra • Ways to Make 10

**Essential Question** How can you use a drawing to make 10 from a given number?

**Listen and Draw**

**Common Core** **Operations and Algebraic Thinking—K.OA.A.4**
*Also K.OA.A.3*
**MATHEMATICAL PRACTICES**
**MP4, MP7**

cubes

cubes

4

6

**DIRECTIONS** Use cubes of two colors to show different ways to make 10. Trace the number of red cubes. Trace the number of cubes in all.

**Chapter 4 • Lesson 3**

one hundred ninety-three **193**

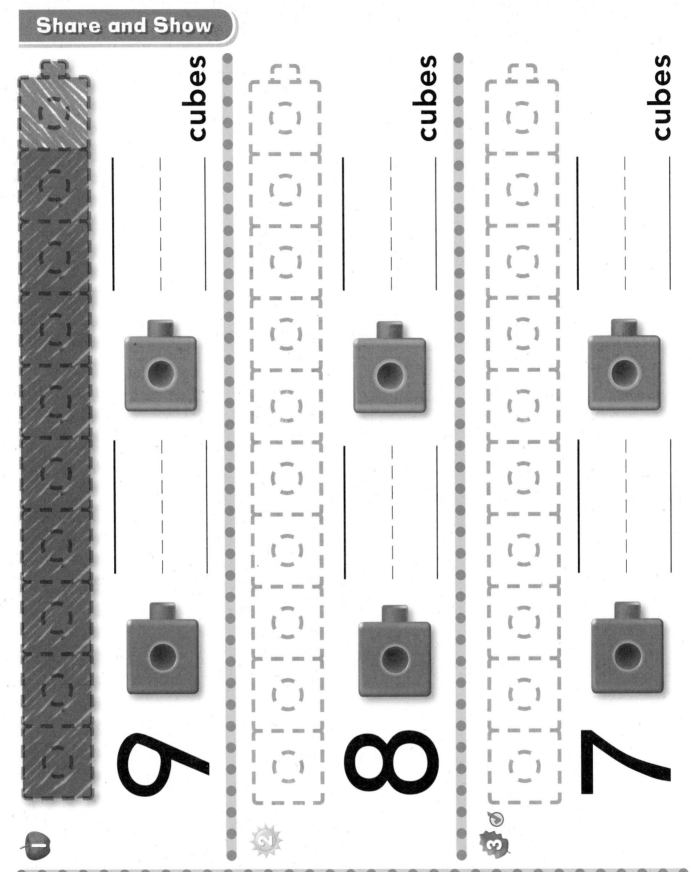

**1.** cubes

**9**

**2.** cubes

**8**

**3.** cubes

**7**

**DIRECTIONS** 1. Count and tell how many cubes of each color there are. Write how many red cubes. Write how many cubes in all. 2–3. Use blue to color the cubes to match the number. Use red to color the other cubes. Write how many red cubes. Write how many cubes in all.

194 one hundred ninety-four

Name _____

cubes

cubes

cubes

5

3

2

**DIRECTIONS** 4–6. Use blue to color the cubes to match the number. Use red to color the other cubes. Write how many red cubes. Write how many cubes in all.

Chapter 4 • Lesson 3

## Problem Solving • Applications

WRITE Math

10

10

10

**DIRECTIONS** 7–9. Jill uses the dot side of two Number Tiles to make 10. Draw the dots on each Number Tile to show a way Jill can make 10. Write the numbers.

 **HOME ACTIVITY •** Ask your child to show a set of 10 objects, using objects of the same kind that are different in one way; for example, large and small paper clips. Then have him or her write the numbers that show how many of each kind are in the set.

196 one hundred ninety-six

# Algebra • Ways to Make 10

Common Core

**COMMON CORE STANDARD—K.OA.A.4**
*Understand addition as putting together and adding to, and understand subtraction as taking apart and taking from.*

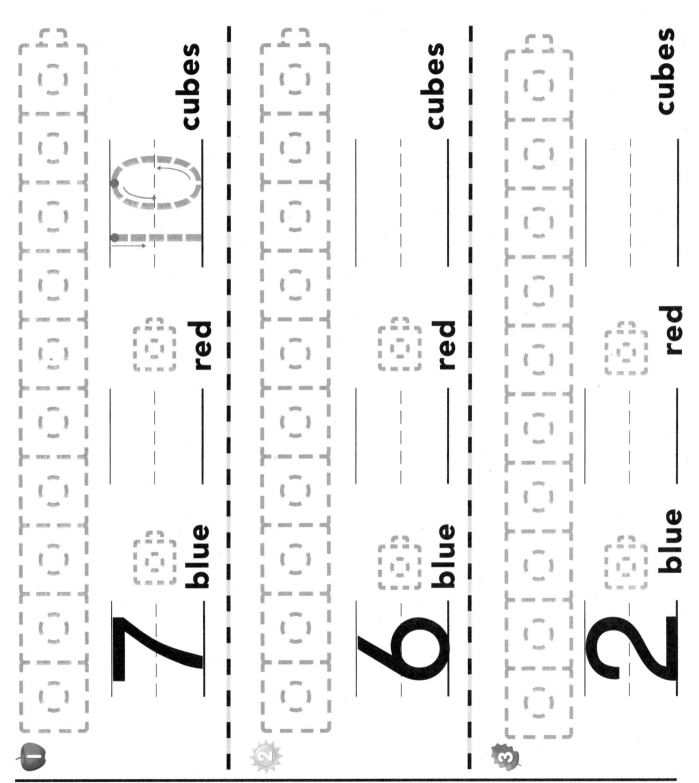

1   _____ cubes  _____ red  7 blue

2   _____ cubes  _____ red  6 blue

3   _____ cubes  _____ red  2 blue

**DIRECTIONS**   1–3. Use blue to color the cubes to match the number. Use red to color the other cubes. Write how many red cubes. Trace or write the number that shows how many cubes in all.

## Lesson Check (K.OA.A.4)

 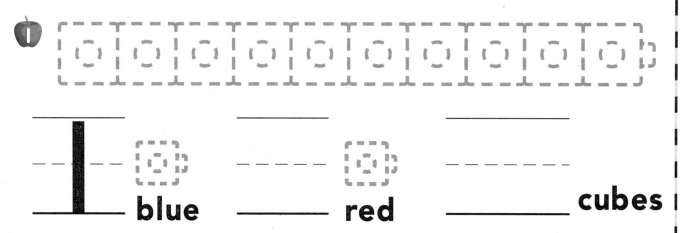

**1** _____  **blue**  _____  **red**  _____ **cubes**

## Spiral Review (K.CC.C.6, K.CC.A.3)

 **2**

_____

- - - - - - -

_____

_____

- - - - - - -

_____

**3**

_____

- - - - - - -

_____

**DIRECTIONS** **1.** Use blue to color the cube to match the number. Use red to color the other cubes. Write how many red cubes. Write the number that shows how many cubes in all. **2.** Count and tell how many are in each set. Write the numbers. Compare the numbers. Circle the number that is greater. **3.** How many birds are there? Write the number.

**198** one hundred ninety-eight

FOR MORE PRACTICE GO TO THE
Personal Math Trainer

Name _____

# Count and Order to 10

**Essential Question** How can you count forward to 10 from a given number?

Common Core · Counting and Cardinality—K.CC.A.2
MATHEMATICAL PRACTICES
MP2

**Listen and Draw**

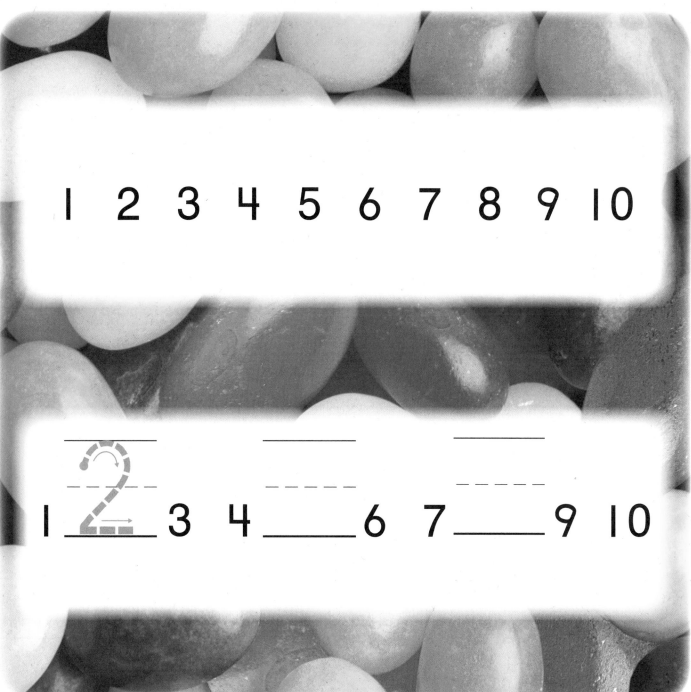

1  2  3  4  5  6  7  8  9  10

1  2  3  4  _  6  7  _  9  10

**DIRECTIONS** Point to the numbers in the top workspace as you count forward to 10. Trace and write the numbers in order in the bottom workspace as you count forward to 10.

**Chapter 4 • Lesson 4**

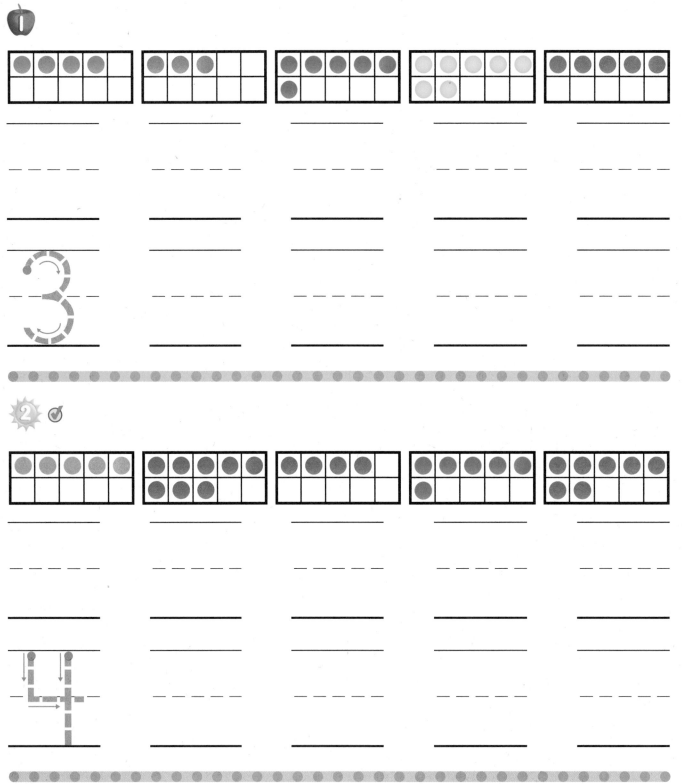

**DIRECTIONS** 1–2. Count the dots of each color in the ten frames. Write the numbers. Look at the next line. Write the numbers in order as you count forward from the dashed number.

Name _____

**3**

_____   _____   _____   _____   _____

- - - - - - - - - - - - - - - - - - - - - - - - - - - - - - - - - - - - - - - - - - - - - -

_____   _____   _____   _____   _____

5

_____   _____   _____   _____   _____

● ● ● ● ● ● ● ● ● ● ● ● ● ● ● ● ● ● ● ● ● ● ● ● ● ● ● ● ● ● ● ● ●

**4** ⊘

_____   _____   _____   _____   _____

- - - - - - - - - - - - - - - - - - - - - - - - - - - - - - - - - - - - - - - - - - - - - -

_____   _____   _____   _____   _____

6

_____   _____   _____   _____   _____

● ● ● ● ● ● ● ● ● ● ● ● ● ● ● ● ● ● ● ● ● ● ● ● ● ● ● ● ● ● ● ● ●

**DIRECTIONS**  3–4. Count the dots of each color in the ten frames. Write the numbers. Look at the next line. Write the numbers in order as you count forward from the dashed number.

**HOME ACTIVITY** • Write the numbers 1 to 10 in order on a piece of paper. Ask your child to point to each number as he or she counts to 10. Repeat beginning with a number other than 1 when counting.

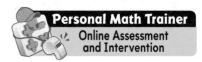

**Concepts and Skills**

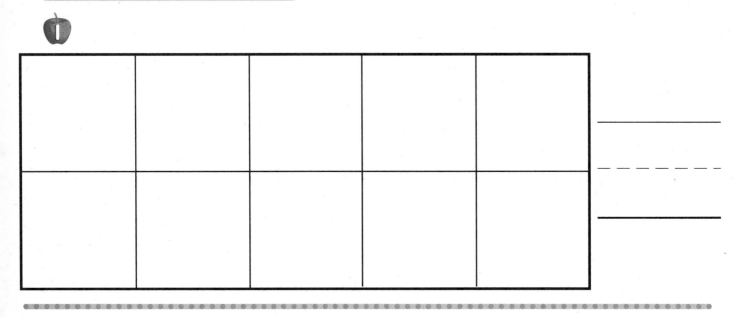

_____
- - - - - - -
_____

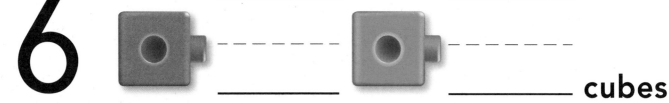

**6**  _____    _____

- - - - - - - -    - - - - - - - -

_____    _____ cubes

**7  8  _____  10**

**DIRECTIONS** **1.** Place counters in the ten frame to model ten. Draw the counters. Write the number. (K.CC.B.5) **2.** Use blue to color the cubes to match the number. Use red to color the other cubes. Write how many red cubes. Write how many cubes in all. (K.OA.A.4) **3.** Count forward. Write the number to complete the counting order. (K.CC.A.2)

# Count and Order to 10

Common Core  **COMMON CORE STANDARD—K.CC.A.2**
*Know number names and the count sequence.*

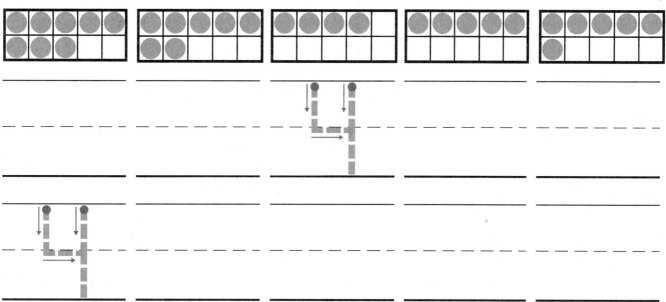

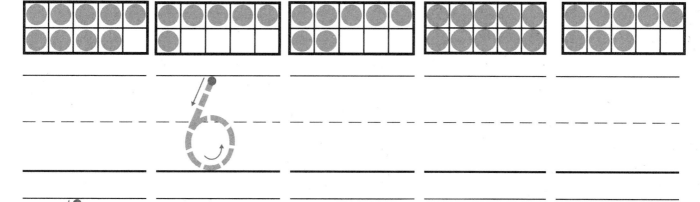

**DIRECTIONS** 1–2. Count the dots in the ten frames. Trace or write the numbers. Look at the next line. Write the numbers in order as you count forward from the dashed number.

# Lesson Check (K.CC.A.2)

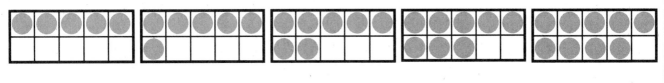

# Spiral Review (K.CC.C.6, K.CC.A.3)

**DIRECTIONS** **I.** Count the dots in the ten frames. Trace the number. Write the numbers in order as you count forward from the dashed number. **2.** Count and tell how many are in each set. Write the numbers. Compare the numbers. Circle the number that is less. **3.** How many counters are there? Write the number.

FOR MORE PRACTICE
GO TO THE
**Personal Math Trainer**

Name _____

# Problem Solving • Compare by Matching Sets to 10

Common Core
Counting and Cardinality—K.CC.C.6
Also K.CC.C.7
MATHEMATICAL PRACTICES
MP4, MP5, MP8

**Essential Question** How can you solve problems using the strategy *make a model*?

**Unlock the Problem**

**DIRECTIONS** Break a ten-cube train into two parts. How can you use matching to compare the parts? Tell a friend about the cube trains. Draw the cube trains.

Chapter 4 • Lesson 5

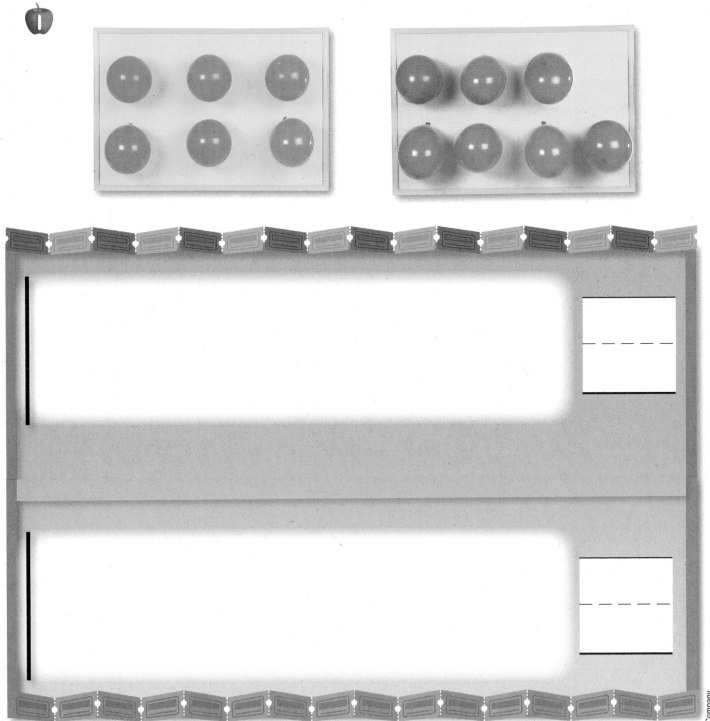

**DIRECTIONS** I. Malia has the red balloons. Andrew has the blue balloons. Who has more balloons? Use *i*Tools or red and blue cube trains to model the sets of balloons. Compare the cube trains by matching. Draw and color the cube trains. Write how many in each set. Which number is greater? Circle that number.

Name _____

**☀2** ✓

_____

– – – – – – – –

_____

_____

– – – – – – – –

_____

**🍁3**

_____

– – – – – – –

_____

_____

– – – – – – –

_____

**DIRECTIONS** **2.** Kyle has 9 tickets. Jared has 7 tickets. Who has fewer tickets? Use cube trains to model the sets of tickets. Compare the cube trains by matching. Draw and color the cube trains. Write how many. Circle the number that is less. **3.** Phil won 8 prizes. Naomi won 5 prizes. Who won fewer prizes? Use cube trains to model the sets of prizes. Compare the cube trains by matching. Draw and color the cube trains. Write how many. Circle the number that is less.

**Chapter 4 • Lesson 5**                                        two hundred seven  **207**

## On Your Own

**WRITE Math**

4

_____

- - - - - - - - - -

_____

_____

- - - - - - - - - -

_____

**DIRECTIONS**  **4.** Ryan has a cube train with red and blue cubes. Does his cube train have more blue cubes or more red cubes? Make cube trains of each color from the cubes in Ryan's cube train. Compare the cube trains by matching. Draw and color the cube trains. Write how many cubes are in each train. Circle the greater number.

**HOME ACTIVITY** • Ask your child to show two sets of up to 10 objects each. Then have him or her compare the sets by matching and tell which set has more objects.

# Problem Solving • Compare by Matching Sets to 10

Common Core

**COMMON CORE STANDARD—K.CC.C.6**
*Compare numbers.*

**1**

_____

- - - - -

_____

- - - - -

_____

**2**

_____

- - - - -

_____

_____

- - - - -

_____

**DIRECTIONS** **1.** Kim has 7 red balloons. Jake has 3 blue balloons. Who has fewer balloons? Use cube trains to model the sets of balloons. Compare the cube trains. Draw and color the cube trains. Write how many. Circle the number that is less. **2.** Meg has 8 red beads. Beni has 5 blue beads. Who has more beads? Use cube trains to model the sets of beads. Compare the cube trains by matching. Draw and color the cube trains. Write how many. Circle the number that is greater.

# Lesson Check (K.CC.C.6)

**1**

_____

_ _ _ _ _ _ _

_____

_____

_ _ _ _ _ _ _

_____

## Spiral Review (K.CC.C.6, K.CC.B.4b)

**2**

_____

_ _ _ _ _ _ _

_____

_____

_ _ _ _ _ _ _

_____

**3**

_____

_ _ _ _ _ _ _

_____

**DIRECTIONS** **1.** Mia has 6 red marbles. Zack has 2 blue marbles. Who has more marbles? Use cube trains to model the sets of marbles. Compare the cube trains by matching. Draw and color the cube trains. Write how many. Circle the number that is greater. **2.** Count and tell how many are in each set. Write the numbers. Compare the numbers. Circle the number that is greater. **3.** Count and tell how many. Write the number.

**210** two hundred ten

**FOR MORE PRACTICE GO TO THE** Personal Math Trainer

Name _____

# Compare by Counting Sets to 10

**Essential Question** How can you use counting strategies to compare sets of objects?

Common Core **Counting and Cardinality—K.CC.C.6**
*Also K.CC.B.5, K.CC.C.7*
**MATHEMATICAL PRACTICES**
**MP6, MP8**

## Listen and Draw Real World

**DIRECTIONS** Look at the sets of objects. Count how many in each set. Trace the numbers that show how many. Compare the numbers.

_____

_ _ _ _ _ _ _ _

_____

_____

_ _ _ _ _ _ _ _

_____

_____

_ _ _ _ _ _ _ _

_____

**DIRECTIONS** 1–3. Count how many in each set. Write the number of objects in each set. Compare the numbers. Circle the greater number.

Name _____

**4**

_____

- - - - - - -

_____

_____

- - - - - - -

_____

**5**

_____

- - - - - - -

_____

_____

- - - - - - -

_____

**6**

_____

- - - - - - -

_____

_____

- - - - - - -

_____

**DIRECTIONS** 4–6. Count how many in each set. Write the number of objects in each set. Compare the numbers. Circle the number that is less.

## Problem Solving • Applications (Real World)

**WRITE Math**

**7**

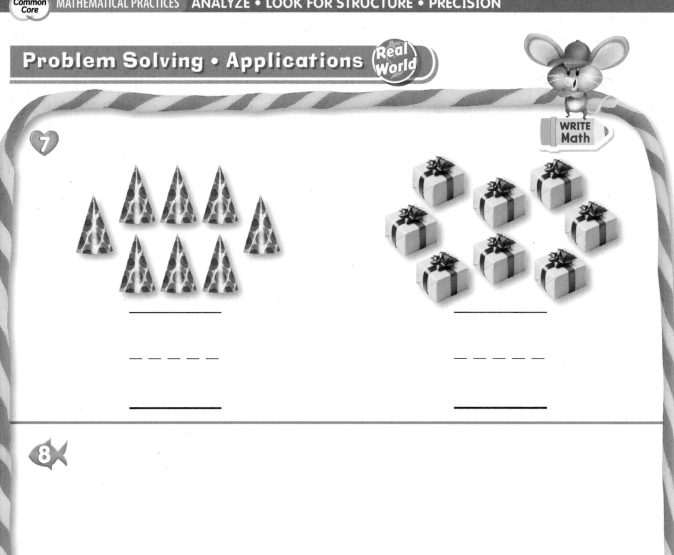

_____

_ _ _ _ _

_____

_____

_ _ _ _ _

_____

**8**

**DIRECTIONS** **7.** Megan bought hats and gifts for a party. How many hats did she buy? How many gifts did she buy? Write the number of objects in each set. Compare the numbers. Tell a friend about the sets. **8.** Draw to show what you know about counting sets to 10 with the same number of objects.

**HOME ACTIVITY •** Show your child two sets of up to 10 objects. Have him or her count the objects in each set. Then have him or her compare the numbers of objects in each set, and tell what he or she knows about those numbers.

Name _____

# Compare by Counting Sets to 10

 COMMON CORE STANDARD—K.CC.C.6
*Compare numbers.*

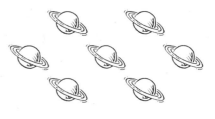

_____

- - - - - - - - -

_____

---

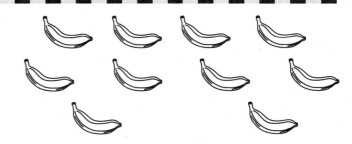

_____

- - - - - - - - -

_____

---

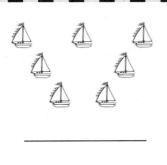

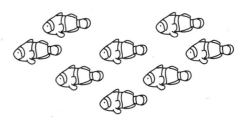

_____

- - - - - - - - -

_____

---

**DIRECTIONS** Count how many in each set. Write the number of objects in each set. Compare the numbers. **1–2.** Circle the number that is less. **3.** Circle the number that is greater.

**Chapter 4**

## Lesson Check (K.CC.C.6)

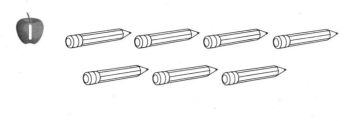

_____

_ _ _ _ _ _ _ _

_____

_____

_ _ _ _ _ _ _ _

_____

## Spiral Review (K.CC.A.3, K.CC.B.5)

_____

_ _ _ _ _ _ _ _

_____

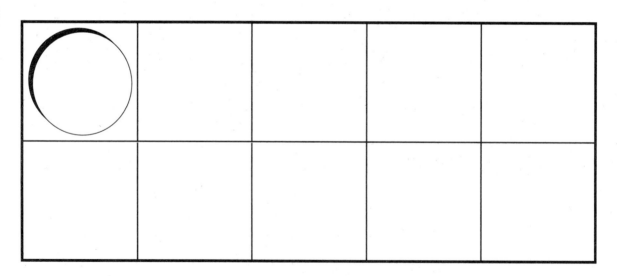

**DIRECTIONS** **1.** Count and tell how many are in each set. Write the numbers. Compare the numbers. Circle the number that is less. **2.** How many whistles are there? Write the number. **3.** How many more counters would you place in the ten frame to show a way to make 6? Draw the counters.

FOR MORE PRACTICE
GO TO THE
**Personal Math Trainer**

Name _____

# Compare Two Numbers

**Essential Question** How can you compare two numbers between 1 and 10?

Counting and Cardinality—
K.CC.C.7
MATHEMATICAL PRACTICES
MP6, MP8

**Listen and Draw** *Real World*

## 7

**7 is less than 8**

**7 is greater than 8**

## 8

**8 is less than 7**

**8 is greater than 7**

**DIRECTIONS** Look at the numbers. As you count forward does 7 come before or after 8? Is it greater or less than 8? Circle the words that describe the numbers when comparing them.

**1**

3          8

**2**

10          5

**3**

6          4

**4** ✓

7          9

**5** ✓

10          8

**DIRECTIONS** 1. Look at the numbers. Think about the counting order as you compare the numbers. Trace the circle around the greater number. 2–5. Look at the numbers. Think about the counting order as you compare the numbers. Circle the greater number.

**6**

2          4

**7**

5          3

**8**

8          9

**9**

10          7

**10**

6          8

**DIRECTIONS** 6–10. Look at the numbers. Think about the counting order as you compare the numbers. Circle the number that is less.

## Problem Solving • Applications

**WRITE Math**

**11.**

_____

— — — — —

_____

_____

— — — — —

_____

**12.**

_____

— — — — —

_____

_____

— — — — —

_____

**DIRECTIONS** **11.** John has a number of apples that is greater than 5 and less than 7. Cody has a number of apples that is two less than 8. Write how many apples each boy has. Compare the numbers. Tell a friend about the numbers. **12.** Write two numbers between 1 and 10. Tell a friend about the two numbers.

**HOME ACTIVITY •** Write the numbers 1 to 10 on individual pieces of paper. Select two numbers and ask your child to compare the numbers and tell which number is greater and which number is less.

**220** two hundred twenty

# Compare Two Numbers

Common Core

**COMMON CORE STANDARD—K.CC.C.7**
Compare numbers.

1.  8          5

2.  10          7

3.  6          9

4.  4          6

5.  8          7

6.  5          3

**DIRECTIONS** 1–3. Look at the numbers. Think about the counting order as you compare the numbers. Circle the greater number. 4–6. Look at the numbers. Think about the counting order as you compare the numbers. Circle the number that is less.

# 7                                    8

**2**

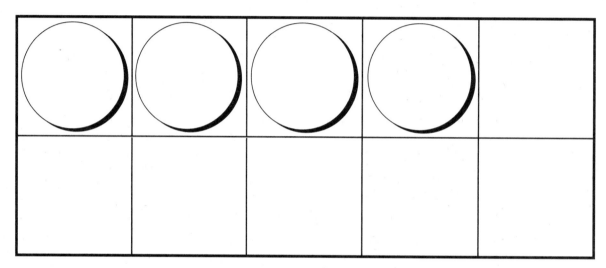

**3**

_____

— — — — — — —

_____

**DIRECTIONS** 1. Look at the numbers. Think about the counting order as you compare the numbers. Circle the greater number. 2. How many more counters would you place in the ten frame to show a way to make 8? Draw the counters. 3. How many birds are there? Write the number.

FOR MORE PRACTICE
GO TO THE
**Personal Math Trainer**

Name _____

 **Chapter 4 Review/Test**

_____
- - - - - - - - - - - - - - -
_____

# 10

| nine |
| ten |

**DIRECTIONS** 1. Circle all the sets that have 10 stars.
2. How many eggs are shown? Write the number.
3. What is another way to write 10? Circle the word.

**Chapter 4**

 **Assessment Options
Chapter Test**

4

______ cubes

______  ______ 

5

3 7

Personal Math Trainer

6 THINK SMARTER +

| | | |
|---|---|---|
| 5 6 7 8 | ○ Yes | ○ No |
| 8 10 9 7 | ○ Yes | ○ No |
| 7 8 9 10 | ○ Yes | ○ No |

**DIRECTIONS** **4.** Write how many red cubes. Write how many blue cubes. Write how many cubes in all. **5.** Look at the numbers. Think about the counting order as you compare the numbers. Circle the number that is less. **6.** Are the numbers in counting order? Choose Yes or No.

Name _____

● ● ● ● ● ● ● ●

_____

🐟 8

_____

🐚 9

# 7  8  9

○        ○        ○

**DIRECTIONS** **7.** Write how many counters are in the set. Use matching lines
to draw a set of counters less than the number of counters shown. Write the
number. Circle the number that is less.   **8.** Count how many in each set. Write
the numbers. Circle the greater number.   **9.** Think about counting order.
Choose the number that is less than 8.

**10**

_____

- - - - - - - - - - -

_____

**11**

_____

- - - - - - - - - - -

_____

_____

- - - - - - - - - - -

_____

**12**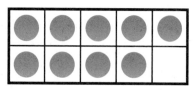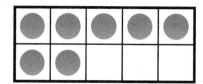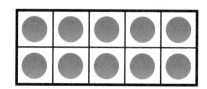

•                  •                  •

•                  •                  •

# 10    9    7

**DIRECTIONS   10.** How many cans of paint are there? Write the number.   **11.** Seth has 10 buttons. Draw Seth's buttons. The number of buttons Tina has is one less than Seth's. Draw Tina's buttons. How many buttons does Tina have? Write how many in each set. Circle the number that is less.   **12.** Match sets to the numbers that show how many counters.

# Chapter 5

# Addition

### Curious About Math with

### Curious George

Most ladybugs have red, orange, or yellow wing covers and black spots.

- How many ladybugs do you see?

Name _____

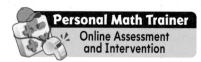 
## More

_ _ _ _ _ _ _ _

_____

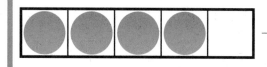

_ _ _ _ _ _ _ _

_____

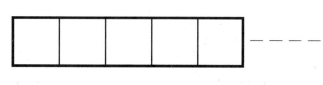

_ _ _ _ _ _ _ _

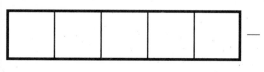

_ _ _ _ _ _ _ _

## Compare Numbers to 10

_____

_ _ _ _ _ _ _ _

_ _ _ _ _ _ _ _

This page checks understanding of important skills needed for success in Chapter 5.

**DIRECTIONS** 1–2. Count and tell how many. Draw a set with one more counter. Write how many in each set. 3. Write the number of cubes in each set. Circle the number that is greater than the other number.

Name _____

ten

**DIRECTIONS** Count and tell how many birds are on the ground. Count and tell how many birds are flying. Write these numbers to show a pair of numbers that make ten.

 • **Interactive Student Edition**
• **Multimedia _eGlossary_**

# Game Pairs That Make 7

**DIRECTIONS** Play with a partner. The first player rolls the number cube and writes the number on the yellow boat. Partners determine what number makes 7 when paired with the number on the yellow boat. Players take turns rolling the number cube until that number is rolled. Write the number beside it on the green boat. Partners continue to roll the number cube finding pairs of numbers that make 7.

**MATERIALS** number cube (1–6)

# Chapter 5 Vocabulary

| | |
|---|---|
| **add**<br>sumar<br>2 | **eight**<br>ocho<br>20 |
| **is equal to**<br>es igual a<br>36 | **nine**<br>nueve<br>45 |
| **plus (+)**<br>más (+)<br>51 | **seven**<br>siete<br>59 |
| **six**<br>seis<br>64 | **ten**<br>diez<br>74 |

8

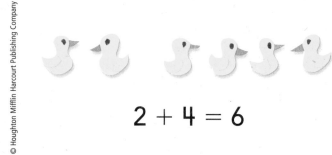

$2 + 4 = 6$

9

$3 + 2 = 5$

**is equal to**

7

$2 + 2 = 4$

**plus** sign

10

6

# Bingo

**Word Box**

add

is equal to

plus

ten

six

seven

eight

nine

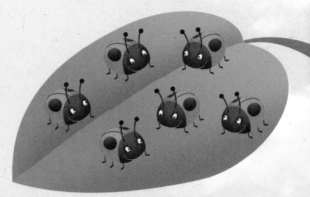

## Player 1

| six | eight | nine | plus | is equal to | add |
|-----|-------|------|------|-------------|-----|

## Player 2

| plus | ten | is equal to | seven | add | eight |
|------|-----|-------------|-------|-----|-------|

**DIRECTIONS** Shuffle the Vocabulary Cards and place in a pile. A player takes the top word card from the pile and tells what they know about the word. The player puts a counter on that word on the board. Players take turns. The first player to cover all the words on his or her board says "Bingo."

**MATERIALS** 2 sets of Vocabulary Cards, 6 two-color counters for each player

# The Write Way

$$5 = \underline{\quad} + \underline{\quad}$$

**DIRECTIONS** Draw and write to show how to find a number pair for 5.
**Reflect** Be ready to tell about your drawing.

Name _____

# Addition: Add To

**Essential Question** How can you show addition as adding to?

Common Core **Operations and Algebraic Thinking—K.OA.A.1**

**MATHEMATICAL PRACTICES**
MP1, MP2

## Listen and Draw *Real World*

**DIRECTIONS** Listen to the addition word problem. Trace the number that shows how many children are on the swings. Trace the number that shows how many children are being added to the group. Trace the number that shows how many children there are now.

Chapter 5 • Lesson I

two hundred thirty-one **231**

 and ____

____

____

____

**DIRECTIONS** 1. Listen to the addition word problem. Trace the number that shows how many children are sitting eating lunch. Write the number that shows how many children are being added to the group. Write the number that shows how many children are having lunch now.

___ ___

___ **and** ___

___

___

___

**DIRECTIONS** 2. Listen to the addition word problem. Write the number that shows how many children are playing with the soccer ball. Write the number that shows how many children are being added to the group. Write the number that shows how many children there are now.

**Problem Solving • Applications**

3

WRITE Math

___ ___ **and** ___ ___

4

___ ___ ___

**DIRECTIONS  3.** Two sheep are in a pen. Two sheep are added to the pen. How can you write the numbers to show the sheep in the pen and the sheep being added?  **4.** Write how many sheep are in the pen now.

**HOME ACTIVITY •** Show your child a set of four objects. Have him or her add one object to the set and tell how many there are now.

## Addition: Add To

Common Core   **COMMON CORE STANDARD—K.OA.A.1**
*Understand addition as putting together and adding to, and understand subtraction as taking apart and taking from.*

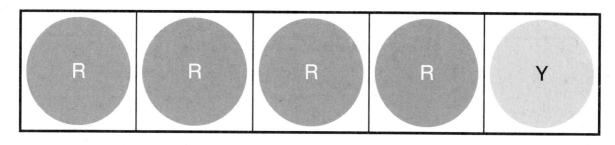

_____

- - - - - -     **and**     - - - - - -

_____                            _____

- - - - - - - - - - - - - - - - - - - - - - - - - - - - - - - - - - -

_____

- - - - -

_____

**DIRECTIONS**  **1.** There are four red counters in the five frame. One yellow counter is added. R is for red, and Y is for yellow. How many are there of each color counter? Write the numbers.  **2.** Write the number that shows how many counters are in the five frame now.

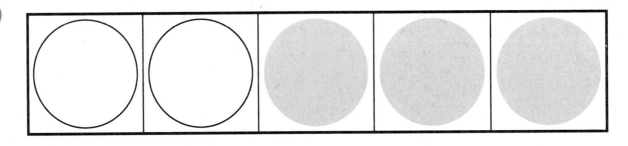

_____          **and**          _____

---

## Spiral Review (K.CC.A.3, K.CC.C.6)

_____

- - - - - - -

_____

_____                                    _____

- - - - - - -                              - - - - - - -

_____                                    _____

---

**DIRECTIONS** **I.** How many of each color counter? Write the numbers. **2.** Count and tell how many balloons. Write the number. **3.** Count and tell how many in each set. Write the numbers. Compare the numbers. Circle the number that is less.

FOR MORE PRACTICE
GO TO THE
Personal Math Trainer

Name _____

# Addition: Put Together

**Essential Question** How can you show addition as putting together?

Common Core

**Operations and Algebraic Thinking—K.OA.A.1**

**MATHEMATICAL PRACTICES**
MP2, MP4, MP5

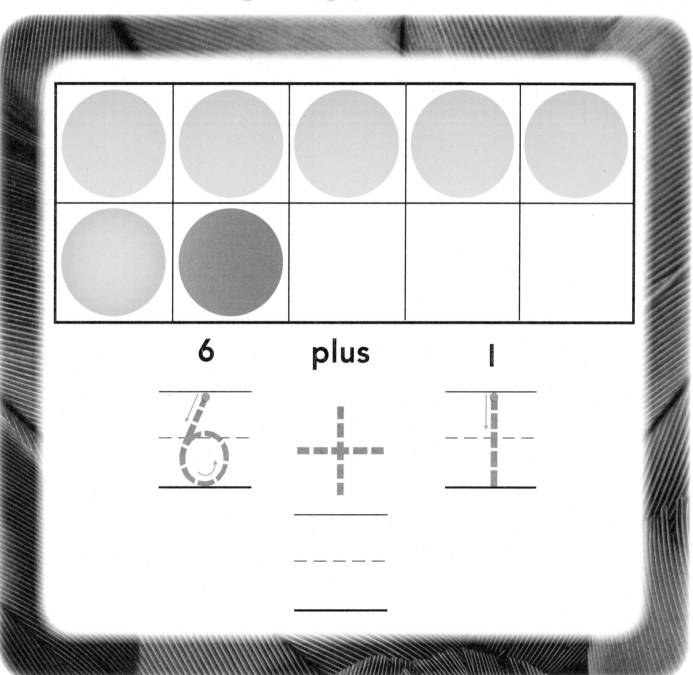

**6**          **plus**          **1**

**DIRECTIONS** Listen to the addition word problem. Place red and yellow counters in the ten frame as shown. Trace the numbers and the symbol to show the sets that are put together. Write the number that shows how many in all.

**Chapter 5 • Lesson 2**

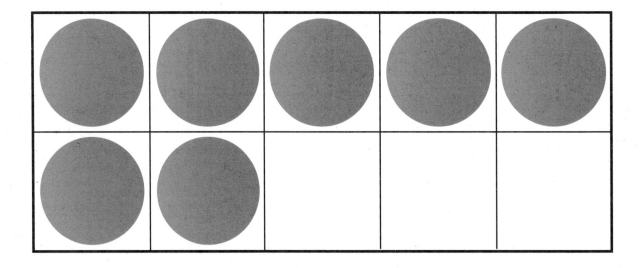

7     plus     2

_____     ╋     _____

_____

**DIRECTIONS** 1. Listen to the addition word problem. Place red counters in the ten frame as shown. Place yellow counters to model the sets that are put together. Write the numbers and trace the symbol. Write the number to show how many in all.

Name _____

<table>
<tr><td></td><td></td><td></td><td></td><td></td></tr>
<tr><td></td><td></td><td></td><td></td><td></td></tr>
</table>

**2**　　　　**plus**　　　　**8**

_____　　　　　　　_____

- - - - -　　　＋　　　- - - - -

_____　　　 ┃ 　　　_____

_____

- - - - -

_____

---

**DIRECTIONS** **2.** Listen to the addition word problem. Place counters in the ten frame to model the sets that are put together. How many are there of each color counter? Write the numbers and trace the symbol. Write the number to show how many in all.

## Problem Solving • Applications

**3**

_____        _____

- - - - -      - - - - -

_____        _____

**4**

_____

- - - - -

_____

**DIRECTIONS  3.** Four red apples and two green apples are on the table. Write the numbers and trace the symbol to show the apples being put together.  **4.** Write the number to show how many apples in all.

**HOME ACTIVITY •** Show your child two sets of four objects. Have him or her put the sets of objects together and tell how many in all.

# Addition: Put Together

Common
Core

**COMMON CORE STANDARD—K.OA.A.1**
*Understand addition as putting together and
adding to, and understand subtraction as
taking apart and taking from.*

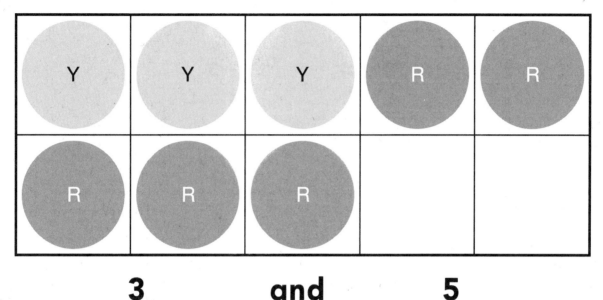

**3**     **and**     **5**

---

**DIRECTIONS**    Roy has three yellow counters and five red counters. How
many counters does he have in all? I.  Place counters in the ten frame to
model the sets that are put together. Y is for yellow, and R is for red. Write the
numbers and trace the symbol. Write the number to show how many in all.

## Lesson Check (K.OA.A.1)

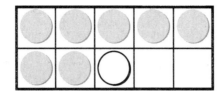

_____     _____
- - - - - - -   ═╬═     - - - - - - -
_____     _____

## Spiral Review (K.CC.A.2, K.CC.C.6)

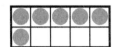 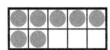 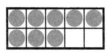 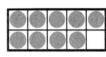 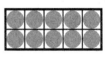

 6 ___  8 ___  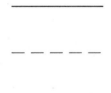 10

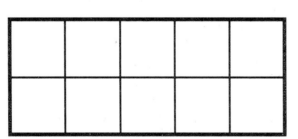

_____
- - - - - - -
_____

**DIRECTIONS** **1.** What numbers show the sets that are put together? Write the numbers and trace the symbol. **2.** Count the dots in the ten frames. Begin with 6. Write the numbers in order as you count forward. **3.** Paul has a number of counters two less than seven. Draw the counters in the ten frame. Write the number.

**242** two hundred forty-two

FOR MORE PRACTICE
GO TO THE
**Personal Math Trainer**

Name _____

# Problem Solving • Act Out Addition Problems

**Essential Question** How can you solve problems using the strategy *act it out*?

Common Core Operations and Algebraic Thinking—K.OA.A.1
MATHEMATICAL PRACTICES
MP1, MP2, MP4

## Unlock the Problem Real World

**DIRECTIONS** Listen to and act out the addition word problem. Trace the addition sentence. Tell a friend how many children in all.

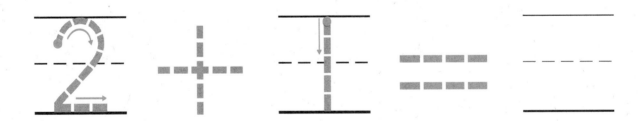

**DIRECTIONS** 1. Listen to and act out the addition word problem. Trace the numbers and the symbols. Write the number that shows how many children in all.

**244** two hundred forty-four

Name _____

**DIRECTIONS** **2.** Listen to and act out the addition word problem.
Trace the numbers and the symbols. Write the number that shows how
many children in all.

**Chapter 5 • Lesson 3**                    two hundred forty-five  **245**

## On Your Own (Real World)

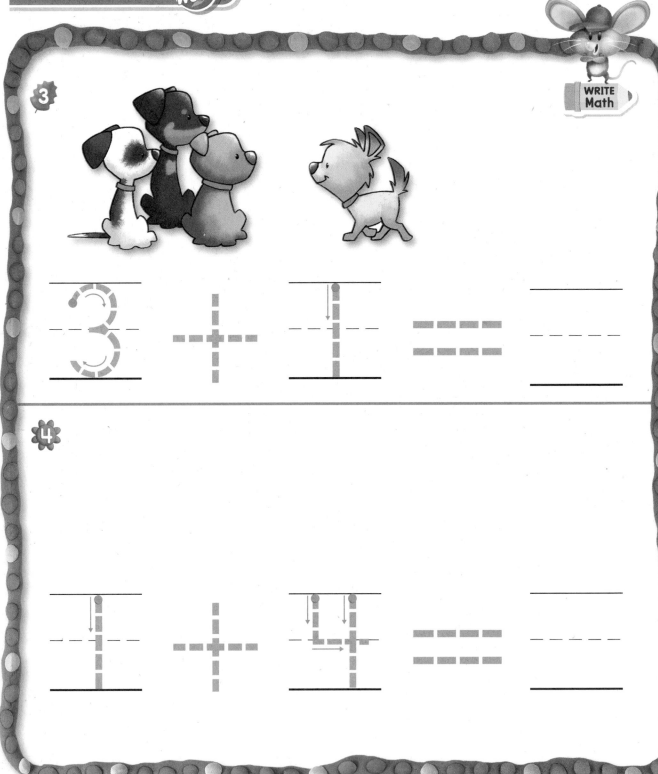

3

$3 + 1 = $ ___

4

$1 + 4 = $ ___

**DIRECTIONS  3.** Tell an addition word problem about the puppies. Trace the numbers and the symbols. Write the number that shows how many puppies there are now.  **4.** Draw a picture to match this addition sentence. Write how many in all. Tell a friend about your drawing.

**HOME ACTIVITY •** Tell your child a short word problem about adding three objects to a set of two objects. Have your child use toys to act out the word problem.

# Problem Solving • Act Out
# Addition Problems

**COMMON CORE STANDARD—K.OA.A.1**
*Understand addition as putting together and
adding to, and understand subtraction as
taking apart and taking from.*

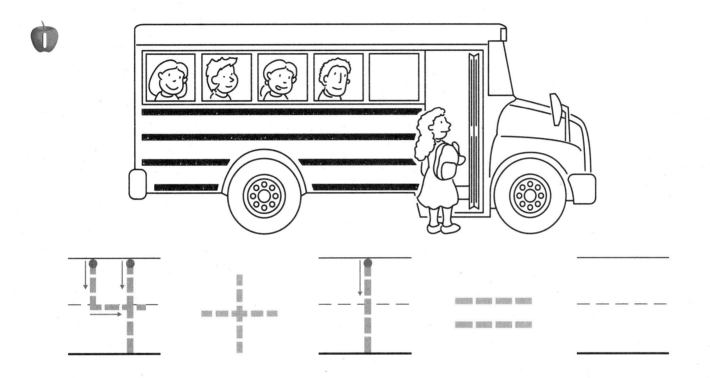

4 + 1 =  _____

3 + 2 =  _____

**DIRECTIONS** 1–2. Tell an addition word problem about the
children. Trace the numbers and the symbols. Write the number
that shows how many children in all.

# Lesson Check (K.OA.A.1)

**1**

$3 + 2 =$ _____

## Spiral Review (K.CC.A.3, K.CC.C.6)

**2**

_____

**3**

_____

**DIRECTIONS 1.** Tell an addition word problem. Trace the numbers and the symbols. Write the number that shows how many cats in all. **2.** Count and tell how many tigers. Write the number. **3.** Count how many bears. Write the number. Draw to show a set of counters that has the same number as the set of bears. Write the number.

FOR MORE PRACTICE
GO TO THE
**Personal Math Trainer**

Name _____

# Algebra • Model and Draw Addition Problems

**Essential Question** How can you use objects and drawings to solve addition word problems?

Common Core  **Operations and Algebraic Thinking—K.OA.A.5**
*Also K.OA.A.1, K.OA.A.2*
**MATHEMATICAL PRACTICES**
**MP1, MP2, MP4**

**Listen and Draw** *Real World*

**DIRECTIONS** Place cubes as shown. Listen to the addition word problem. Model to show the cubes put together in a cube train. Color to show how the cube train looks. Trace to complete the addition sentence.

**Chapter 5 • Lesson 4**

1

1 + 2 = 3

2 ✓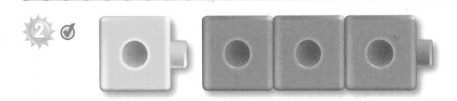

1 + 3 = ___

**DIRECTIONS** 1–2. Place cubes as shown. Listen to the addition word problem. Model to show the cubes put together. Draw the cube train. Trace and write to complete the addition sentence.

Name _____

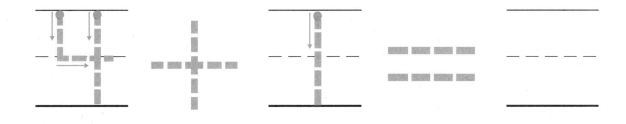

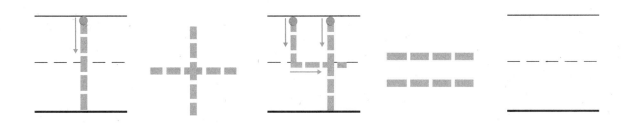

**DIRECTIONS** 3–4. Place cubes as shown. Listen to the addition word problem. Model to show the cubes put together. Draw the cube train. Trace and write to complete the addition sentence.

**Chapter 5 • Lesson 4**

two hundred fifty-one **251**

**Mid-Chapter Checkpoint**

**Concepts and Skills**

 **1**

_____          _____

— — — — —          — — — — —

**and**

•  •  •  •  •  •  •  •  •  •  •  •  •  •  •  •  •  •  •  •  •  •  •  •  •  •  •

 **2**

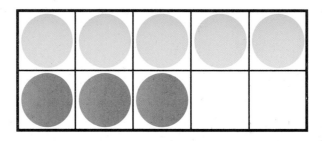

_____          _____

— — — —    **+**    — — — —

 **3** **THINK** SMARTER

I plus 3

I + 2

I plus 2

**DIRECTIONS** 1. Write the number that shows how many puppies are sitting. Write the number that shows how many puppies are being added to them. (K.OA.A.1) 2. Write the numbers and trace the symbol to show the sets that are put together. (K.OA.A.1) 3. Circle all the ways that show how many in all. (K.OA.A.1)

**252** two hundred fifty-two

# Algebra • Model and Draw
# Addition Problems

**COMMON CORE STANDARD—K.OA.A.5**
*Understand addition as putting together and adding to, and understand subtraction as taking apart and taking from.*

 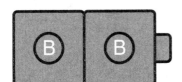 

  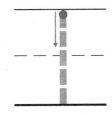

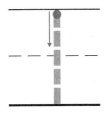  

**DIRECTIONS** 1–2. Place cubes as shown. B is for blue, and Y is for yellow. Tell an addition word problem. Model to show the cubes put together. Draw the cube train. Trace and write the numbers to complete the addition sentence.

**Chapter 5**

## Lesson Check (K.OA.A.5)

## Spiral Review (K.CC.A.3, K.CC.B.5)

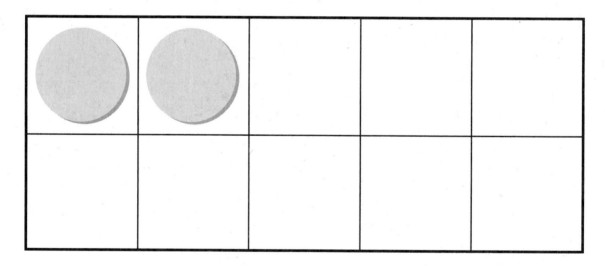

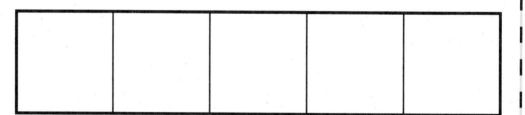

**DIRECTIONS** **1.** Look at the cube train. Tell an addition word problem. Trace and write to complete the addition sentence. **2.** How many more counters would you place to model a way to make 7? Draw the counters. **3.** Draw counters to make a set that shows the number.

FOR MORE PRACTICE
GO TO THE
**Personal Math Trainer**

# Algebra • Write Addition Sentences for 10

**Essential Question** How can you use a drawing to find the number that makes a ten from a given number?

Common Core

**Operations and Algebraic Thinking—K.OA.A.4**
*Also K.OA.A.1, K.OA.A.2*

**MATHEMATICAL PRACTICES**
**MP2, MP7, MP8**

## Listen and Draw

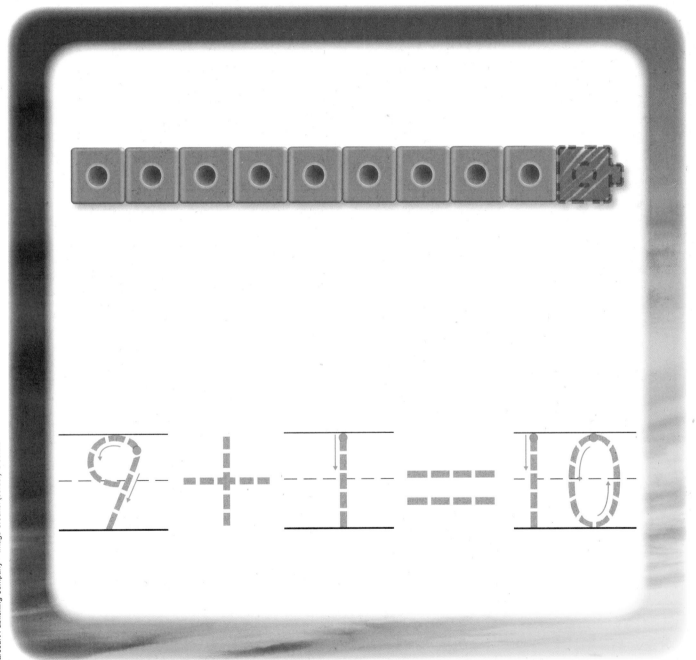

**DIRECTIONS** Look at the cube train. How many red cubes do you see? How many blue cubes do you need to add to make 10? Trace the blue cube. Trace to show this as an addition sentence.

**Share and Show**

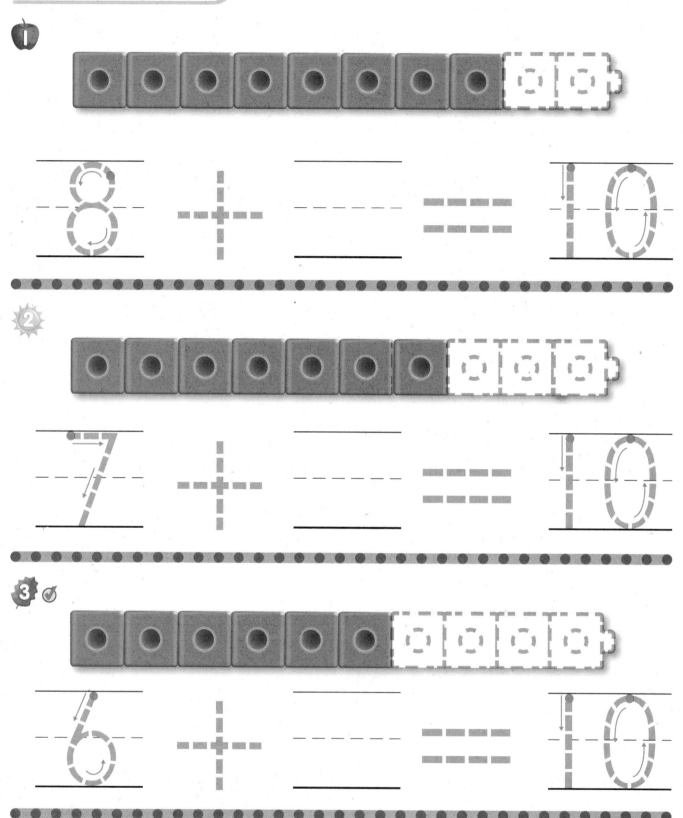

**1**

8 + ___ = 10

**2**

7 + ___ = 10

**3**

6 + ___ = 10

**DIRECTIONS** 1–3. Look at the cube train. How many red cubes do you see? How many blue cubes do you need to add to make 10? Use blue to color those cubes. Write and trace to show this as an addition sentence.

Name _____

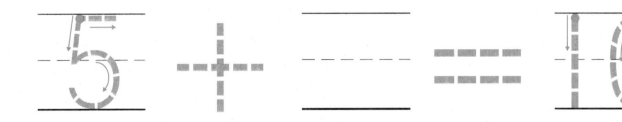

5 + ____ = 10

4 + ____ = 10

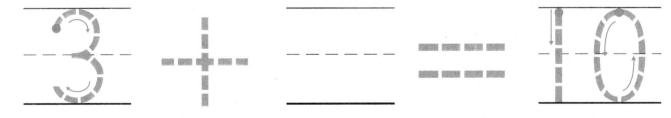

3 + ____ = 10

**DIRECTIONS** 4–6. Look at the cube train. How many red cubes do you see? How many blue cubes do you need to add to make 10? Use blue to draw those cubes. Write and trace to show this as an addition sentence.

Chapter 5 • Lesson 5 two hundred fifty-seven **257**

# Problem Solving • Applications (Real World)

WRITE Math

**7**

$$2 + \underline{\phantom{0}} = 10$$

**8**

$$1 + \underline{\phantom{0}} = 10$$

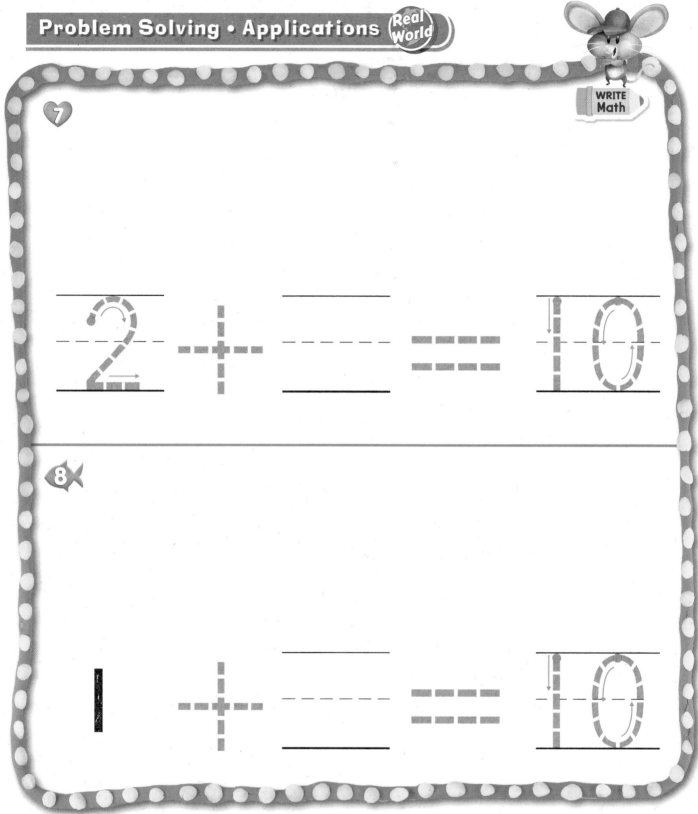

**DIRECTIONS  7.** Troy has 2 ducks. How many more ducks does he need to get to have 10 ducks in all? Draw to solve the problem. Trace and write to show this as an addition sentence.  **8.** Draw to find the number that makes 10 when put together with the given number. Trace and write to show this as an addition sentence.

**HOME ACTIVITY** • Show your child a number from 1 to 9. Ask him or her to find the number that makes 10 when put together with that number. Then have him or her tell a story to go with the problem.

Name _____

# Algebra • Write Addition Sentences for 10

COMMON CORE STANDARD—K.OA.A.4
*Understand addition as putting together and adding to, and understand subtraction as taking apart and taking from.*

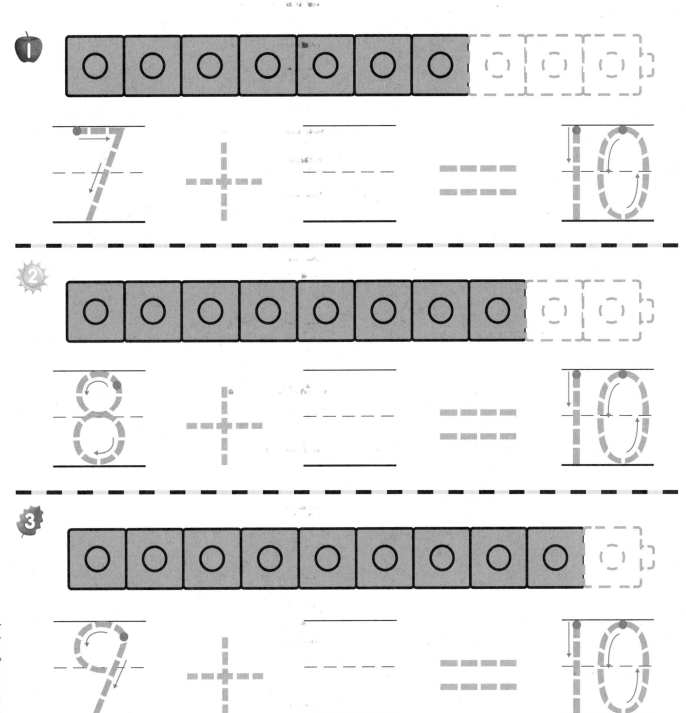

**DIRECTIONS** 1–3. Look at the cube train. How many gray cubes do you see? How many blue cubes do you need to add to make 10? Use blue to color those cubes. Write and trace to show this as an addition sentence.

© Houghton Mifflin Harcourt Publishing Company

## Lesson Check (K.OA.A.4)

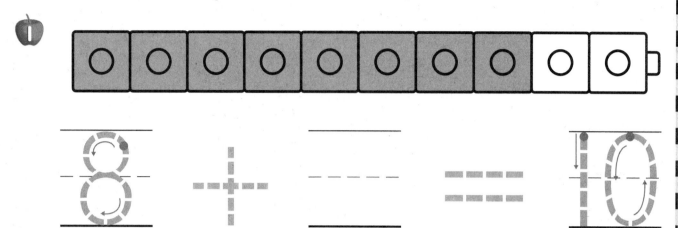

## Spiral Review (K.CC.C.6, K.CC.C.7)

5        4

---

**DIRECTIONS** 1. Look at the cube train. How many white cubes are added to the gray cubes to make 10? Write and trace to show this as an addition sentence.   2. Which number is less? Circle the number.   3. How many cubes are there? Write the number. Model a cube train that has the same number of cubes. Draw the cube train. Write how many.

**260** two hundred sixty

**FOR MORE PRACTICE GO TO THE**
**Personal Math Trainer**

Name _____

# Algebra • Write Addition Sentences

**Essential Question** How can you solve addition word problems and complete the addition sentence?

Common Core

**Operations and Algebraic Thinking—K.OA.A.5**
*Also K.OA.A.1, K.OA.A.2*

**MATHEMATICAL PRACTICES**
**MP1, MP2**

**Listen and Draw** *Real World*

$$2 + 1 = 3$$

**DIRECTIONS** Listen to the addition word problem. Circle the set you start with. How many are being added to the set? How many are there now? Trace the addition sentence.

**Chapter 5 • Lesson 6**

two hundred sixty-one **261**

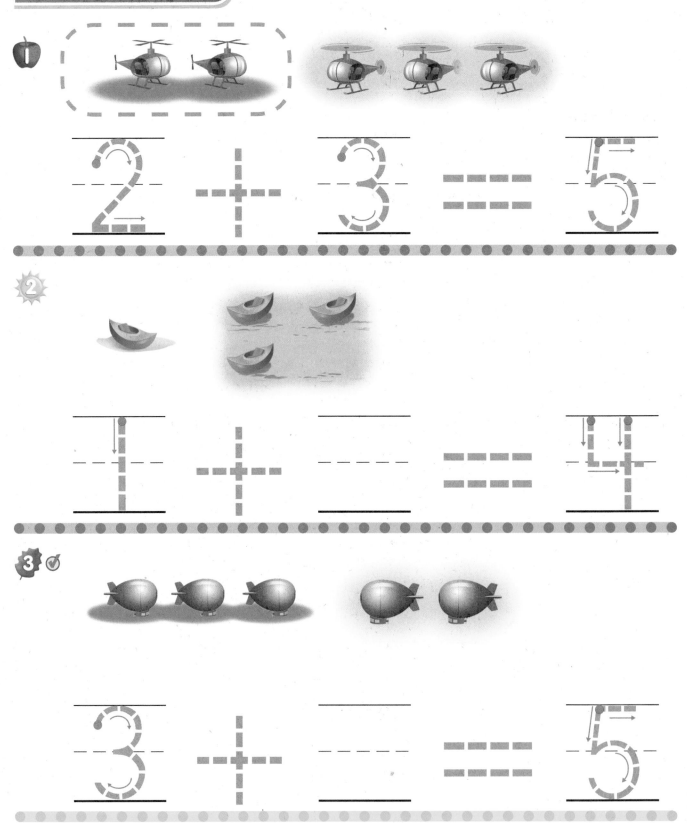

1
$$2 + 3 = 5$$

2
$$1 + \_\_ = 4$$

3
$$3 + \_\_ = 5$$

**DIRECTIONS** **I.** Listen to the addition word problem. Trace the circle around the set you start with. How many are being added to the set? How many are there now? Trace the addition sentence. **2–3.** Listen to the addition word problem. Circle the set you start with. How many are being added to the set? How many are there now? Write and trace the numbers and symbols to complete the addition sentence.

**4**

$$1 + \underline{\phantom{4}} = 5$$

**5**

$$3 + \underline{\phantom{4}} = 4$$

**6**

$$2 + \underline{\phantom{4}} = 5$$

**DIRECTIONS   4–6.** Tell an addition word problem about the sets. Circle the set you start with. How many are being added to the set? How many are there now? Write and trace the numbers and symbols to complete the addition sentence.

# Problem Solving • Applications Real World

WRITE Math

**7**

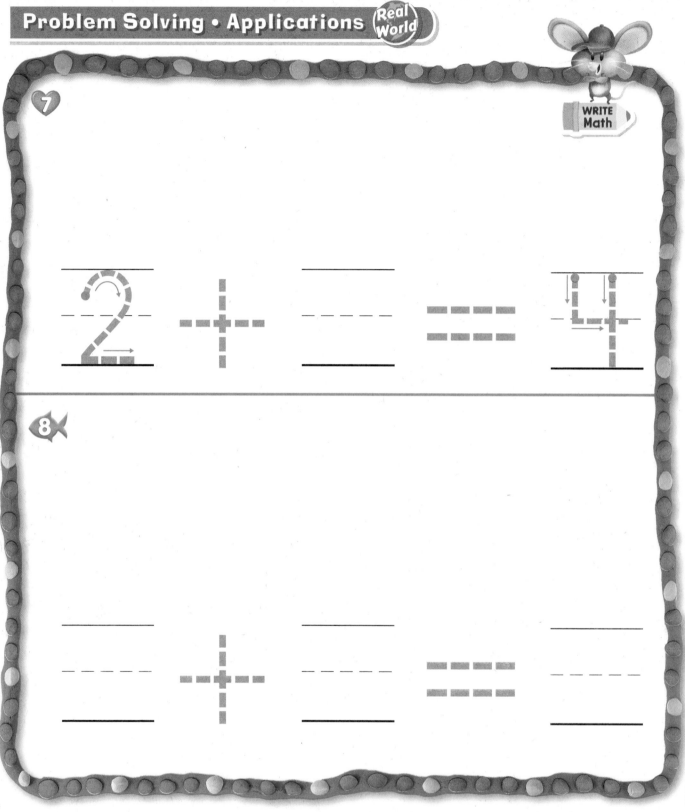

$$2 + \underline{\hspace{1cm}} = 4$$

**8**

$$\underline{\hspace{1cm}} + \underline{\hspace{1cm}} = \underline{\hspace{1cm}}$$

**DIRECTIONS** **7.** Bill catches two fish. Jake catches some fish. They catch four fish in all. How many fish does Jake catch? Draw to show the fish. Trace and write to complete the addition sentence. **8.** Tell a different addition word problem about fish. Draw to show the fish. Tell about your drawing. Complete the addition sentence.

**HOME ACTIVITY** • Have your child show three fingers. Have him or her show more fingers to make five fingers in all. Then have him or her tell how many more fingers he or she showed.

# Algebra • Write Addition Sentences

Common Core

**COMMON CORE STANDARD—K.OA.A.5**
*Understand addition as putting together and adding to, and understand subtraction as taking apart and taking from.*

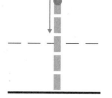  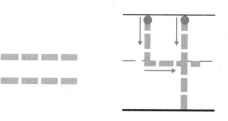

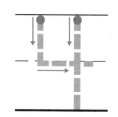    

**DIRECTIONS** 1–3. Tell an addition word problem about the sets. Circle the set you start with. How many are being added to the set? How many are there now? Write and trace to complete the addition sentence.

**Chapter 5**

## Spiral Review (K.CC.A.3, K.CC.B.5)

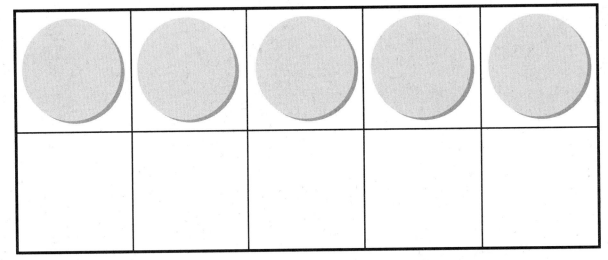

**DIRECTIONS 1.** Tell an addition word problem about the sets. Write and trace to complete the addition sentence. **2.** How many more counters would you place to model a way to make 8? Draw the counters. **3.** How many paintbrushes are there? Write the number.

**FOR MORE PRACTICE
GO TO THE
Personal Math Trainer**

Name _____

# Algebra • Write More Addition Sentences

**Essential Question** How can you solve addition word problems and complete the addition sentence?

Common Core

**Operations and Algebraic Thinking—K.OA.A.2**
*Also K.OA.A.1*
MATHEMATICAL PRACTICES
MP1, MP2

## Listen and Draw (Real World)

$$4 + 1 = 5$$

**DIRECTIONS** Listen to the addition word problem about the birds. Circle the bird joining the other birds. Trace the circle around the number that shows how many birds are being added. Now how many birds are on the branch? Trace the addition sentence.

**Chapter 5 • Lesson 7**

two hundred sixty-seven **267**

**1**

$$4 + 3 = 7$$

**2**

$$2 + \underline{\phantom{0}} = \underline{\phantom{0}}$$

**3** ✓

$$6 + \underline{\phantom{0}} = \underline{\phantom{0}}$$

**DIRECTIONS** **1.** Listen to the addition word problem. How many ants are being added? Circle the set being added. How many ants are there now? Trace to complete the addition sentence. **2–3.** Listen to the addition word problem. Circle the set being added. Write and trace to complete the addition sentence.

**268** two hundred sixty-eight

**4**

$$3 \;+\; \text{-----} \;=\; \text{-----}$$

**5**

$$6 \;+\; \text{-----} \;=\; \text{-----}$$

**6**

$$2 \;+\; \text{-----} \;=\; \text{-----}$$

**DIRECTIONS  4–6.** Tell an addition word problem. Circle the set being added. Write and trace to complete the addition sentence.

© Houghton Mifflin Harcourt Publishing Company

# Problem Solving • Applications Real World

**7**

WRITE Math

_____ + _____ = _____

**DIRECTIONS 7.** Tell an addition word problem. Complete the addition sentence. Draw a picture of real objects to show the problem. Tell a friend about your drawing.

**HOME ACTIVITY •** Tell your child an addition word problem such as: There are four socks in the drawer. I added some more socks. Now there are ten socks in the drawer. How many socks did I add to the drawer?

Name _____

# Algebra • Write More
# Addition Sentences

**COMMON CORE STANDARD—K.OA.A.2**
*Understand addition as putting together and
adding to, and understand subtraction as
taking apart and taking from.*

**1**

_____  _____  ▯ _____  ▯▯▯  _____
    ▮       +              = = =

**2**

_____  _____  ▯ _____  ▯▯▯  _____
    ▮       +              = = =

**3**

_____  _____  ▯ _____  ▯▯▯  _____
    ▮       +              = = =

**4**

_____  _____  ▯ _____  ▯▯▯  _____
    ▮       +              = = =

---

**DIRECTIONS  1–4.** Tell an addition word problem. How many are being added to
the set? Circle the set being added. How many are there now? Write and trace to
complete the addition sentence.

**Chapter 5**

## Lesson Check (K.OA.A.2)

 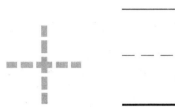

## Spiral Review (K.CC.B.4b, K.CC.B.5)

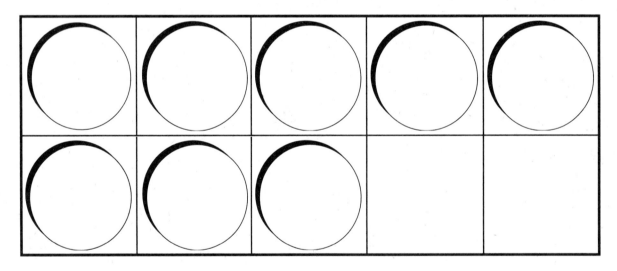

_____

- - - - -

_____

**DIRECTIONS** **1.** Tell an addition word problem about the sets. Circle the set being added. Trace and write to complete the addition sentence. **2.** How many more counters would you place to model a way to make 9? Draw the counters. **3.** Count and tell how many trumpets. Write the number.

**FOR MORE PRACTICE GO TO THE Personal Math Trainer**

# Algebra • Number Pairs to 5

**Essential Question** How can you model and write addition sentences for number pairs for sums to 5?

Common Core **Operations and Algebraic Thinking—K.OA.A.3**
**MATHEMATICAL PRACTICES**
MP2, MP7

**Listen and Draw**

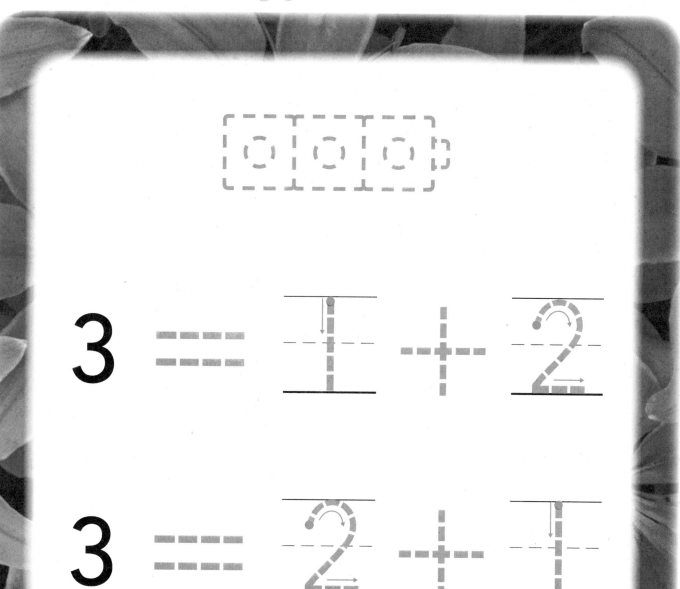

**DIRECTIONS** Place two colors of cubes on the cube train to show the number pairs that make 3. Trace the addition sentences to show some of the number pairs.

**1** 4 == 3 + 1

**2** 4 == ___ = ___ + ___

**3** ✓ 4 == ___ = ___ + ___

**DIRECTIONS** Place two colors of cubes on the cube train to show the number pairs that make 4. **1.** Trace the addition sentence to show one of the pairs. **2–3.** Complete the addition sentence to show another number pair. Color the cube train to match the addition sentence in Exercise 3.

Name _____

**✿ 4**

5

**❀ 5**

5

**🌰 6**

5

**♥ 7**

5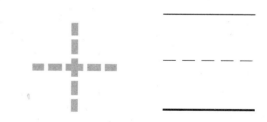

**DIRECTIONS**  Place two colors of cubes on the cube train to show the number pairs that make 5.  **4–7.** Complete the addition sentence to show a number pair. Color the cube train to match the addition sentence in Exercise 7.

© Houghton Mifflin Harcourt Publishing Company

# Problem Solving • Applications

WRITE Math

**8.**

$$5 = \underline{\phantom{0}} \quad \underline{\phantom{0}} + \underline{\phantom{0}}$$

**9.**

**DIRECTIONS** **8.** Peyton and Ashley have five red apples. Peyton is holding five of the apples. How many is Ashley holding? Color the cube train to show the number pair. Complete the addition sentence. **9.** Draw to show what you know about a number pair to 5.

**HOME ACTIVITY** • Have your child tell you the number pairs for a set of objects up to five. Have him or her tell an addition sentence for one of the number pairs.

# Algebra • Number Pairs to 5

Common Core

**COMMON CORE STANDARD—K.OA.A.3**
*Understand addition as putting together and adding to, and understand subtraction as taking apart and taking from.*

**1**

**3**

**2**

**4**

**3**

**5**

**DIRECTIONS** 1–3. Look at the number at the beginning of the addition sentence. Place two colors of cubes on the cube train to show a number pair for that number. Complete the addition sentence to show a number pair. Color the cube train to match the addition sentence.

## Lesson Check (K.OA.A.3)

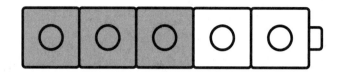

$$5 = \underline{\hspace{1.5cm}} + \underline{\hspace{1.5cm}}$$

## Spiral Review (K.CC.B.5, K.CC.C.6)

    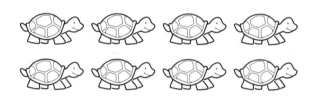

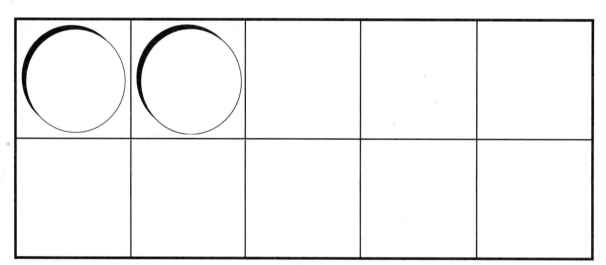

**DIRECTIONS 1.** Complete the addition sentence to show the numbers that match the cube train. **2.** Count the number of turtles in each set. Circle the set that has the greater number of turtles. **3.** How many more counters would you place to model a way to make 6? Draw the counters.

**278** two hundred seventy-eight

FOR MORE PRACTICE
GO TO THE
**Personal Math Trainer**

Name _____

# Algebra • Number Pairs for 6 and 7

**Essential Question** How can you model and write addition sentences for number pairs for each sum of 6 and 7?

Common Core **Operations and Algebraic Thinking—K.OA.A.3**
**MATHEMATICAL PRACTICES**
MP2, MP7

**Listen and Draw**

$$6 = 5 + 1$$

$$7 = 6 + 1$$

**DIRECTIONS** Place two colors of cubes on the cube trains to match the addition sentences. Color the cube trains. Trace the addition sentences.

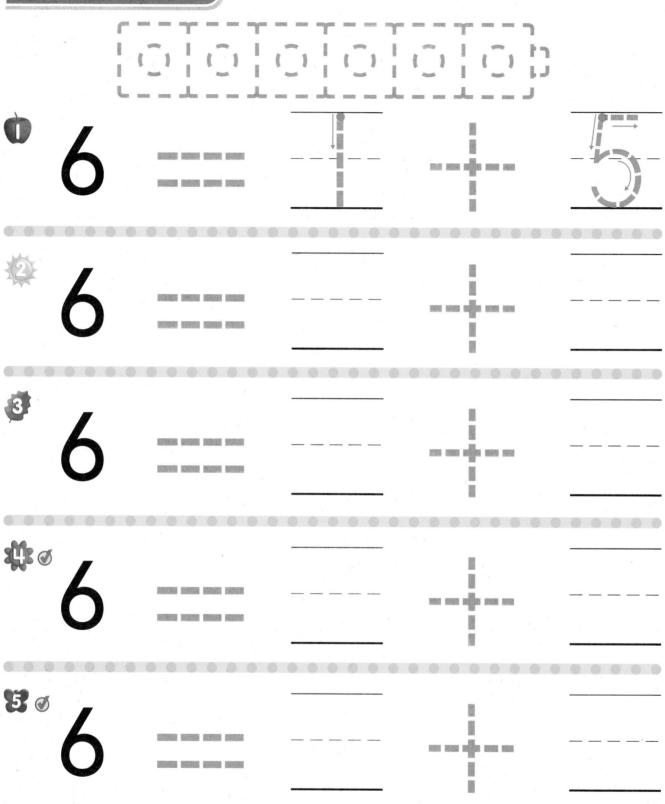

**1** 6 = ___ + 5

**2** 6 = ___ + ___

**3** 6 = ___ + ___

**4** 6 = ___ + ___

**5** 6 = ___ + ___

**DIRECTIONS** Place two colors of cubes on the cube train to show the number pairs that make 6. **1.** Trace the addition sentence to show one of the pairs. **2–5.** Complete the addition sentence to show a number pair for 6. Color the cube train to match the addition sentence in Exercise 5.

Name _____

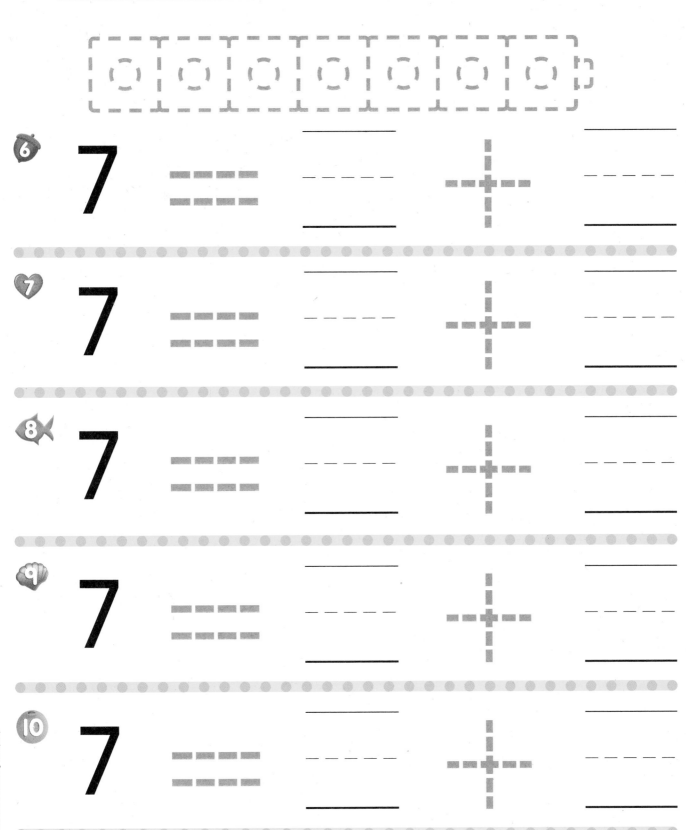

6. 7  ___ = ___ + ___

7. 7  ___ = ___ + ___

8. 7  ___ = ___ + ___

9. 7  ___ = ___ + ___

10. 7  ___ = ___ + ___

**DIRECTIONS** Place two colors of cubes on the cube train to show the number pairs that make 7. **6–10.** Complete the addition sentence to show a number pair for 7. Color the cube train to match the addition sentence in Exercise 10.

## Problem Solving • Applications  Real World

**11.**

6 === ___ ___ + ___

**12.**

7 === ___ ___ + ___

**DIRECTIONS** 11. Peter and Grant have six toy cars. Peter has no cars. How many cars does Grant have? Color the cube train to show the number pair. Complete the addition sentence. 12. Draw to show what you know about a number pair for 7 when one number is 0. Complete the addition sentence.

 **HOME ACTIVITY** • Have your child use his or her fingers on two hands to show a number pair for 6.

**282** two hundred eighty-two

# Algebra • Number Pairs for 6 and 7

Common Core

**COMMON CORE STANDARD—K.OA.A.3**
*Understand addition as putting together and
adding to, and understand subtraction as
taking apart and taking from.*

$$6 = \underline{\hspace{2cm}} + \underline{\hspace{2cm}}$$

$$7 = \underline{\hspace{2cm}} + \underline{\hspace{2cm}}$$

**DIRECTIONS  1–2.** Look at the number at the beginning of the addition
sentence. Place two colors of cubes on the cube train to show a number
pair for that number. Complete the addition sentence to show a number
pair. Color the cube train to match the addition sentence.

## Lesson Check (K.OA.A.3)

7 = ___  ___ + ___

## Spiral Review (K.CC.B.5, K.CC.A.3)

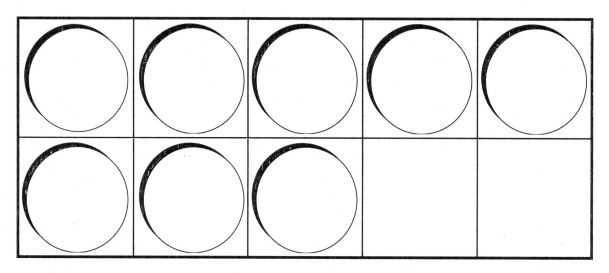

___ ___

**DIRECTIONS  1.** Complete the addition sentence to show the numbers that match the cube train.  **2.** How many more counters would you place to model a way to make 10? Draw the counters.  **3.** Count and tell how many hats. Write the number.

**284** two hundred eighty-four

FOR MORE PRACTICE GO TO THE Personal Math Trainer

# Algebra • Number Pairs for 8

**Essential Question** How can you model and write addition sentences for number pairs for sums of 8?

 **Common Core** Operations and Algebraic Thinking—K.OA.A.3

**MATHEMATICAL PRACTICES**
MP2, MP7

 Listen and Draw *Real World*  Hands On

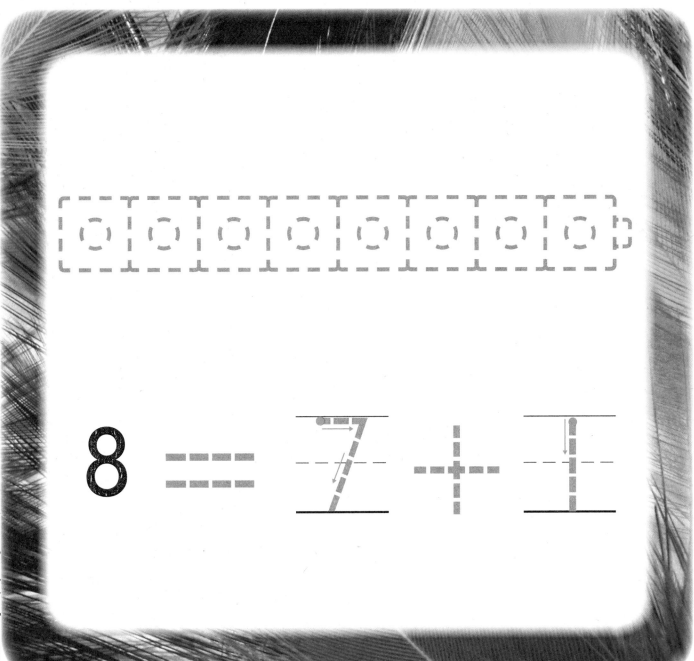

$$8 = 7 + 1$$

**DIRECTIONS** Use two colors of cubes to make a cube train to match the addition sentence. Color the cube train to show your work. Trace the addition sentence.

© Houghton Mifflin Harcourt Publishing Company • Image Credits: (border) ©Artville/Getty Images

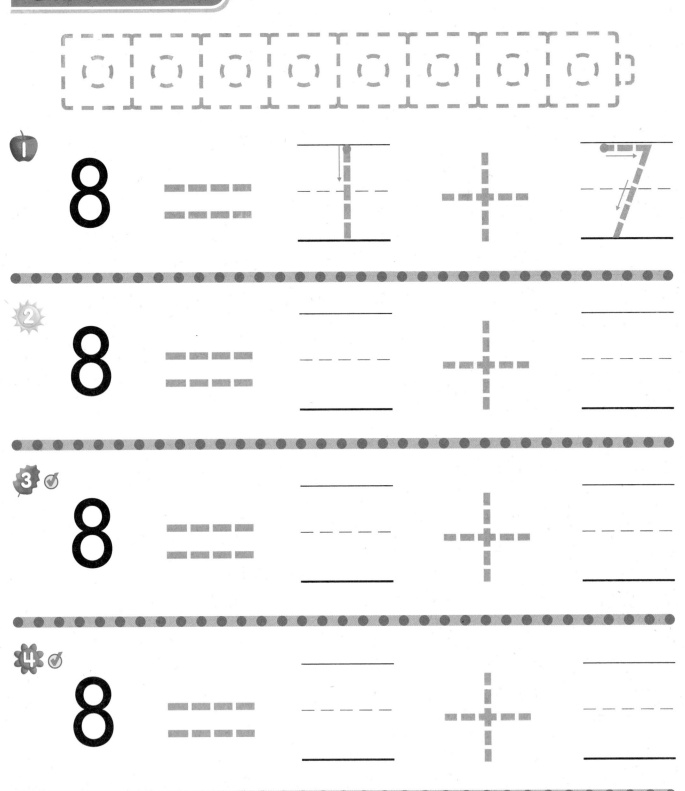

**1** 8 ▬▬▬ = I + 7

**2** 8 ▬▬▬ = ___ + ___

**3** 8 ▬▬▬ = ___ + ___

**4** 8 ▬▬▬ = ___ + ___

**DIRECTIONS** Use two colors of cubes to make a cube train to show the number pairs that make 8. **1.** Trace the addition sentence to show one of the pairs. **2–4.** Complete the addition sentence to show a number pair for 8. Color the cube train to match the addition sentence in Exercise 4.

Name _____

**5**

**8** === = ___ ___ + ___

**6**

**8** === = ___ ___ + ___

**7**

**8** === = ___ ___ + ___

**DIRECTIONS** Use two colors of cubes to make a cube train to
show the number pairs that make 8. **5–7.** Complete the addition
sentence to show a number pair for 8. Color the cube train to match
the addition sentence in Exercise 7.

**Chapter 5 • Lesson 10**

two hundred eighty-seven **287**

## Problem Solving • Applications

**8**

$$8 = \underline{\quad\quad} + \underline{\quad\quad}$$

**9**

$$8 = \underline{\quad\quad} + \underline{\quad\quad}$$

**DIRECTIONS** **8.** There are eight crayons in a packet. Eight of the crayons are red. How many are not red? Draw and color to show how you solved. Complete the addition sentence. **9.** Draw to show what you know about a different number pair for 8. Complete the addition sentence.

**HOME ACTIVITY •** Have your child tell you the number pairs for a set of eight objects. Have him or her tell the addition sentence to match one of the number pairs.

Name _____

# Algebra • Number Pairs for 8

 **COMMON CORE STANDARD—K.OA.A.3**
*Understand addition as putting together and adding to, and understand subtraction as taking apart and taking from.*

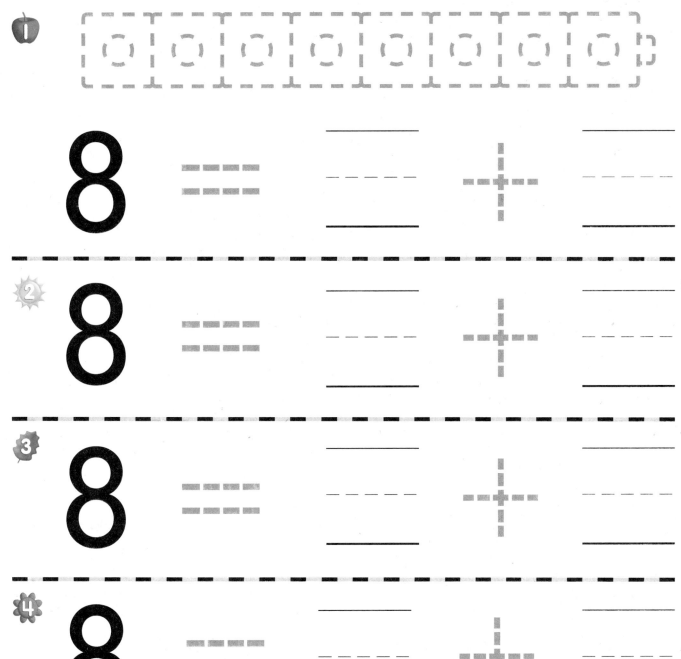

**DIRECTIONS** Use two colors of cubes to make a cube train to show the number pairs that make 8. **1–4.** Complete the addition sentence to show a number pair for 8. Color the cube train to match the addition sentence in Exercise 4.

## Lesson Check (K.OA.A.3)

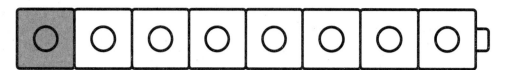

8 === ____ ____ + ____

......................................................

## Spiral Review (K.CC.A.3, K.CC.C.6)

____

---

____

____

---

**DIRECTIONS** **I.** Complete the addition sentence to show the numbers that match the cube train. **2.** Count and tell how many in each set. Write the numbers. Compare the numbers. Circle the number that is greater. **3.** How many more counters would you place in the five frame to show a way to make 5? Draw the counters.

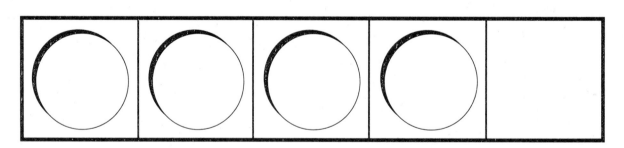

FOR MORE PRACTICE
GO TO THE
**Personal Math Trainer**

Name _____

# Algebra • Number Pairs for 9

**Essential Question** How can you model and write addition sentences for number pairs for sums of 9?

Common Core — **Operations and Algebraic Thinking—K.OA.A.3**
**MATHEMATICAL PRACTICES**
MP2, MP7

## Listen and Draw

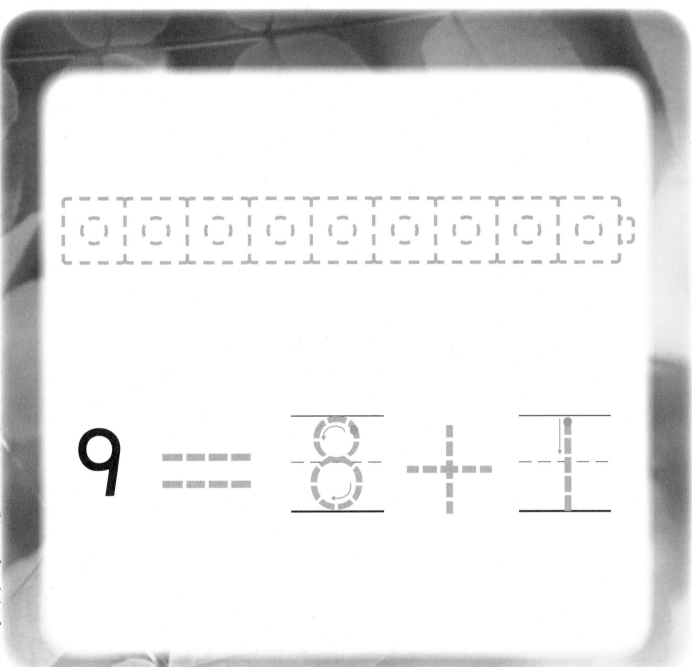

$$9 = 8 + 1$$

**DIRECTIONS** Use two colors of cubes to make a cube train to match the addition sentence. Color the cube train to show your work. Trace the addition sentence.

Chapter 5 • Lesson II

two hundred ninety-one **291**

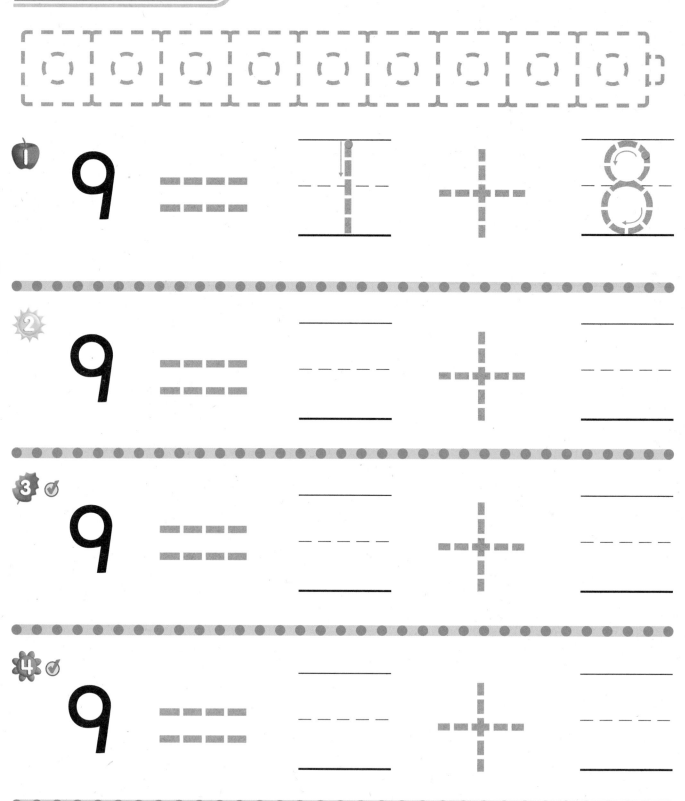

**1** 9 == ‖ + 8

**2** 9 ==

**3** ✓ 9 ===

**4** ✓ 9 ==

**DIRECTIONS** Use two colors of cubes to make a cube train to show the number pairs that make 9. **1.** Trace the addition sentence to show one of the pairs. **2–4.** Complete the addition sentence to show a number pair for 9. Color the cube train to match the addition sentence in Exercise 4.

Name _____

**5** 9 = ___  ___ + ___

**6** 9 = ___  ___ + ___

**7** 9 = ___  ___ + ___

**8** 9 = ___  ___ + ___

**DIRECTIONS** Use two colors of cubes to make a cube train to show the number pairs that make 9. **5–8.** Complete the addition sentence to show a number pair for 9. Color the cube train to match the addition sentence in Exercise 8.

**Chapter 5 • Lesson 11**                          two hundred ninety-three **293**

## Problem Solving • Applications Real World

**WRITE Math**

**9**

9 === ------ + ------

**10**

9 === ------ + ------

**DIRECTIONS 9.** Shelby has nine friends. None of them are boys. How many are girls? Complete the addition sentence to show the number pair. **10.** Draw to show what you know about a different number pair for 9. Complete the addition sentence.

**HOME ACTIVITY •** Have your child use his or her fingers on two hands to show a number pair for 9.

# Algebra • Number Pairs for 9

**Common Core**

**COMMON CORE STANDARD—K.OA.A.3**
*Understand addition as putting together and adding to, and understand subtraction as taking apart and taking from.*

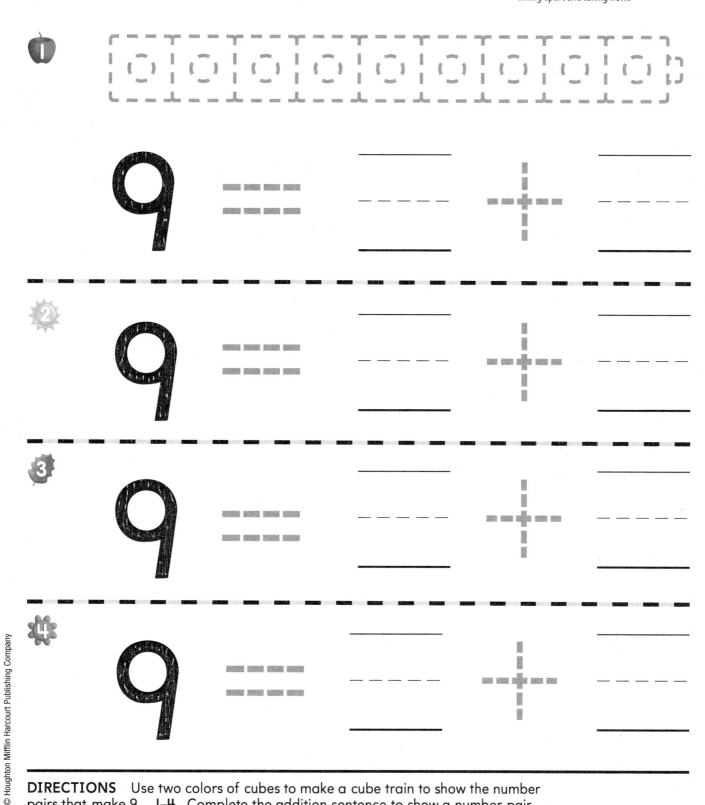

**DIRECTIONS** Use two colors of cubes to make a cube train to show the number pairs that make 9. **1–4.** Complete the addition sentence to show a number pair for 9. Color the cube train to match the addition sentence in Exercise 4.

**Chapter 5**

two hundred ninety-five **295**

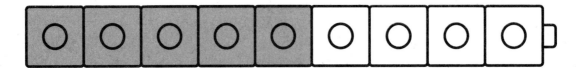

**9**

**DIRECTIONS   1.** Complete the addition sentence to show the numbers that match the cube train.   **2.** Count how many birds. Write the number. **3.** Count and tell how many in each set.  Write the numbers. Compare the numbers.  Circle the number that is less.

**FOR MORE PRACTICE
GO TO THE
Personal Math Trainer**

Name _____

# Algebra • Number Pairs for 10

**Essential Question** How can you model and write addition sentences for number pairs for sums of 10?

Common Core **Operations and Algebraic Thinking—K.OA.A.3**
MATHEMATICAL PRACTICES
MP2, MP7

**Listen and Draw**

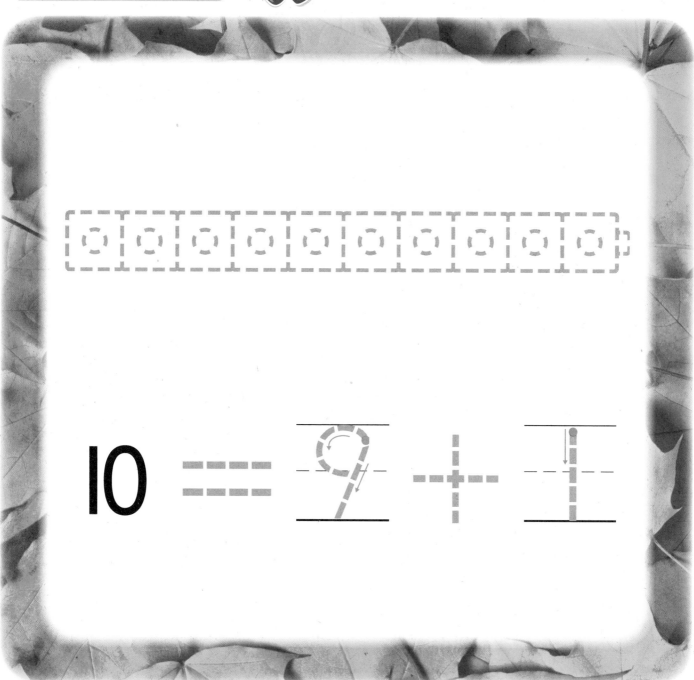

$$10 = 9 + 1$$

**DIRECTIONS** Use two colors of cubes to make a cube train to match the addition sentence. Color the cube train to show your work. Trace the addition sentence.

**1** 10 === <u>1</u> + <u>9</u>

**2** 10 === ____ + ____

**3** ✓ 10 === ____ + ____

**4** ✓ 10 === ____ + ____

**DIRECTIONS** Use two colors of cubes to build a cube train to show the number pairs that make 10. **1.** Trace the addition sentence to show one of the pairs. **2–4.** Complete the addition sentence to show a number pair for 10. Color the cube train to match the addition sentence in Exercise 4.

Name _____

**5** 10 === _ _ _ _ _ + _ _ _ _ _

**6** 10 ==== _ _ _ _ _ + _ _ _ _ _

**7** 10 === _ _ _ _ _ + _ _ _ _ _

**8** 10 === _ _ _ _ _ + _ _ _ _ _

**DIRECTIONS** Use two colors of cubes to build a cube train to show the number pairs that make 10. **5–8.** Complete the addition sentence to show a number pair for 10. Color the cube train to match the addition sentence in Exercise 8.

Chapter 5 • Lesson 12

two hundred ninety-nine **299**

## Problem Solving • Applications  Real World

WRITE Math

**9.**

10 === _____ + _____

**10**

10 === _____ + _____

**DIRECTIONS  9.** There are ten children in the cafeteria. Ten of them are drinking water. How many children are drinking milk? Complete the addition sentence to show the number pair.  **10.** Draw to show what you know about a different number pair for 10. Complete the addition sentence.

 **HOME ACTIVITY •** Have your child tell you the number pairs for a set of ten objects. Have him or her tell the addition sentence to match one of the number pairs.

© Houghton Mifflin Harcourt Publishing Company

# Algebra • Number Pairs for 10

Common Core

**COMMON CORE STANDARD—K.OA.A.3**
*Understand addition as putting together and adding to, and understand subtraction as taking apart and taking from.*

**1** 10 = ___ + ___

**2** 10 = ___ + ___

**3** 10 = ___ + ___

**4** 10 = ___ + ___

**DIRECTIONS** Use two colors of cubes to build a cube train to show the number pairs that make 10. **1–4.** Complete the addition sentence to show a number pair for 10. Color the cube train to match the addition sentence in Exercise 4.

## Lesson Check (K.OA.A.3)

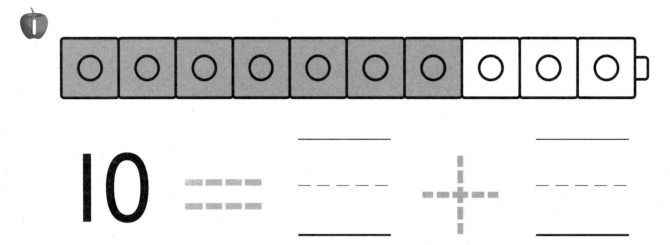

$$10 = \underline{\hspace{3em}} + \underline{\hspace{3em}}$$

· · · · · · · · · · · · · · · · · · · · · · · · · · · · · · · · · · · · · · · · · · · · · · · · · · · · · · · · · · · · · · · · · · · · · · · · · · · · · · · · · ·

## Spiral Review (K.CC.B.4c, K.OA.A.4)

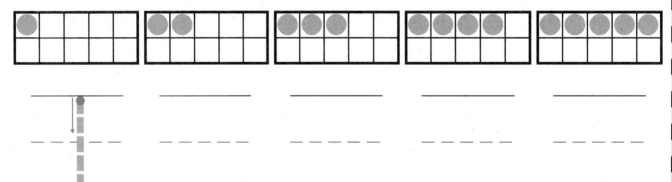

**DIRECTIONS** 1. Complete the addition sentence to show the numbers that match the cube train. 2. Count the dots in the ten frames. Trace the number. Write the numbers in order as you count forward from the dashed number. 3. Use blue and red to color the cubes to show a way to make 10.

FOR MORE PRACTICE
GO TO THE
**Personal Math Trainer**

**Chapter 5 Review/Test**

_____ **and** _____

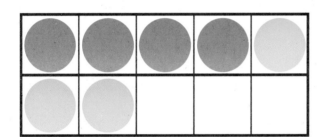

○ 4 plus 3

○ 4 plus 1

○ 4 + 3

 +  =

**DIRECTIONS** **1.** How many puppies are sitting? How many puppies are being added to the group? Write the numbers. **2.** Sonja put 4 red counters in the ten frame. Then she put 3 yellow counters in the ten frame. Choose all the ways that show the counters being put together. **3.** How many of each color cube is being added? Trace the numbers and symbols. Write the number that shows how many cubes in all.

**4.**

**5.**

**6.**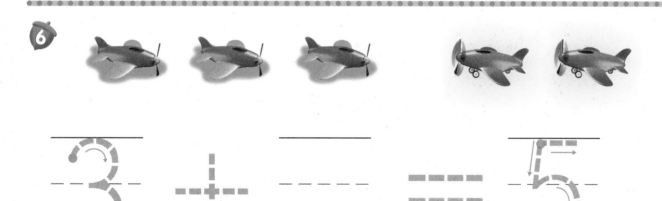

**DIRECTIONS** **4.** Annabelle has 2 red cubes. She has 2 yellow cubes. How many cubes does she have? Draw the cubes. Trace the numbers and symbols. Write how many in all. **5.** Look at the cube train. How many red cubes do you see? How many more cubes do you need to add to make 10? Draw the cubes. Color them blue. Write and trace to show this as an addition sentence. **6.** Write and trace the numbers to complete the addition sentence.

Name _____

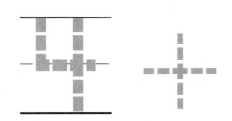 + ___  6

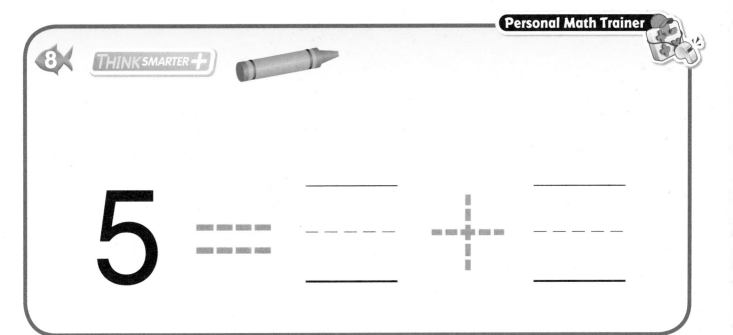

8 THINK SMARTER +

5 = ___ + ___

| 5 + 2 | ○ Yes | ○ No |
| 4 + 3 | ○ Yes | ○ No |
| 2 + 4 | ○ Yes | ○ No |

**DIRECTIONS** **7.** Trace and write the numbers and trace the symbols to complete the addition sentence. **8.** Nora has 1 green crayon. Gary has some red crayons. Together they have 5 crayons. Draw to show how many red crayons Gary has. Complete the number pair. **9.** Does this show a number pair for 7? Choose Yes or No.

$$4 + 5 \qquad 2 + 6 \qquad 1 + 7$$

**11.**

$$9 = \underline{\phantom{00}} + \underline{\phantom{00}}$$

**12.**

$$10 = \underline{\phantom{00}} + \underline{\phantom{00}}$$

**DIRECTIONS** **10.** Circle all the number pairs for 8.  **11.** Larry counted out 9 cubes. The cubes were either red or blue. How many red and blue cubes could he have? Color the cubes to show the number of red and blue cubes. Write the numbers to complete the addition sentence.  **12.** Complete the addition sentence to show a number pair for 10.

# Chapter 6 Subtraction

## Curious About Math with Curious George

Penguins are birds with black and white feathers.

- There are 4 penguins on the ice. One penguin jumps in the water. How many penguins are on the ice now?

Name _____

## Fewer

1 🍎

2 ☀

---

## Compare Numbers to 10

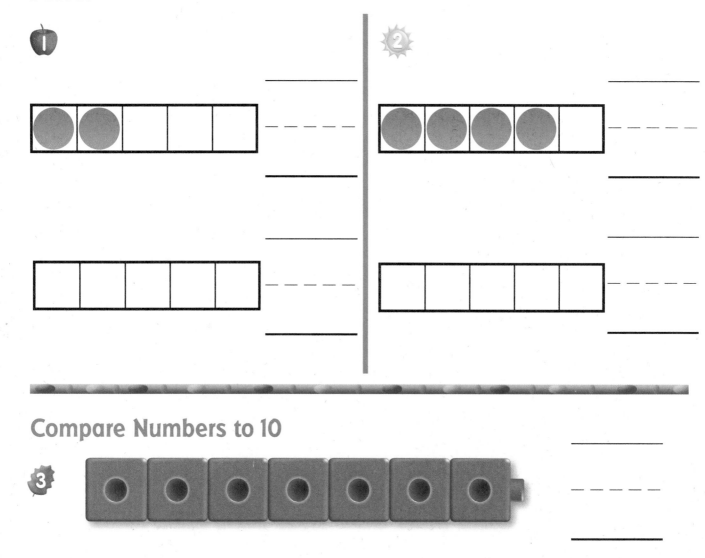

3

---

This page checks understanding of important skills needed for success in Chapter 6.

**DIRECTIONS** 1–2. Count and tell how many. Draw a set with one fewer counter. Write how many in each set. 3. Write the number of cubes in each set. Circle the number that is less than the other number.

Name _____

add

**DIRECTIONS** Add the set of bees and the set of butterflies. Write how many insects altogether.

• **Interactive Student Edition**
• **Multimedia eGlossary**

## Game

# Spin for More

| Spin for More | | | | |
|---|---|---|---|---|
| Player 1 | | | | |
| Player 2 | | | | |

**DIRECTIONS** Play with a partner. Decide who goes first. Take turns spinning to get a number from each spinner. Use cubes to model a cube train with the number from the first spin. Say the number. Add the cubes from the second spin. Compare your number with your partner's. Mark an X on the table for the player who has the greater number. The first player to have five Xs wins the game.

**MATERIALS** two paper clips, connecting cubes

# Chapter 6 Vocabulary

**add**

sumar

2

**fewer**

menos

23

**is equal to**

es igual a

36

**minus (−)**

menos (−)

42

**pairs**

pares

50

**plus (+)**

más (+)

51

**subtract**

restar

72

**zero**

cero, ninguno

86

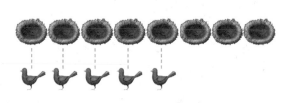

## 3 **fewer** birds

$2 + 4 = 6$

$6 - 3 = 3$

**minus** sign

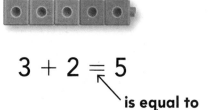

$3 + 2 = 5$

**is equal to**

$2 + 2 = 4$

**plus** sign

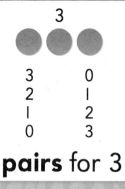

3

| 3 | 0 |
| 2 | 1 |
| 1 | 2 |
| 0 | 3 |

**pairs** for 3

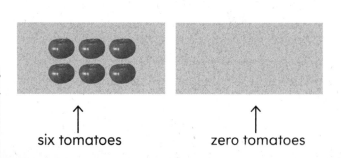

six tomatoes          zero tomatoes

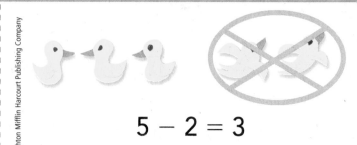

$5 - 2 = 3$

# Picture It

**Word Box**

minus

subtract

is equal to

plus

add

fewer

zero

pair

## Secret Words

| Player 1 | | | | | |
|---|---|---|---|---|---|
| Player 2 | | | | | |

**DIRECTIONS** Players take turns. A player chooses a secret word from the Word Box and then sets the timer. The player draws pictures to give hints about the secret word. If the other player guesses the secret word before time runs out, he or she puts a counter in the chart. The first player who has counters in all his or her boxes is the winner.

**MATERIALS** timer, drawing paper, two-color counters for each player

# The Write Way

© Houghton Mifflin Harcourt Publishing Company • Image Credits: ©pablo_hernan/Fotolia

**DIRECTIONS** Draw to show how to solve a subtraction problem. Write a subtraction sentence.
**Reflect** Be ready to tell about your drawing.

Name _____

# Subtraction: Take From

**Essential Question** How can you show subtraction as taking from?

Common Core **Operations and Algebraic Thinking—K.OA.A.1**

**MATHEMATICAL PRACTICES**
MP1, MP2

## Listen and Draw *Real World*

 take away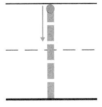

⬤⬤⬤⬤⬤⬤⬤⬤⬤⬤⬤⬤⬤⬤⬤⬤⬤⬤⬤⬤⬤⬤⬤⬤⬤⬤⬤⬤⬤⬤

**DIRECTIONS** Listen to the subtraction word problem. Trace the number that shows how many children in all. Trace the number that shows how many children are leaving. Trace the number that shows how many children are left.

**Chapter 6 • Lesson 1**

three hundred eleven **311**

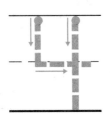 take away

**312** three hundred twelve

Name _____

_____                               _____

\_ \_ \_ \_ \_                             \_ \_ \_ \_ \_

_____   **take away**   \_\_\_\_\_

_____

\_ \_ \_ \_ \_

_____

**DIRECTIONS  2.** Listen to the subtraction word problem. Write the number that shows how many children in all. Write the number that shows how many children are leaving. Write the number that shows how many children are left.

## Problem Solving • Applications Real World

**3**   WRITE Math

_____    _____

- - - - -    - - - - -

_____  **take away**  _____

**4**

_____

- - - - -

_____

**DIRECTIONS**   **3.** Blair has two marbles. His friend takes one marble from him. Draw to show the subtraction. Write the numbers.   **4.** Write the number that shows how many marbles Blair has now.

**HOME ACTIVITY •** Show your child a set of four small objects. Have him or her tell how many objects there are. Take one of the objects from the set. Have him or her tell you how many objects there are now.

## Subtraction: Take From

Common Core

**COMMON CORE STANDARD—K.OA.A.1**
*Understand addition as putting together and adding to, and understand subtraction as taking apart and taking from.*

_____

- - - - -

_____

**take away**

_____

- - - - -

_____

_____

- - - - -

_____

---

**DIRECTIONS  I.** Tell a subtraction word problem about the children. Write the number that shows how many children in all. Write the number that shows how many children are leaving. Write the number that shows how many children are left.

## Lesson Check (K.OA.A.1)

# 3 take away 1

_____

- - - - -

_____

## Spiral Review (K.CC.B.5, K.OA.A.2)

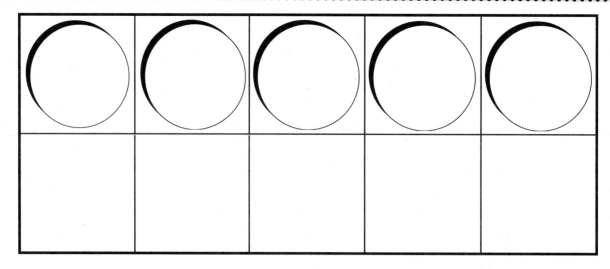

**DIRECTIONS** **1.** Tell a subtraction word problem about the frogs. Write the number that shows how many frogs are left. **2.** Tell an addition word problem about the birds. Circle the birds joining the set. Trace and write to complete the addition sentence. **3.** How many more counters would you place to model a way to make 8? Draw the counters.

Name _____

# Subtraction: Take Apart

**Essential Question** How can you show subtraction as taking apart?

Common Core **Operations and Algebraic Thinking—K.OA.A.1**
**MATHEMATICAL PRACTICES**
MP2, MP4, MP5

**Listen and Draw** Real World  Hands On

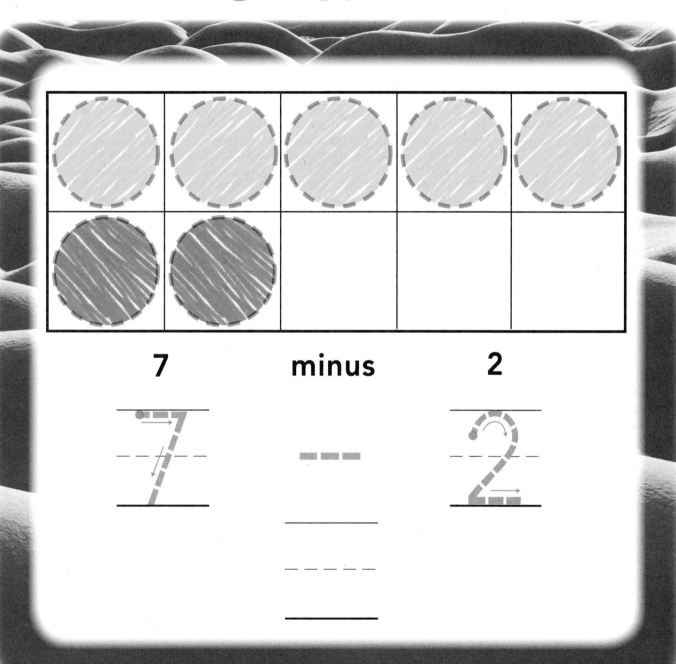

7       minus       2

**DIRECTIONS** Listen to the subtraction word problem. Place seven counters in the ten frame as shown. Trace the counters. Trace the number that shows how many in all. Trace the number that shows how many are red. Write the number that shows how many are yellow.

**Chapter 6 • Lesson 2**

three hundred seventeen **317**

| | | | | |
|---|---|---|---|---|
| | | | | |
| | | | | |

8          minus          I

8          ---          I

\_\_\_\_\_

---

◦◦◦◦◦◦◦◦◦◦◦◦◦◦◦◦◦◦◦◦◦◦◦◦◦◦◦◦◦◦◦◦◦◦◦◦◦

**DIRECTIONS** I. Listen to the subtraction word problem. Place eight counters in the ten frame. Draw and color the counters. Trace the number that shows how many in all. Write the number that shows how many are yellow. Write the number that shows how many are red.

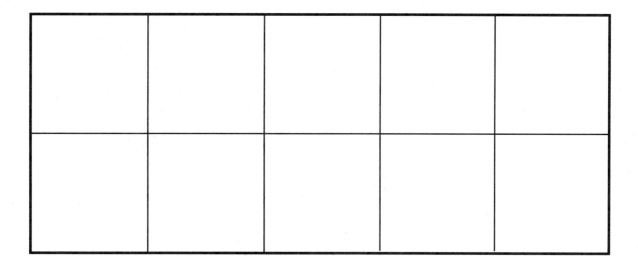

10          minus          4

_____          _____

- - - - -     ▬ ▬ ▬     - - - - -

_____          _____

_____

- - - - - -

_____

**DIRECTIONS  2.** Listen to the subtraction word problem. Place ten counters in the ten frame. Draw and color the counters. Write the number that shows how many in all. Write the number that shows how many are red. Write the number that shows how many are yellow.

## Problem Solving • Applications

**WRITE Math**

**3**

_____

- - - - -          ▪ ▪ ▪          - - - - -

_____                                  _____

 **4**

_____

- - - - -

_____

**DIRECTIONS** **3.** Juanita has nine apples. One apple is red. The rest of the apples are yellow. Draw the apples. Write the numbers and trace the symbol. **4.** Write the number that shows how many apples are yellow.

 **HOME ACTIVITY** • Show your child a set of seven small objects. Now take away four objects. Have him or her tell a subtraction word problem about the objects.

# Subtraction: Take Apart

**Common Core** COMMON CORE STANDARD—K.OA.A.1
*Understand addition as putting together and
adding to, and understand subtraction as
taking apart and taking from.*

**1**

| | | | | |
|---|---|---|---|---|
| | | | | |
| | | | | |

## 9    minus    3

\_\_\_\_\_

\- \- \- \- \-      ▬ ▬ ▬      \- \- \- \- \-

\_\_\_\_\_

\_\_\_\_\_

\- \- \- \- \-

\_\_\_\_\_

---

**DIRECTIONS   I.** Listen to the subtraction word problem. Jane has
nine counters. Three of her counters are red. The rest of her counters
are yellow. How many are yellow? Place nine counters in the ten frame.
Draw and color the counters. Write the number that shows how many in
all. Write the number that shows how many are red. Write the number
that shows how many are yellow.

# Lesson Check (K.OA.A.1)

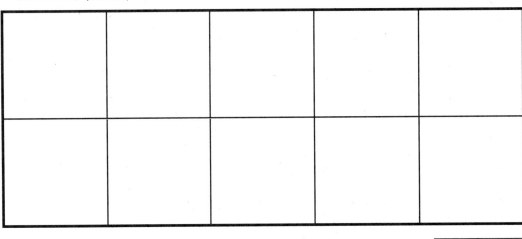

$$8 - 2$$

____

- - - -

____

## Spiral Review (K.CC.C.6)

- - - -

____

____

- - - -

____

**DIRECTIONS** 1. Clyde has eight counters. Two of his counters are yellow. The rest of his counters are red. How many are red? Draw and color the counters. Write the number that shows how many are red. **2.** Count the number of leaves in each set. Circle the set that has the greater number of leaves. **3.** Compare the cube trains. Write how many. Circle the number that is greater.

FOR MORE PRACTICE
GO TO THE
**Personal Math Trainer**

Name _____

# Problem Solving • Act Out Subtraction Problems

**Essential Question** How can you solve problems using the strategy *act it out*?

Common Core

**Operations and Algebraic Thinking—K.OA.A.1**
*Also K.OA.A.2, K.OA.A.5*

**MATHEMATICAL PRACTICES**
MP1, MP2, MP4

## Unlock the Problem
Real World

   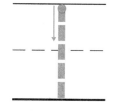      

**DIRECTIONS** Listen to and act out the subtraction word problem. Trace the subtraction sentence. How can you use subtraction to tell how many children are left?

Chapter 6 • Lesson 3

three hundred twenty-three **323**

 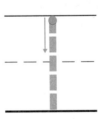 

**DIRECTIONS** I. Listen to and act out the subtraction word problem. Trace the numbers and the symbols. Write the number that shows how many children are left.

**324** three hundred twenty-four

Name _____

2 ✓

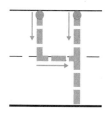 —  =

**DIRECTIONS** 2. Listen to and act out the subtraction word problem. Trace the numbers and the symbols. Write the number that shows how many children are left.

**Chapter 6 • Lesson 3**

three hundred twenty-five **325**

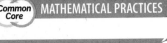

## On Your Own (Real World)

WRITE Math

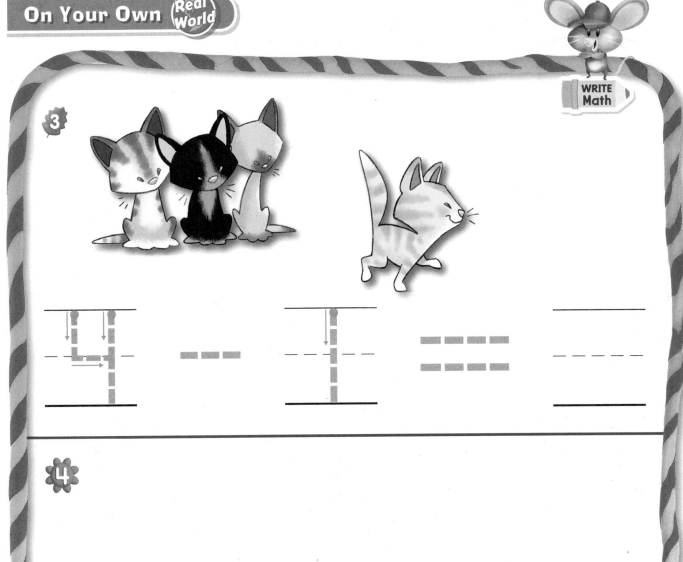

**3**

4 − 1 === _____

**4**

4 − 3 === _____

**DIRECTIONS  3.** Tell a subtraction word problem about the kittens. Trace the numbers and the symbols. Write the number that shows how many kittens are left.  **4.** Draw to show what you know about the subtraction sentence. Write how many are left. Tell a friend a subtraction word problem to match.

**HOME ACTIVITY** • Tell your child a short subtraction word problem. Have him or her use objects to act out the word problem.

# Problem Solving • Act Out
# Subtraction Problems

**Common Core**
**COMMON CORE STANDARD—K.OA.A.1**
*Understand addition as putting together and
adding to, and understand subtraction as
taking apart and taking from.*

 — 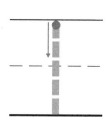 = _____

---

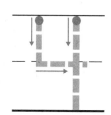 —  = _____

---

**DIRECTIONS** **1.** Tell a subtraction word problem about the beavers.
Trace the numbers and the symbols. Write the number that shows how
many beavers are left. **2.** Draw to tell a story about the subtraction
sentence. Trace the numbers and the symbols. Write how many are left.
Tell a friend about your drawing.

 $5 -- $ 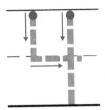 $4 == $ _____

_____

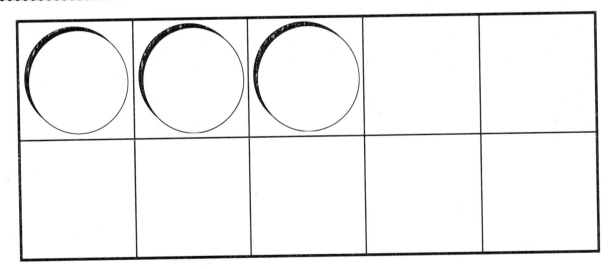

**DIRECTIONS** **1.** Tell a subtraction word problem about the birds. Trace the numbers and the symbols. Write the number that shows how many birds are left. **2.** Count and tell how many bees. Write the number. **3.** How many more counters would you place to model a way to make 7? Draw the counters.

**328** three hundred twenty-eight

FOR MORE PRACTICE
GO TO THE
Personal Math Trainer

Name _____

# Algebra • Model and Draw Subtraction Problems

**Essential Question** How can you use objects and drawings to solve subtraction word problems?

**Common Core** Operations and Algebraic Thinking—K.OA.A.5
*Also K.OA.A.1, K.OA.A.2*
**MATHEMATICAL PRACTICES**
**MP1, MP2, MP4**

**Listen and Draw**

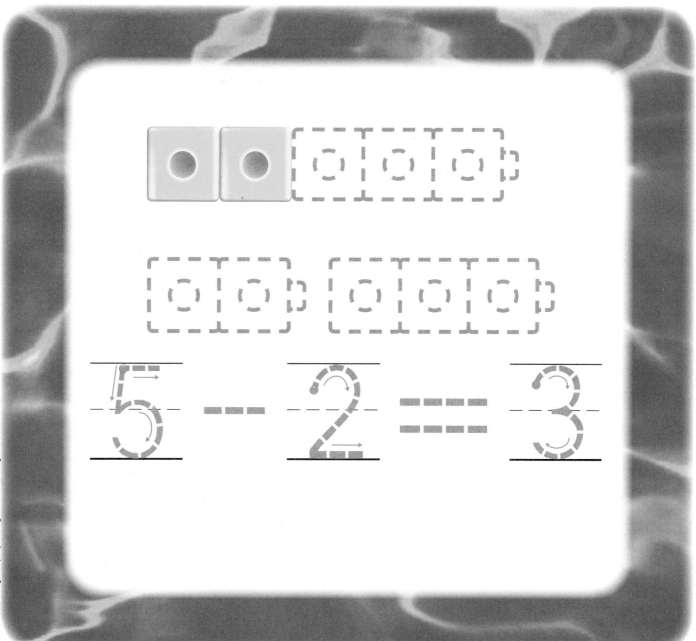

**DIRECTIONS** Model a five-cube train. Two cubes are yellow and the rest are red. Take apart the train to show how many cubes are red. Draw and color the cube trains. Trace the subtraction sentence.

**Chapter 6 • Lesson 4**

three hundred twenty-nine **329**

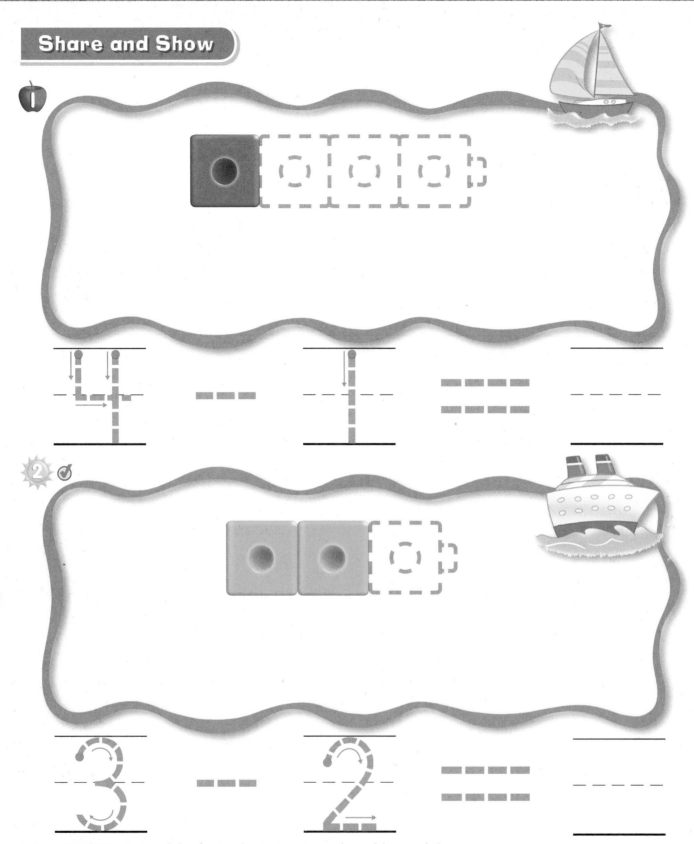

**DIRECTIONS** 1. Model a four-cube train. One cube is blue and the rest are green. Take apart the train to show how many cubes are green. Draw and color the cube trains. Trace and write to complete the subtraction sentence. 2. Model a three-cube train. Two cubes are orange and the rest are blue. Take apart the train to show how many cubes are blue. Draw and color the cube trains. Trace and write to complete the subtraction sentence.

Name _____

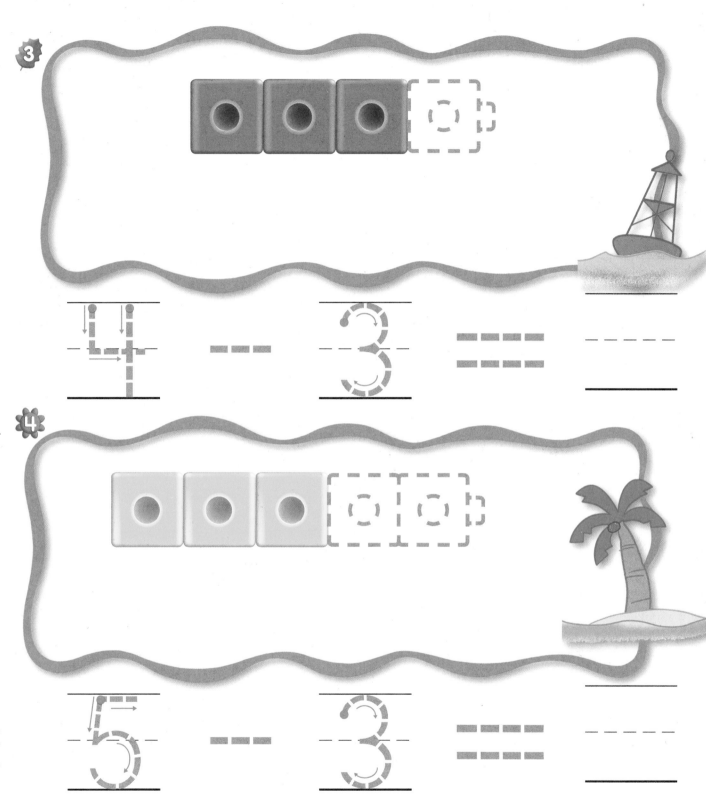

**3**

$$4 - 3 =$$ _____

**4**

$$5 - 3 =$$ _____

© Houghton Mifflin Harcourt Publishing Company

**DIRECTIONS  3.** Model a four-cube train. Three cubes are red and the rest are blue. Take apart the train to show how many cubes are blue. Draw and color the cube trains. Trace and write to complete the subtraction sentence.  **4.** Model a five-cube train. Three cubes are yellow and the rest are green. Take apart the train to show how many cubes are green. Draw and color the cube trains. Trace and write to complete the subtraction sentence.

 **HOME ACTIVITY •** Show your child two small objects. Take apart the set of objects. Have him or her tell a word problem to match the subtraction.

**Concepts and Skills**

**1**

6        minus        1

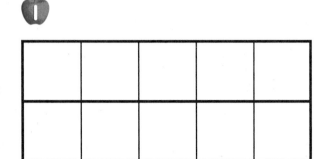

_____        _____        _____

_ _ _ _ _        ▬ ▬ ▬        _ _ _ _ _

_____        _____        _____

 **2**

$$5 - 4 =$$

**3** THINK SMARTER

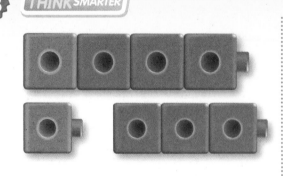

$$4 - 2 = 2 \quad \text{Yes} \circ \quad \text{No} \circ$$

$$4 - 3 = 1 \quad \text{Yes} \circ \quad \text{No} \circ$$

$$3 - 1 = 2 \quad \text{Yes} \circ \quad \text{No} \circ$$

**DIRECTIONS** 1. Choi has 6 counters. One of his counters is yellow. The rest are red. Draw and color the six counters in the ten frame. Write the number that shows how many in all. Write the number that shows how many are yellow. (K.OA.A.1)  2. Model a five-cube train. Four cubes are blue and the rest are orange. Take apart the cube train to show how many are orange. Draw and color the cube trains. Trace and write to complete the subtraction sentence. (K.OA.A.5)  3. Choose Yes or No. Does the subtraction sentence match the model? (K.OA.A.5)

# Algebra • Model and Draw
# Subtraction Problems

 **COMMON CORE STANDARD—K.OA.A.5**
*Understand addition as putting together and adding to, and understand subtraction as taking apart and taking from.*

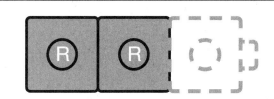

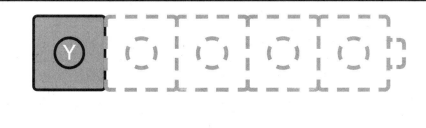

**DIRECTIONS** **1.** Model a three-cube train. Two cubes are red and the rest are blue. Take apart the cube train to show how many cubes are blue. Draw and color the cube trains. Trace and write to complete the subtraction sentence. **2.** Model a five-cube train. One cube is yellow and the rest are green. Take apart the train to show how many cubes are green. Draw and color the cube trains. Trace and write to complete the subtraction sentence.

## Lesson Check (K.OA.A.5)

 --  == _____

## Spiral Review (K.CC.A.2, K.OA.A.3)

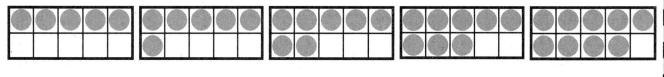

 ___  ___ 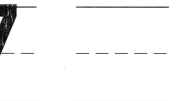 ___

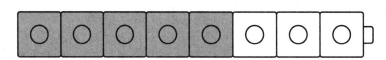

**8** == _____

_____ + _____

**DIRECTIONS** 1. Ellie makes the cube train shown. She takes the cube train apart to show how many cubes are gray. Trace and write to show the subtraction sentence for Ellie's cube train. **2.** Count the dots in the ten frames. Begin with 5. Write the numbers in order as you count forward. **3.** Complete the addition sentence to show the numbers that match the cube train.

**334** three hundred thirty-four

**FOR MORE PRACTICE
GO TO THE**
Personal Math Trainer

Name _____

# Algebra • Write Subtraction Sentences

**Essential Question** How can you solve subtraction word problems and complete the equation?

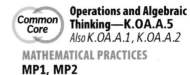

**Common Core** Operations and Algebraic Thinking—K.OA.A.5
*Also K.OA.A.1, K.OA.A.2*
**MATHEMATICAL PRACTICES**
MP1, MP2

**Listen and Draw** *Real World*

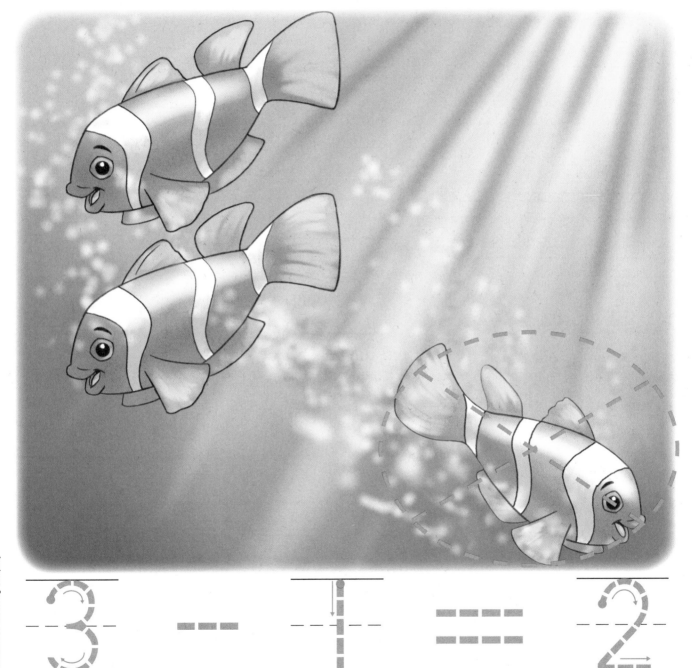

$$3 - 1 = 2$$

**DIRECTIONS** There are three fish. Some fish swim away. Now there are two fish. Trace the circle and X to show the fish swimming away. Trace the subtraction sentence.

**Chapter 6 • Lesson 5**

three hundred thirty-five **335**

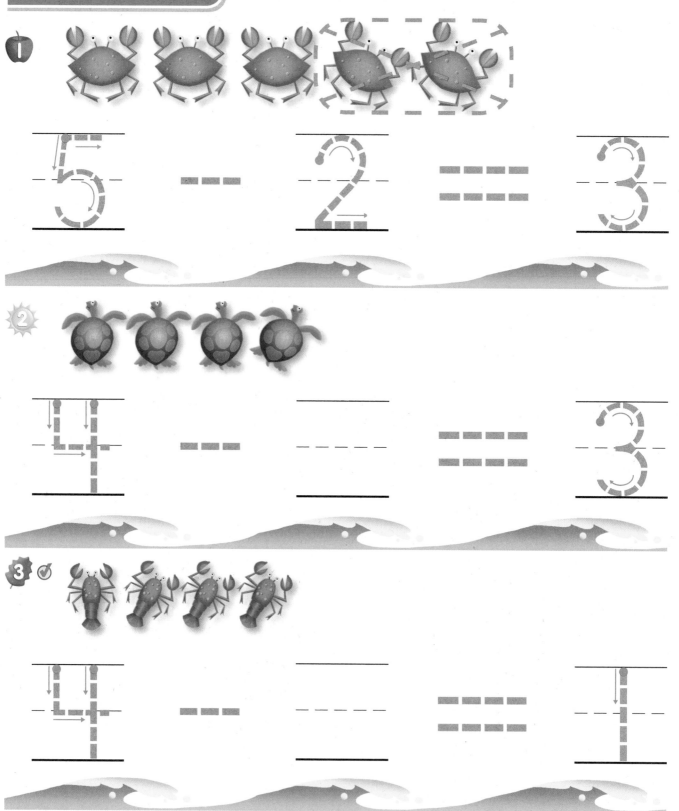

**1**

5 − 2 = 3

**2**

4 − 1 = 3

**3** ✓

4 − 3 = 1

**DIRECTIONS** 1. Listen to the subtraction word problem. Trace the circle and X to show how many are being taken from the set. Trace to complete the subtraction sentence. 2–3. Listen to the subtraction word problem. How many are being taken from the set? Circle and mark an X to show how many are being taken from the set. Trace and write to complete the subtraction sentence.

**4**

$$5 - \_\_\_ = 2$$

**5**

$$3 - \_\_\_ = 1$$

**6**

$$5 - \_\_\_ = 1$$

**DIRECTIONS** 4–6. Listen to the subtraction word problem. How many are being taken from the set? Circle and mark an X to show how many are being taken from the set. Trace and write to complete the subtraction sentence.

# Problem Solving • Applications Real World

WRITE Math

❤️ 7

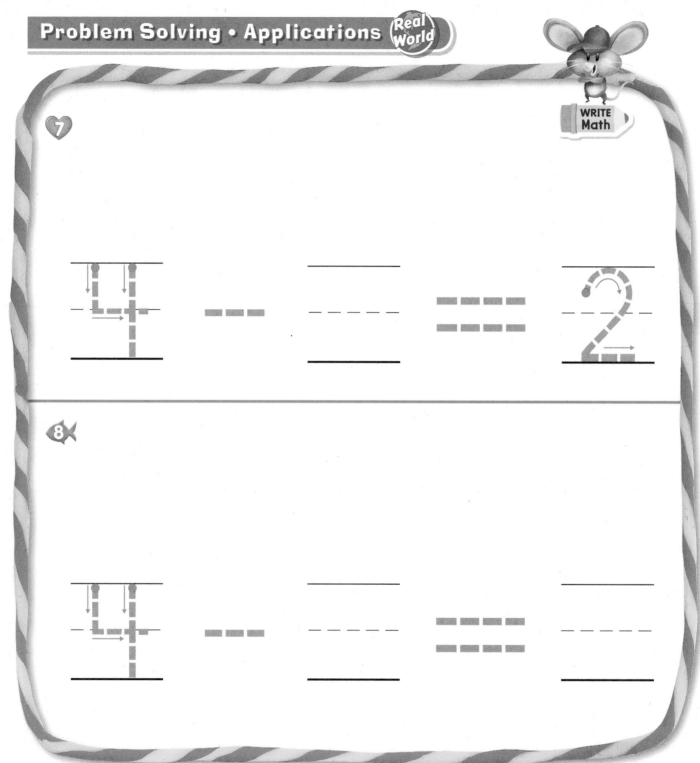

4 - ___ ___ = 2

🐟 8

4 - ___ = ___ = ___

**DIRECTIONS** **7.** Kristen has four flowers. She gives her friend some flowers. Now Kristen has two flowers. How many did Kristen give her friend? Draw to solve the problem. Complete the subtraction sentence. **8.** Tell a different subtraction word problem about the flowers. Draw to solve the problem. Tell a friend about your drawing. Complete the subtraction sentence.

**HOME ACTIVITY** • Have your child draw a set of five or fewer balloons. Have him or her circle and mark an X on some balloons to show that they have popped. Then have your child tell a word problem to match the subtraction.

**338** three hundred thirty-eight

# Algebra • Write Subtraction Sentences

**COMMON CORE STANDARD—K.OA.A.5**
*Understand addition as putting together and adding to, and understand subtraction as taking apart and taking from.*

4 − ___ = 1

---

3 − ___ = 2

---

5 − ___ = 1

---

**DIRECTIONS** 1–3. Listen to the subtraction word problem about the animals. There are ____ ____. Some are taken from the set. Now there are ____. How many are taken from the set? Circle and mark an X to show how many are being taken from the set. Trace and write to complete the subtraction sentence.

## Lesson Check (K.OA.A.5)

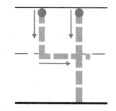   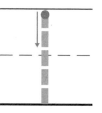

## Spiral Review (K.CC.B.5, K.CC.C.6)

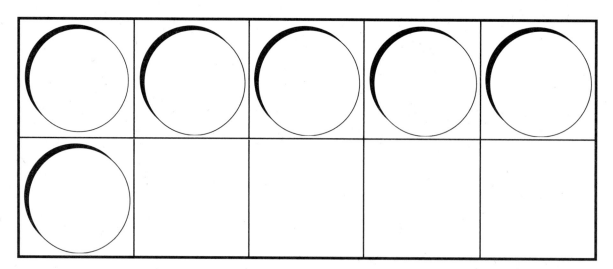

**DIRECTIONS 1.** Trace and write to show the subtraction sentence for the set. **2.** Count the number of counters in each set. Circle the set that has the greater number of counters. **3.** How many more counters would you place to model a way to make 9? Draw the counters.

FOR MORE PRACTICE
GO TO THE
**Personal Math Trainer**

Name _____

# Algebra • Write More Subtraction Sentences

**Essential Question** How can you solve subtraction word problems and complete the equation?

**Common Core** Operations and Algebraic Thinking—K.OA.A.2
*Also K.OA.A.1*
**MATHEMATICAL PRACTICES**
**MP1, MP2**

**Listen and Draw** *Real World*

**DIRECTIONS** There are six birds. A bird flies away. Trace the circle and X around that bird. How many birds are left? Trace the subtraction sentence.

**Chapter 6 • Lesson 6**

three hundred forty-one **341**

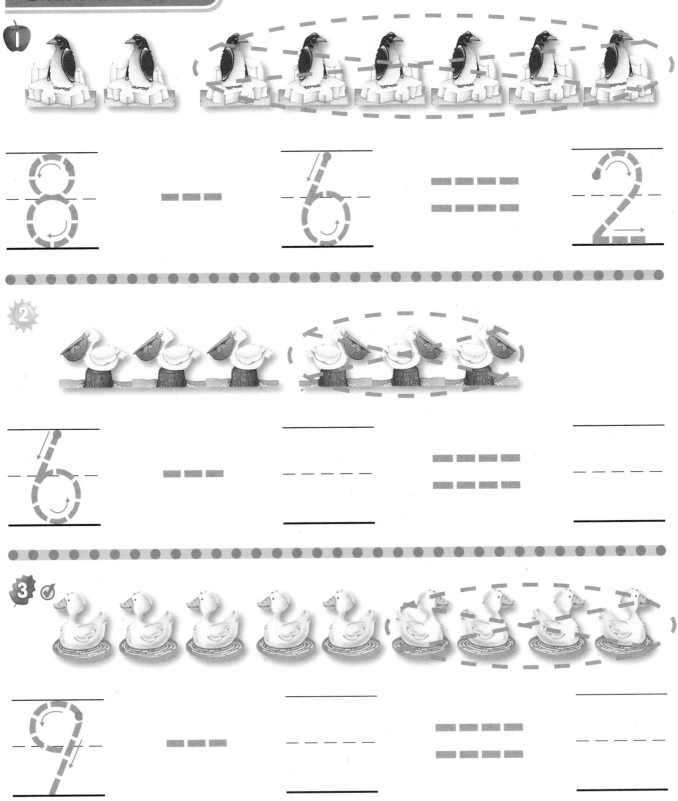

1.    8   –   6   =   2

2.    6   –   ___   =   ___

3.    9   –   ___   =   ___

**DIRECTIONS** Listen to the subtraction word problem.   **1.** How many birds are taken from the set? Trace the circle and X. How many birds are left? Trace the subtraction sentence.   **2–3.** How many birds are taken from the set? Trace the circle and X. How many birds are left? Trace and write to complete the subtraction sentence.

**❋ 4**

6   - -   _ _ _   == ==   _ _ _

**❋ 5**

9   - -   _ _ _   == ==   _ _ _

**❋ 6**

8   - -   _ _ _   == ==   _ _ _

**DIRECTIONS** **4–6.** Listen to the subtraction word problem. How many birds are taken from the set? Trace the circle and X. How many birds are left? Trace and write to complete the subtraction sentence.

## Problem Solving • Applications  Real World

WRITE Math

7

$$8 - \_\_\_ = \_\_\_$$

**DIRECTIONS** 7. Complete the subtraction sentence. Draw a picture of real objects to show what you know about this subtraction sentence. Tell a friend about your drawing.

**HOME ACTIVITY** • Tell your child you have ten small objects in your hand. Tell him or her that you are taking two objects from the set. Ask him or her to tell you how many objects are in your hand now.

# Algebra • Write More
# Subtraction Sentences

**COMMON CORE STANDARD—K.OA.A.2**
*Understand addition as putting together and
adding to, and understand subtraction as
taking apart and taking from.*

Common
Core

**❶**

___ ___ = ___

**❷**

___ ___ = ___

**❸**

___ ___ = ___

**DIRECTIONS    1–3.** Listen to a subtraction word problem about the birds. There
are seven birds. _____ birds are taken from the set. Now there are _____ birds. How
many birds are taken from the set? How many birds are there now? Trace and write
to complete the subtraction sentence.

**Chapter 6**

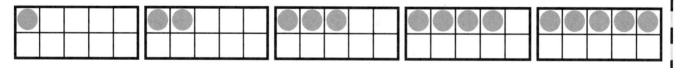

**DIRECTIONS** 1. Trace and write to show the subtraction sentence for the buses. **2.** How many lunch boxes are there? Write the number. **3.** Count the dots in the ten frames. Begin with 1. Write the numbers in order as you count forward.

346 three hundred forty-six

FOR MORE PRACTICE
GO TO THE
**Personal Math Trainer**

Name _____

# Algebra • Addition and Subtraction

**Essential Question** How can you solve word problems using addition and subtraction?

**Common Core** Operations and Algebraic Thinking—K.OA.A.2
*Also K.OA.A.1*
**MATHEMATICAL PRACTICES**
**MP2, MP5, MP8**

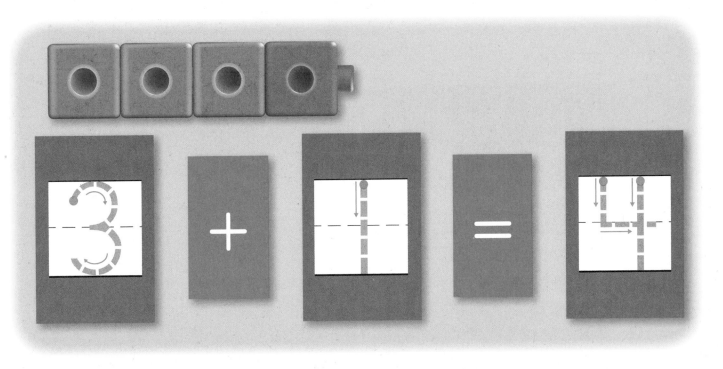

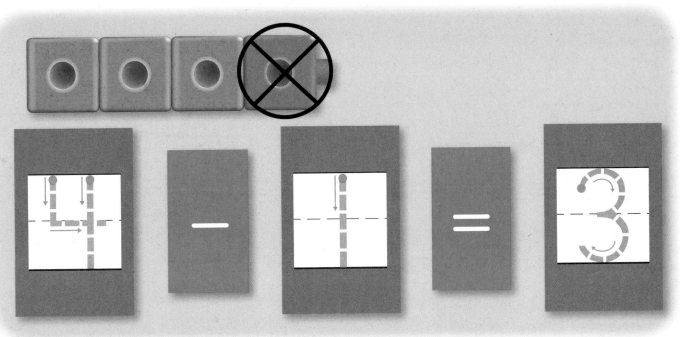

**DIRECTIONS** Listen to the addition and subtraction word problems. Use cubes and Number and Symbol Tiles as shown to match the word problems. Trace to complete the number sentences.

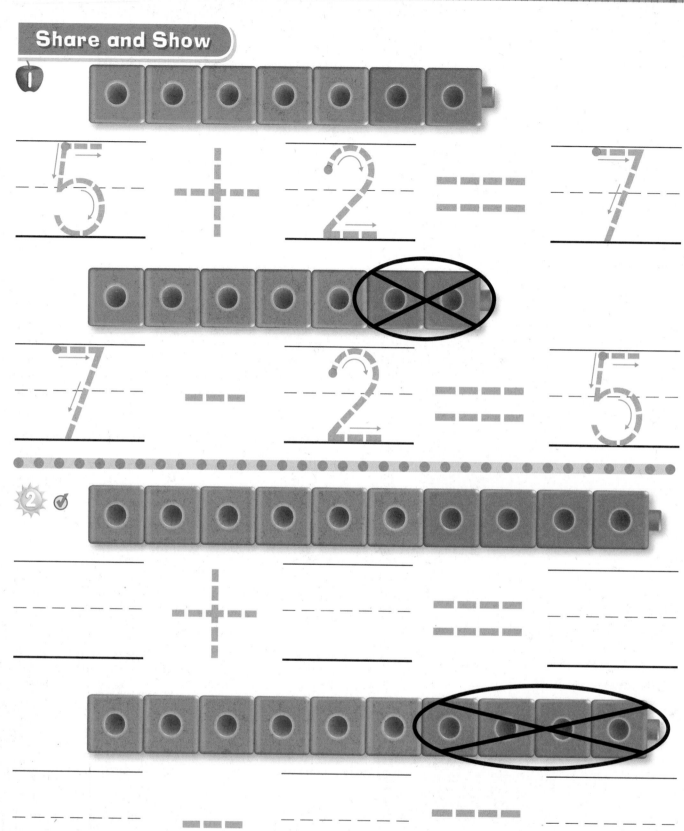

**DIRECTIONS** Tell addition and subtraction word problems.
Use cubes to add and to subtract.   **I.** Trace the number
sentences.   **2.** Complete the number sentences.

Name _____

**3**

_ _ _ _      **+**      _ _ _ _      **=**      _ _ _ _

_____      _____      _____

_ _ _ _      **–**      _ _ _ _      **=**      _ _ _ _

_____      _____      _____

**4**

_ _ _ _      **+**      _ _ _ _      **=**      _ _ _ _

_____      _____      _____

_ _ _ _      **–**      _ _ _ _      **=**      _ _ _ _

_____      _____      _____

**DIRECTIONS** 3–4. Tell addition and subtraction word problems. Use cubes to add and subtract. Complete the number sentences.

**Chapter 6 • Lesson 7**                    three hundred forty-nine **349**

## Problem Solving • Applications  Real World

WRITE Math

$$6 + 3 = 9$$

**5**

_____    \_ \_ \_ \_ \_    ▭▭▭▭    \_ \_ \_ \_

\_ \_ \_    ▭▭

_____    \_\_\_\_\_    \_\_\_\_\_    \_\_\_\_\_

**6**

_____    \_\_\_\_\_    ▭▭▭

\_ \_ \_ \_    \_ \_ \_ \_    ▭▭▭

\_ \_ \_    \_ \_ \_ \_

_____    \_\_\_\_\_    \_\_\_\_\_

**DIRECTIONS** Look at the addition sentence at the top of the page. **5–6.** Tell a related subtraction word problem. Complete the subtraction sentence.

**HOME ACTIVITY** • Ask your child to use objects to model a simple addition problem. Then have him or her explain how to make it into a subtraction problem.

Name _____

# Algebra • Addition and Subtraction

 **COMMON CORE STANDARD—K.OA.A.2**
*Understand addition as putting together and adding to, and understand subtraction as taking apart and taking from.*

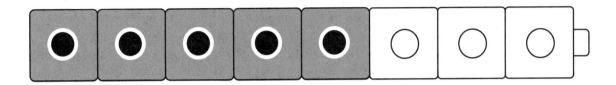

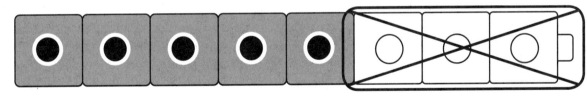

**DIRECTIONS** 1–2. Tell an addition or subtraction word problem. Use cubes to add or subtract. Complete the number sentence.

**Chapter 6**

## Lesson Check  (K.OA.A.2)

**1**

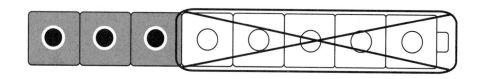

_____      _____  =  _____      _____  =  _____

## Spiral Review (K.CC.C.7, K.OA.A.3)

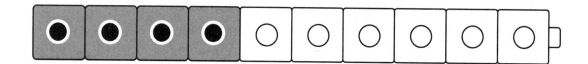

  =  _____  +  _____

# 8                              9

**DIRECTIONS  1.** Tell a subtraction word problem. Use cubes to subtract. Complete the number sentence.  **2.** Complete the addition sentence to show the numbers that match the cube train.  **3.** Compare the numbers. Circle the number that is greater.

**352** three hundred fifty-two

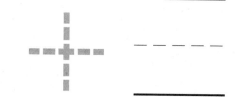
FOR MORE PRACTICE
GO TO THE
**Personal Math Trainer**

Name _____

**①**

4 take away _____

_____

_____

_____

**②**

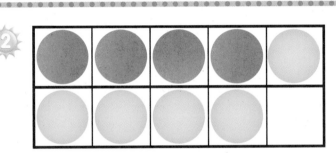

9 – 1   ○ Yes   ○ No

9 – 5   ○ Yes   ○ No

8 – 3   ○ Yes   ○ No

**Personal Math Trainer**

**③** THINK SMARTER +

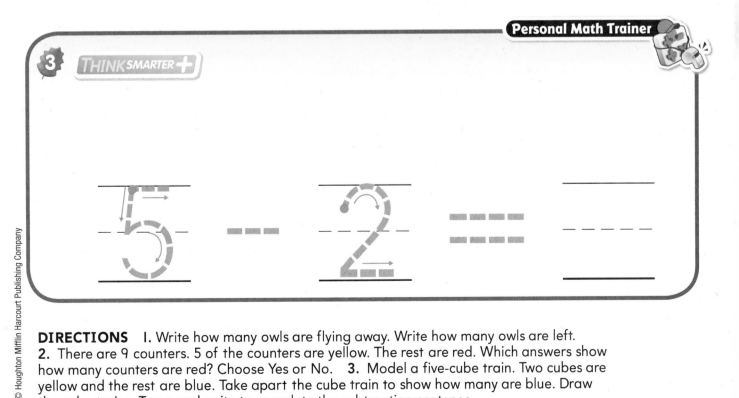

5 – 2 = _____

**DIRECTIONS** 1. Write how many owls are flying away. Write how many owls are left.
2. There are 9 counters. 5 of the counters are yellow. The rest are red. Which answers show how many counters are red? Choose Yes or No. 3. Model a five-cube train. Two cubes are yellow and the rest are blue. Take apart the cube train to show how many are blue. Draw the cube trains. Trace and write to complete the subtraction sentence.

**4**

$$4 - 2 = \underline{\qquad}$$

**5**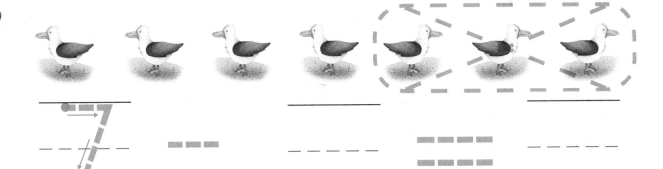

$$7 - \underline{\quad} = \underline{\qquad}$$

**6**

5 − 4 = 1    Yes    No

4 + 1 = 5    Yes    No

5 − 2 = 3    Yes    No

**7**

9 = 3 + 6     10 = 3 + 7     3 + 7 = 10

○         ○         ○

**DIRECTIONS** **4.** There are 4 penguins. Two penguins are taken from the set. How many penguins are left? Trace and write to complete the subtraction sentence. **5.** There are seven birds. Some birds are taken from the set. How many birds are left? Trace and write to complete the subtraction sentence. **6.** Does the number sentence match the picture? Circle Yes or No. **7.** Mark under all the number sentences that match the cubes.

Name _____

4 - 3 = ___

8 - 1 = ___

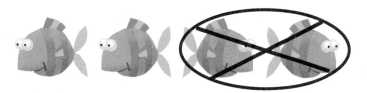

4 - ___ = 2

**DIRECTIONS   8.** Model a four-cube train. Three cubes are red and the rest are blue. Take apart the train to show how many cubes are blue. Draw the cube trains. Complete the subtraction sentence.   **9–10.** Complete the subtraction sentence to match the picture.

**11**  **THINK SMARTER +**

_____  _____
- - - - - - = - - - - - - = 0
_____  _____

**12**

_____  _____  _____
5 - - _____ = _____
_____  _____  _____

**13**

_____  _____
6 - - _____ = 4
_____  _____

**DIRECTIONS** **11.** There were some apples on a tree. Some were taken away. Now there are zero apples left. Draw to show how many apples there could have been to start. Cross out apples to show how many were taken away. Complete the subtraction sentence. **12.** There are five birds. Some birds are taken from the set. How many birds are left? Trace and write to complete the subtraction sentence. **13.** Erica has 6 balloons. She gives some of her balloons to a friend. Now Erica has 4 balloons. How many did Erica give to her friend? Draw to solve the problem. Complete the subtraction sentence.

# Represent, Count, and Write 11 to 19

**Curious About Math with**

## Curious George

Shells come in many colors and patterns.

- Is the number of shells greater than or less than 10?

Name _____

## Draw Objects to 10

 **1**

# 10

**2**

# 9

## Write Numbers to 10

**3**

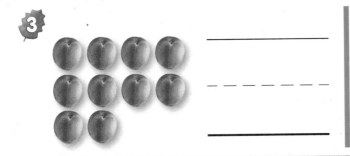

_____

- - - - - - - - - - - - - - -

_____

**4**

_____

- - - - - - - - - - - - - - -

_____

**5**

_____

- - - - - - - - - - - - - - -

_____

**6**

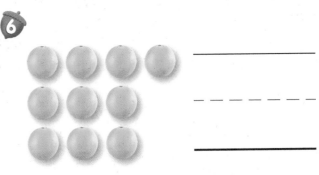

_____

- - - - - - - - - - - - - - -

_____

This page checks understanding of important skills needed for success in Chapter 7.

**DIRECTIONS** **1.** Draw 10 oranges. **2.** Draw 9 apples. **3–6.** Count and tell how many. Write the number.

Name _____

FINISH

three

four

one 1

two

3

4

five

5

eight 8

seven 7

six 6

CABBAGE PARK RUN

9

10

nine

ten

**DIRECTIONS** Circle the number word that is greater than nine.

**GO DIGITAL**
• **Interactive Student Edition**
• **Multimedia eGlossary**

## Game

# Sweet and Sour Path

**DIRECTIONS** Play with a partner. Place game markers on START. Take turns. Toss the number cube. Move that number of spaces. If a player lands on a lemon, the player reads the number and moves back that many spaces. If a player lands on a strawberry, the player reads the number and moves forward that many spaces. If a player lands on a space without a lemon or strawberry, it is the other player's turn. The first player to reach END wins.

**MATERIALS** two game markers, number cube (1–6)

# Chapter 7 Vocabulary

**eighteen**
dieciocho
21

**eleven**
once
22

**fifteen**
quince
24

**fourteen**
catorce
29

**nineteen**
diecinueve
46

**ones**
unidades
49

**seventeen**
diecisiete
60

**sixteen**
dieciséis
65

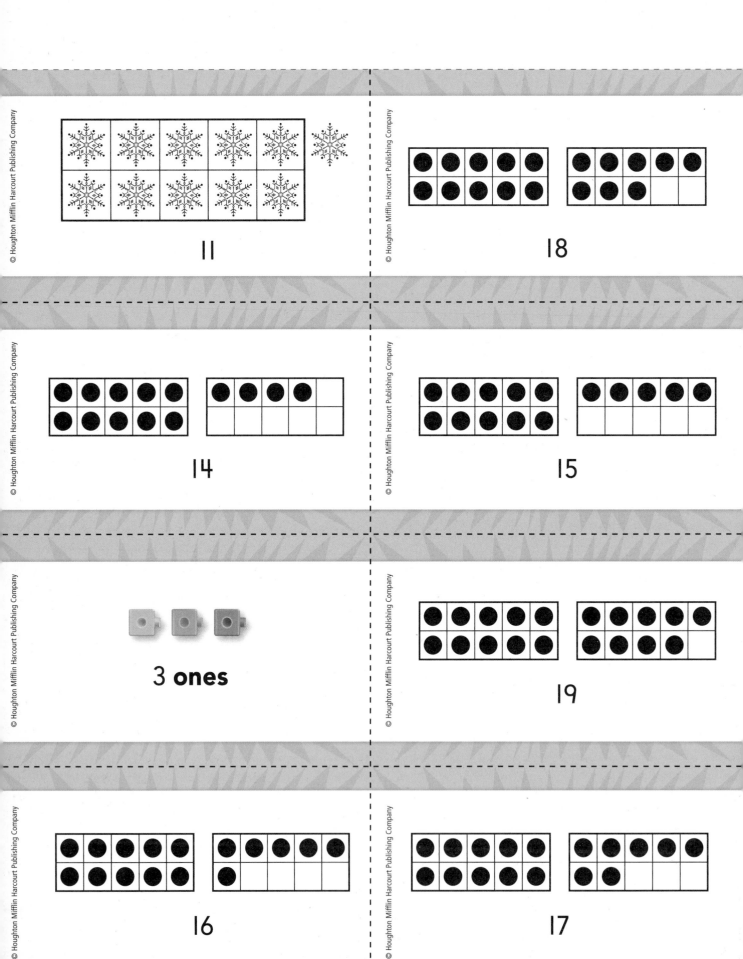

11

18

14

15

**3 ones**

19

16

17

**thirteen**

trece

76

**twelve**

doce

80

**two**

dos

82

**zero**

cero, ninguno

86

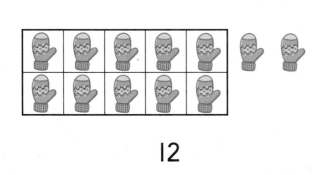

12

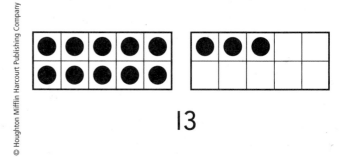

13

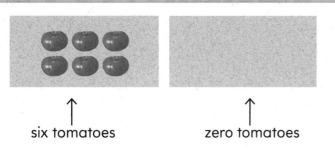

↑         ↑

six tomatoes     zero tomatoes

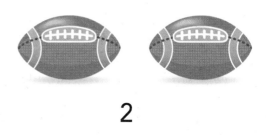

2

# Guess the Word

### Word Box
eleven
twelve
thirteen
fourteen
fifteen
sixteen
seventeen
eighteen
nineteen
ones

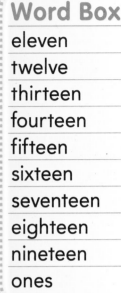

## Secret Words

| Player 1 | | | | | |
|---|---|---|---|---|---|
| | | | | | |
| **Player 2** | | | | | |
| | | | | | |

**DIRECTIONS** Players take turns. A player chooses a secret word from the Word Box and then sets the timer. The player gives hints about the secret word. If the other player guesses the secret word before time runs out, he or she puts a connecting cube in the chart. The first player who has connecting cubes in all his or her boxes is the winner.

**MATERIALS** timer, connecting cubes for each player

# The Write Way

**DIRECTIONS** Trace 17. Draw to show what you know about 17.
**Reflect** Be ready to tell about your drawing.

Name _____

# Model and Count 11 and 12

**Essential Question** How can you use objects to show 11 and 12 as ten ones and some more ones?

**Common Core** Number and Operations in Base Ten—K.NBT.A.1
*Also K.CC.B.4b, K.CC.B.4c, K.CC.B.5*

MATHEMATICAL PRACTICES
**MP2, MP3, MP7**

**DIRECTIONS** Use counters to show the number 11. Add more to show the number 12. Draw the counters. Tell a friend what you know about these numbers.

**Chapter 7 • Lesson 1**

three hundred sixty-one **361**

1 eleven

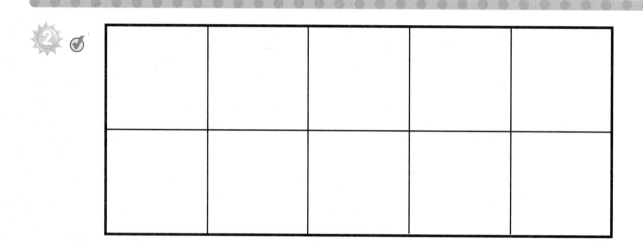

2 ✓

3

ones and _____ one

**DIRECTIONS** 1. Count and tell how many. Trace the number. 2. Use counters to show the number 11. Draw the counters. 3. Look at the counters you drew. How many ones are in the ten frame? Trace the number. How many more ones are there? Write the number.

Name _____

**4**

# 12
## twelve

**5**

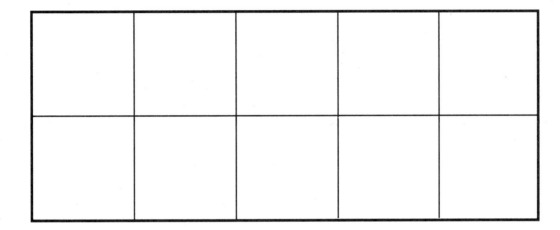

**6**

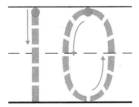    _____

ones and    _____ **ones**

**DIRECTIONS** **4.** Count and tell how many. Trace the number.   **5.** Use counters to show the number 12. Draw the counters.   **6.** Look at the counters you drew. How many ones are in the ten frame? Trace the number. How many more ones are there? Write the number.

# Problem Solving · Applications · Real World

WRITE Math

**7**

**8**

**9**

**11** == == == — — — + — — —

**DIRECTIONS** **7.** Maria makes a bracelet with 11 beads. She starts with the blue bead on the left. Circle to show the beads Maria uses to make her bracelet. **8.** Are there more blue beads or more yellow beads in those 11 beads? Circle the color bead that has more. **9.** Draw a set of 11 objects. If you circle 10 of the objects, how many more objects are there? Complete the addition sentence to match.

**HOME ACTIVITY** • Draw a ten frame on a sheet of paper. Have your child use small objects, such as buttons, pennies, or dried beans, to show the numbers 11 and 12.

**Practice and Homework**
**Lesson 7.1**

# Model and Count 11 and 12

**Common Core**

**COMMON CORE STANDARD—K.NBT.A.1**
*Work with numbers 11–19 to gain foundations for place value.*

## 12
**twelve**

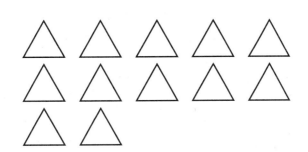

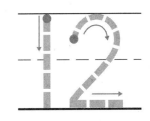

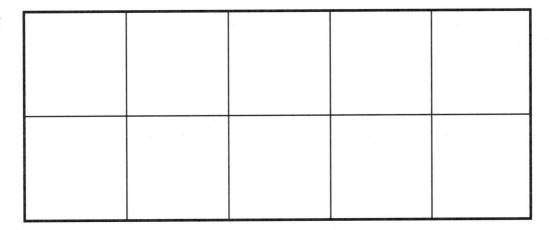

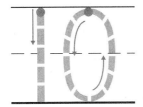

_____
- - - - - -

**ones and** _____ **ones**

**DIRECTIONS** 1. Count and tell how many. Trace the number. 2. Use counters to show the number 12. Draw the counters. 3. Look at the counters you drew. How many ones are in the ten frame? Trace the number. How many more ones are there? Write the number.

**Chapter 7**

# Lesson Check (K.NBT.A.1)

 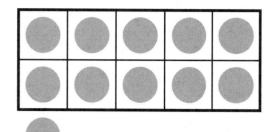

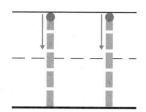

# Spiral Review (K.CC.C.6, K.OA.A.5)

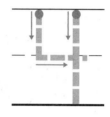 

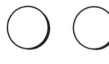

**DIRECTIONS** **1.** Count and tell how many. Trace the number. **2.** Write and trace to show the addition sentence for the sets of airplanes. **3.** Count and tell how many in each set. Write the numbers. Compare the numbers. Circle the number that is less.

FOR MORE PRACTICE
GO TO THE
**Personal Math Trainer**

Name _____

# Count and Write 11 and 12

**Essential Question** How can you count and write 11 and 12 with words and numbers?

**Common Core** Number and Operations in Base Ten—K.NBT.A.1
Also K.CC.A.3, K.CC.B.4b
**MATHEMATICAL PRACTICES**
MP2, MP7, MP8

**Listen and Draw**

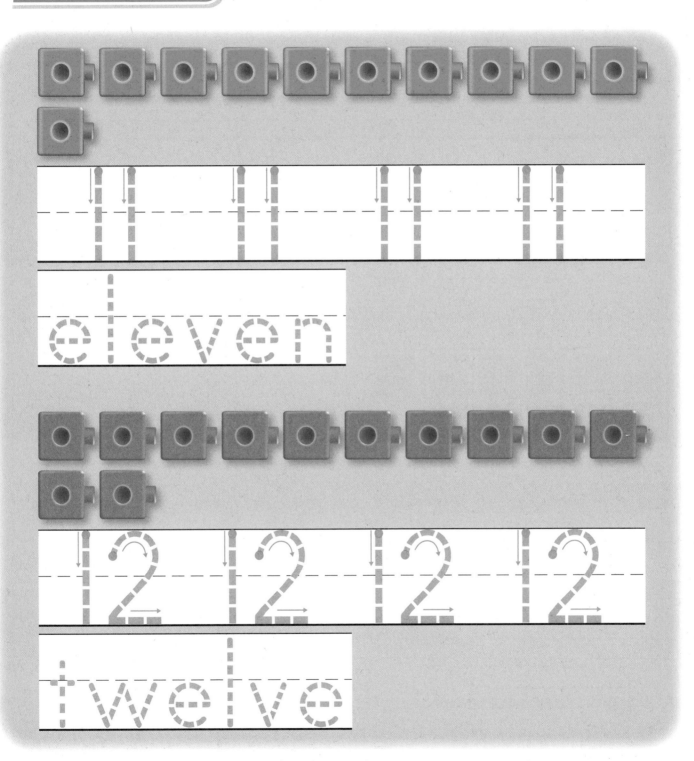

**DIRECTIONS** Count and tell how many. Trace the numbers and the words.

Chapter 7 • Lesson 2

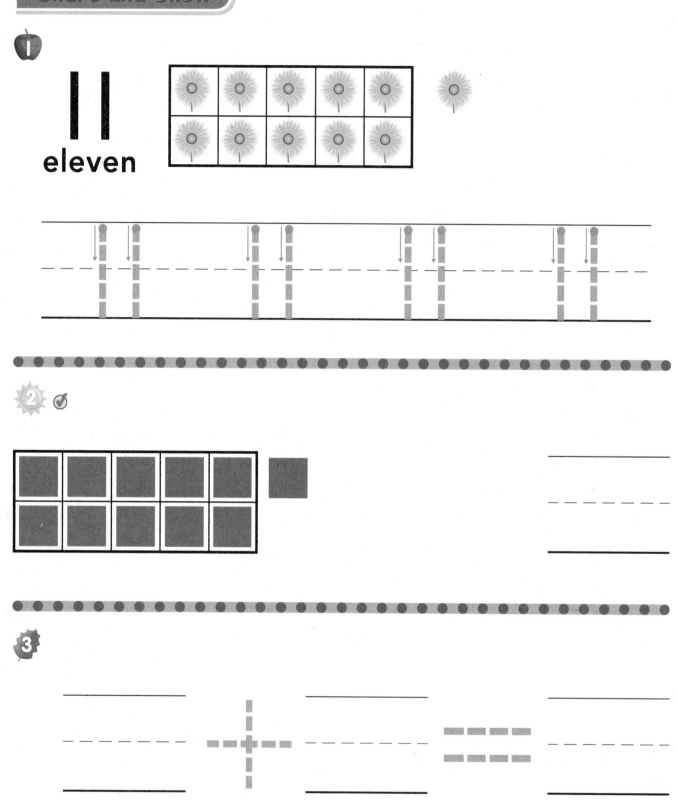

**1**

11
eleven

**2** ✓

**3**

**DIRECTIONS** 1. Count and tell how many. Trace the numbers. 2. Count and tell how many. Write the number. 3. Look at the ten ones and some more ones in Exercise 2. Complete the addition sentence to match.

**368** three hundred sixty-eight

## 4

# 12
## twelve

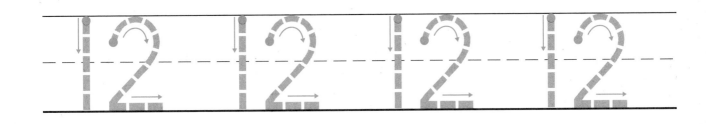

## 5

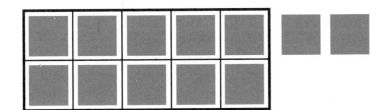

_____

- - - - - - - - - - -

_____

## 6

_____        _____        _____

- - - - - -  +  - - - - - -  =  - - - - - -

_____        _____        _____

**DIRECTIONS** **4.** Count and tell how many. Trace the numbers.   **5.** Count and tell how many. Write the number.   **6.** Look at the ten ones and some more ones in Exercise 5. Complete the addition sentence to match.

## Problem Solving • Applications  Real World

**WRITE Math**

**7**

11

12

13

**8**

12 = __ __ = ___ ___ + ___

**DIRECTIONS** **7.** Brooke picked a number of flowers. Circle the number of flowers Brooke picked. Draw more flowers to show that number.   **8.** Draw a set of 12 objects. If you circle 10 of the objects, how many more objects are there? Complete the addition sentence to match.

**HOME ACTIVITY •** Ask your child to count and write the number for a set of 11 or 12 objects, such as coins or buttons.

© Houghton Mifflin Harcourt Publishing Company

# Count and Write 11 and 12

Common Core

**COMMON CORE STANDARD—K.NBT.A.1**
*Work with numbers 11–19 to gain foundations for place value.*

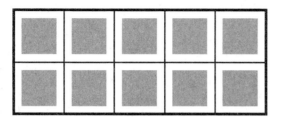 

_____

_  _  _  _  _  _

_____

_____  _____  _____

_____  _____  _____

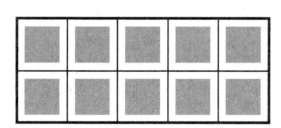 

_____

_  _  _  _  _  _

_____

_____  _____  _____

_____  _____  _____

**DIRECTIONS 1.** Count and tell how many. Write the number.
**2.** Look at the ten ones and some more ones in Exercise 1.
Complete the addition sentence to match. **3.** Count and tell how
many. Write the number. **4.** Look at the ten ones and some more
ones in Exercise 3. Complete the addition sentence to match.

**Chapter 7**

## Lesson Check

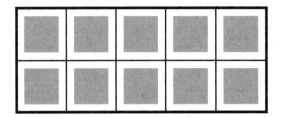

_____   +   _____   =   _____

## Spiral Review

---

**DIRECTIONS** **1.** Look at the ten ones and some more ones. Complete the addition sentence to match. **2.** Trace and write to show the subtraction sentence for the fish. **3.** How many birds are there? Write the number.

© Houghton Mifflin Harcourt Publishing Company

**FOR MORE PRACTICE GO TO THE Personal Math Trainer**

Name _____

# Model and Count 13 and 14

**Essential Question** How can you use objects to show 13 and 14 as ten ones and some more ones?

**Listen and Draw**

**Common Core** **Number and Operations in Base Ten—K.NBT.A.1**
*Also K.CC.B.4b, K.CC.B.4c, K.CC.B.5*

**MATHEMATICAL PRACTICES**
**MP2, MP3, MP7**

**DIRECTIONS** Use counters to show the number 13. Add more to show the number 14. Draw the counters. Tell a friend what you know about these numbers.

**Chapter 7 • Lesson 3**

**13**
**thirteen**

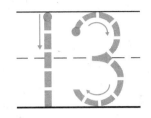

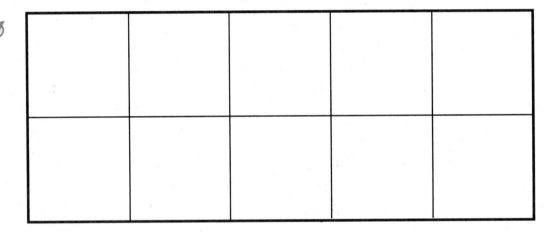

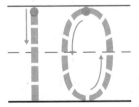 **ones and** _____ **ones**

**DIRECTIONS** 1. Count and tell how many. Trace the number. 2. Use counters to show the number 13. Draw the counters. 3. Look at the counters you drew. How many ones are in the ten frame? Trace the number. How many more ones are there? Write the number.

**374** three hundred seventy-four

Name _____

 **14**
**fourteen**

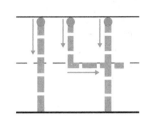

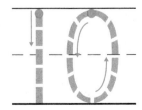

_____  _ _ _ _ _ _

**ones and** _____ **ones**

**DIRECTIONS** 4. Count and tell how many. Trace the number. 5. Use counters to show the number 14. Draw the counters. 6. Look at the counters you drew. How many ones are in the ten frame? Trace the number. How many more ones are there? Write the number.

## Problem Solving • Applications Real World

**7**

**8**

**9**

13 === ___ ___ + ___

**DIRECTIONS** **7.** Erika makes a bracelet with 13 beads. She starts with the blue bead on the left. Circle to show the beads Erika uses to make her bracelet. **8.** Are there more blue beads or more yellow beads in those 13 beads? Circle the color bead that has more. **9.** Draw a set of 13 objects. If you circle 10 of the objects, how many more objects are there? Complete the addition sentence to match.

**HOME ACTIVITY** • Draw a ten frame on a sheet of paper. Have your child use small objects, such as buttons, pennies, or dried beans, to show the numbers 13 and 14.

## Model and Count 13 and 14

 **COMMON CORE STANDARD—K.NBT.A.1**
Work with numbers 11–19 to gain foundations for place value.

# 14
## fourteen

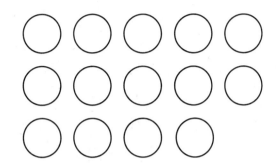

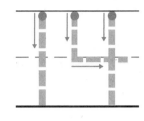

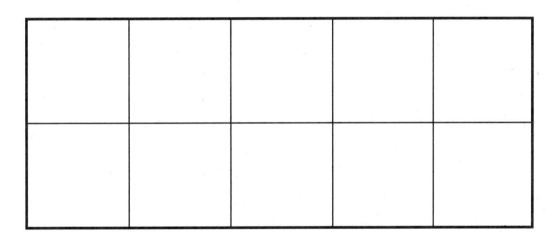

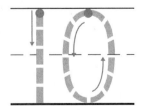

**ones and** _____ **ones**

**DIRECTIONS** 1. Count and tell how many. Trace the number. 2. Use counters to show the number 14. Draw the counters. 3. Look at the counters you drew. How many ones are in the ten frame? Trace the number. How many more ones are there? Write the number.

# Lesson Check (K.NBT.A.1)

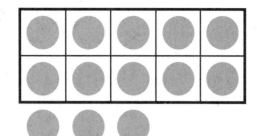
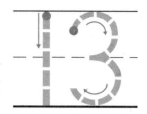

# Spiral Review (K.OA.A.1, K.OA.A.2)

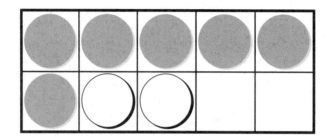

**DIRECTIONS** 1. Count and tell how many. Trace the number. 2. Show the sets that are put together. Write the numbers and trace the symbol. 3. Trace and write to show the subtraction sentence.

FOR MORE PRACTICE
GO TO THE
**Personal Math Trainer**

Name _____

# Count and Write 13 and 14

**Essential Question** How can you count and write 13 and 14 with words and numbers?

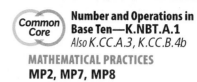

Common Core — **Number and Operations in Base Ten—K.NBT.A.1** *Also K.CC.A.3, K.CC.B.4b*
**MATHEMATICAL PRACTICES**
MP2, MP7, MP8

**Listen and Draw**

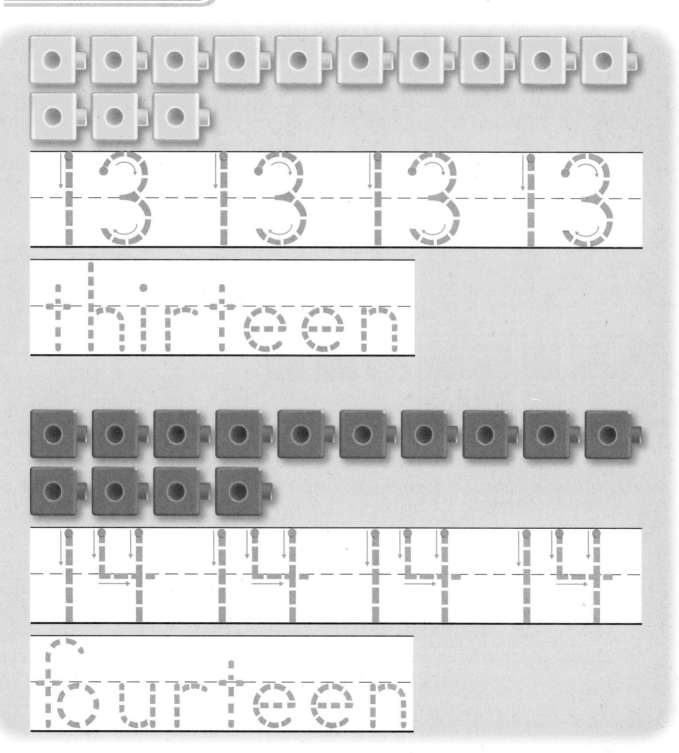

**DIRECTIONS** Count and tell how many. Trace the numbers and the words.

Chapter 7 • Lesson 4

three hundred seventy-nine **379**

## Share and Show

**1**

# 13
## thirteen

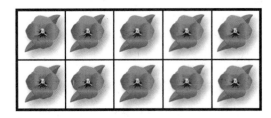 

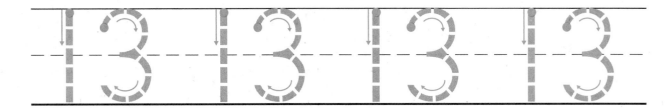

**2** ✓

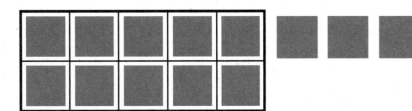 

_____
- - - - - - - - - - - - -
_____

**3**

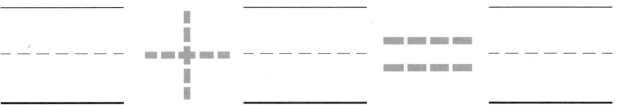

_____   +   _____   =   _____

**DIRECTIONS** 1. Count and tell how many. Trace the numbers. **2.** Count and tell how many. Write the number. **3.** Look at the ten ones and some more ones in Exercise 2. Complete the addition sentence to match.

**380** three hundred eighty

**4**

# 14
## fourteen

14  14  14  14

**5**

_____

- - - - - - - - - -

_____

**6**

_____  +  _____  =  _____

**DIRECTIONS** 4. Count and tell how many. Trace the numbers. 5. Count and tell how many. Write the number. 6. Look at the ten ones and some more ones in Exercise 5. Complete the addition sentence to match.

## Problem Solving • Applications

**7**

12

13

14

**8**

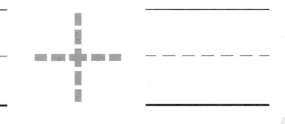

14 = ___ ___ + ___

**DIRECTIONS 7.** Eva picked 13 flowers. Circle the number of flowers Eva picked. Draw more flowers to show that number. **8.** Draw a set of 14 objects. If you circle 10 of the objects, how many more objects are there? Complete the addition sentence to match.

**HOME ACTIVITY •** Ask your child to count and write the number for a set of 13 or 14 objects, such as coins or buttons.

Name _____

# Count and Write 13 and 14

Common Core    **COMMON CORE STANDARD—K.NBT.A.1**
*Work with numbers 11–19 to gain foundations
for place value.*

**1**

_____

- - - - - - - - -

_____

**2**

_____   +   _____   =   _____

_____       _____       _____

**3**

_____

- - - - - - - - -

**4**

_____   +   _____   =   _____

_____       _____       _____

---

**DIRECTIONS**  **1.** Count and tell how many. Write the number.  **2.** Look at the ten ones and some more ones in Exercise 1. Complete the addition sentence to match.  **3.** Count and tell how many. Write the number.  **4.** Look at the ten ones and some more ones in Exercise 3. Complete the addition sentence to match.

**Chapter 7**

three hundred eighty-three **383**

## Lesson Check (K.NBT.A.1)

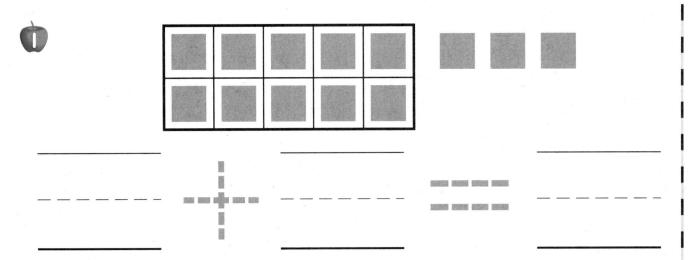

## Spiral Review (K.CC.B.4C, K.OA.A.1)

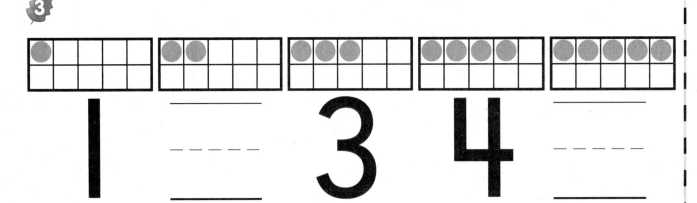

**DIRECTIONS 1.** Look at the ten ones and some more ones. Complete the addition sentence to match. **2.** Tell a subtraction word problem about the cats. Write and trace to complete the subtraction sentence. **3.** Count the dots in the ten frames. Begin with I. Write the numbers in order as you count forward.

FOR MORE PRACTICE
GO TO THE
**Personal Math Trainer**

Name _____

# Model, Count, and Write 15

**Essential Question** How can you use objects to show 15 as ten ones and some more ones and show 15 as a number?

**Listen and Draw**

Common Core — **Number and Operations in Base Ten—K.NBT.A.1**
Also K.CC.A.3, K.CC.B.4b, K.CC.B.5
**MATHEMATICAL PRACTICES**
MP2, MP5, MP7

**DIRECTIONS** Use counters to show the number 15. Draw the counters. Tell a friend about the counters.

three hundred eighty-five **385**

**15**

fifteen

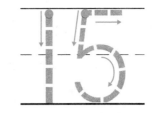

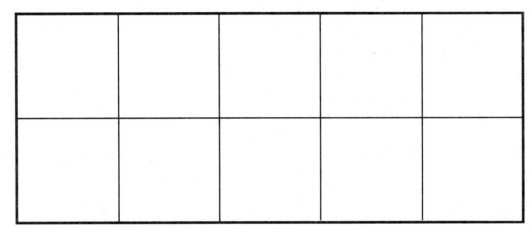

**ones and** _____ **ones**

**DIRECTIONS** 1. Count and tell how many. Trace the number.   2. Use counters to show the number 15. Draw the counters.   3. Look at the counters you drew. How many ones are in the ten frame? Trace the number. How many more ones? Write the number.

Name _____

15
fifteen

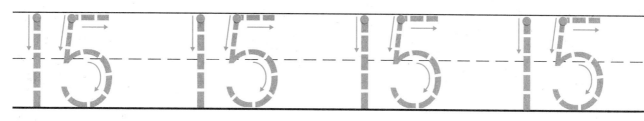

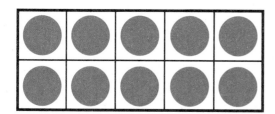

_____

- - - - - - - - - - - - -

_____

**DIRECTIONS** 4. Count and tell how many. Trace the numbers.
5. Count and tell how many. Write the number. 6. Look at the ten
ones and some more ones in Exercise 5. Complete the addition sentence
to match.

**Chapter 7 • Lesson 5**

three hundred eighty-seven **387**

## Problem Solving • Applications (Real World)

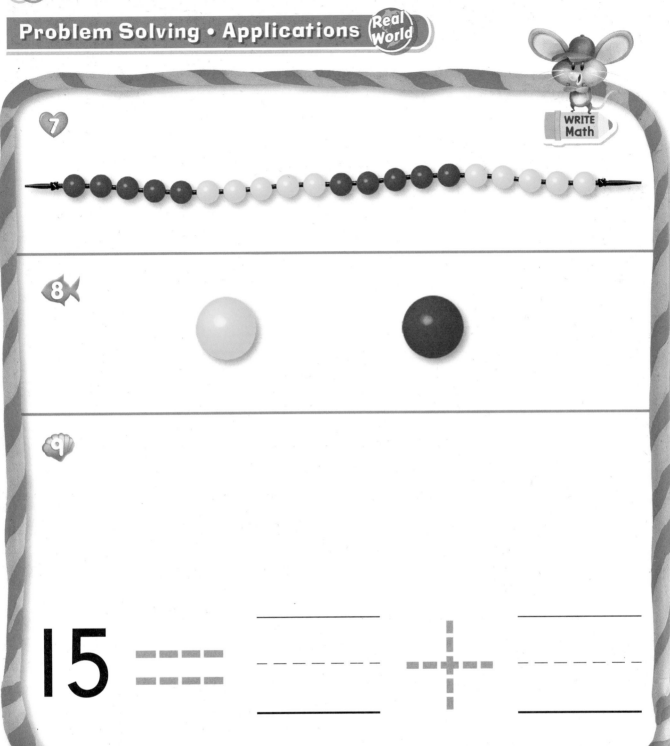

**7**

**8**

**9**

$$15 = \underline{\hspace{2cm}} + \underline{\hspace{2cm}}$$

**DIRECTIONS** **7.** Martha makes a necklace with 15 beads. She starts with the blue bead on the left. Circle to show the beads Martha uses to make her necklace.   **8.** Are there more blue beads or more yellow beads in those 15 beads? Circle the color bead that has more.   **9.** Draw a set of 15 objects. If you circle 10 of the objects, how many more objects are there? Complete the addition sentence to match.

**HOME ACTIVITY •** Have your child use two different kinds of objects to show all the ways he or she can make 15, such as 8 coins and 7 buttons.

# Model, Count, and Write 15

**COMMON CORE STANDARD—K.NBT.A.1**
Work with numbers 11–19 to gain foundations
for place value.

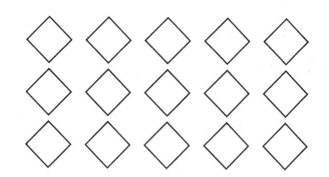

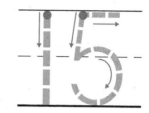

15
fifteen

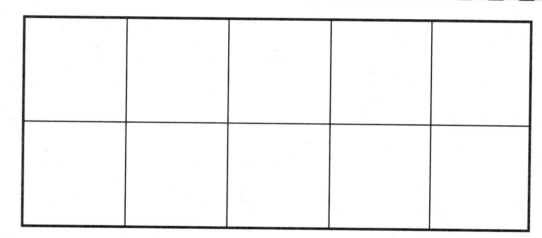

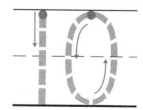

**ones and** _____ **ones**

---

**DIRECTIONS** 1. Count and tell how many. Trace the number. 2. Use counters to show the number 15. Draw the counters. 3. Look at the counters you drew. How many ones are in the ten frame? Trace the number. How many more ones? Write the number.

Chapter 7

# Lesson Check (K.NBT.A.1)

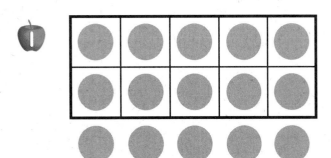 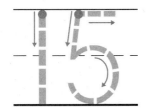

# Spiral Review (K.CC.C.6, K.OA.A.5)

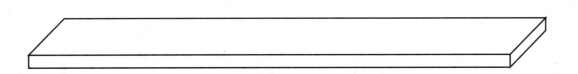

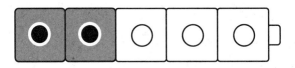

**DIRECTIONS** **1.** Count and tell how many. Trace the number. **2.** Draw to solve this problem. The number of plates on the shelf is two less than 8. How many plates are on the shelf? Draw the plates. Write the number. **3.** Complete the addition sentence to show the numbers that match the cube train.

Name _____

# Problem Solving • Use Numbers to 15

**Essential Question** How can you solve problems using the strategy *draw a picture*?

 **Counting and Cardinality—K.CC.A.3**

MATHEMATICAL PRACTICES
**MP1, MP2, MP4**

 **Unlock the Problem** *Real World*

_____

- - - - - - -

_____ chairs

**DIRECTIONS** There are 14 children sitting on chairs. There is one chair with no child on it. How many chairs are there? Draw to show how you solved the problem.

**Chapter 7 • Lesson 6**

three hundred ninety-one **391**

I

_____

_ _ _ _ _

___ more bees

**DIRECTIONS** 1. There are 15 flowers. Ten flowers have 1 bee on them. How many more bees would you need to have one bee on each flower? Draw to solve the problem. Write how many more bees.

Name _____

_____
_ _ _ _
____ **boys**

**DIRECTIONS** **2.** There are 15 children in Miss Sully's class. There are 5 children in each row. There are 3 boys and 2 girls in each row. How many boys are in the class? Draw to solve the problem.

**HOME ACTIVITY** • Draw a ten frame on a sheet of paper. Have your child use small objects, such as buttons, pennies, or dried beans, to show the number 15.

**Chapter 7 • Lesson 6**

three hundred ninety-three **393**

# ✓ Mid-Chapter Checkpoint

## Concepts and Skills

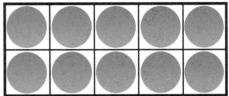

_____

- - - - - - - - - - -

_____

$$14 = \text{\_\_\_\_\_} + \text{\_\_\_\_\_}$$

_____

- - - - - - - - - - -

_____

_____

- - - - - - - - - - -

_____

**5. THINK SMARTER**

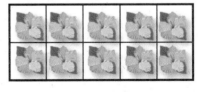

_____

- - - - - - - - - - -

_____

**DIRECTIONS** 1. Count and tell how many. Write the number.
(K.CC.A.3) **2.** Draw a set of 14 objects. If you circle 10 of the objects, how many more objects are there? Complete the addition sentence to match.
(K.NBT.A.1) **3–4.** Count and tell how many. Write the number. (K.CC.A.3)
**5.** Write the number that shows how many flowers. (K.CC.A.3)

**394** three hundred ninety-four

Name _____

## Problem Solving • Use
## Numbers to 15

**COMMON CORE STANDARD—K.CC.A.3**
*Know number names and the count sequence.*

_____

_ _ _ _ _ _ _

_____ **carrot plants**

**DIRECTIONS** There are 15 vegetables in the garden. They are planted in rows of 5. There are 2 carrot plants and 3 potato plants in each row. How many carrot plants are in the garden? Draw to solve the problem.

**Chapter 7**

three hundred ninety-five **395**

© Houghton Mifflin Harcourt Publishing Company

# Lesson Check (K.CC.A.3)

———

——— **caps**

## Spiral Review (K.OA.A.2, K.OA.A.4)

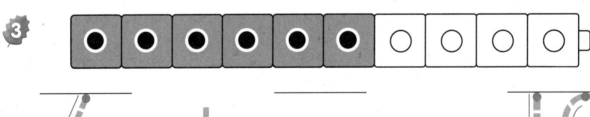

---

**DIRECTIONS** 1. There are 15 children. Ten children are each wearing 1 cap. How many more caps would you need to have one cap on each child?. Draw to solve the problem. Write how many more caps. 2. Trace and write to show the subtraction sentence for the penguins. 3. Look at the cube train. How many white cubes are added to the gray cubes to make 10? Write and trace to show this as an addition sentence.

**FOR MORE PRACTICE GO TO THE Personal Math Trainer**

# Model and Count 16 and 17

**Essential Question** How can you use objects to show 16 and 17 as ten ones and some more ones?

**Listen and Draw**

Common Core
**Number and Operations in Base Ten—K.NBT.A.1**
*Also K.CC.B.4b, K.CC.B.4c, K.CC.B.5*
**MATHEMATICAL PRACTICES**
**MP2, MP3, MP7**

**DIRECTIONS** Use counters to show the number 16. Add more to show the number 17. Draw the counters. Tell a friend what you know about these numbers.

**1** ## 16
sixteen

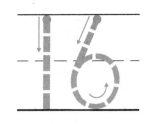

 **2** ☑

 **3**

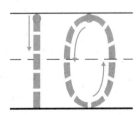

**ones and** _____ **ones**

**DIRECTIONS** 1. Count and tell how many. Trace the number. **2.** Place counters in the ten frames to show the number 16. Draw the counters. **3.** Look at the counters you drew in the ten frames. How many ones are in the top ten frame? Trace the number. How many ones are in the bottom ten frame? Write the number.

Name _____

**4**

# 17
**seventeen**

**6**

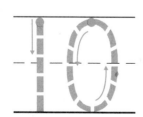

_____

**ones and**  _____  **ones**

**DIRECTIONS** **4.** Count and tell how many. Trace the number. **5.** Place counters in the ten frames to show the number 17. Draw the counters. **6.** Look at the counters you drew in the ten frames. How many ones are in the top ten frame? Trace the number. How many ones are in the bottom ten frame? Write the number.

**Chapter 7 • Lesson 7**

## Problem Solving • Applications (Real World)

WRITE Math

**7**

**8**

**9**

16 = ___ ___ ___  +  ___

**DIRECTIONS  7.** Chloe makes a necklace with 16 beads. She starts with the blue bead on the left. Circle to show the beads Chloe uses to make her necklace.  **8.** Are there more blue beads or more yellow beads in those 16 beads? Circle the color bead that has more.  **9.** Draw a set of 16 objects. If you circle 10 of the objects, how many more objects are there? Complete the addition sentence to match.

**HOME ACTIVITY** • Draw two ten frames on a sheet of paper. Have your child use small objects, such as buttons, pennies, or dried beans, to show the numbers 16 and 17.

## Model and Count 16 and 17

Common Core

**COMMON CORE STANDARD—K.NBT.A.1**
*Work with numbers 11–19 to gain foundations for place value.*

**17**
**seventeen**

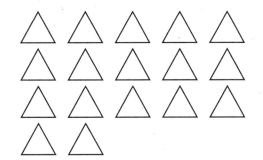

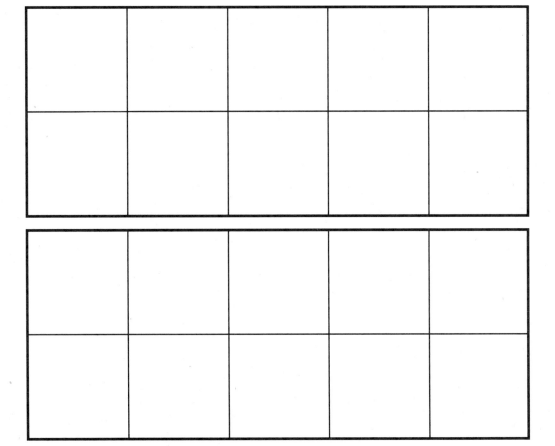

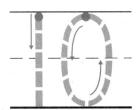 **ones and** _____ **ones**

**DIRECTIONS** 1. Count and tell how many. Trace the number. 2. Place counters in the ten frames to show the number 17. Draw the counters. 3. Look at the counters you drew in the ten frames. How many ones are in the top ten frame? Trace the number. How many ones are in the bottom ten frame? Write the number.

## Lesson Check (K.NBT.A.1)

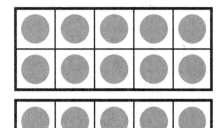

## Spiral Review (K.CC.B.4b, K.OA.A.1)

$2 + \_\_\_ = 3$

5

**DIRECTIONS** 1. Count and tell how many. Trace the number. **2.** Tell an addition word problem about the dogs. Write and trace to complete the addition sentence. **3.** How many counters would you place in the five frame to show the number? Draw the counters.

**402** four hundred two

FOR MORE PRACTICE
GO TO THE
**Personal Math Trainer**

Name _____

# Count and Write 16 and 17

**Essential Question** How can you count and write 16 and 17 with words and numbers?

Common Core **Number and Operations in Base Ten—K.NBT.A.1** *Also K.CC.A.3, K.CC.B.4b* **MATHEMATICAL PRACTICES** **MP2, MP7, MP8**

## Listen and Draw

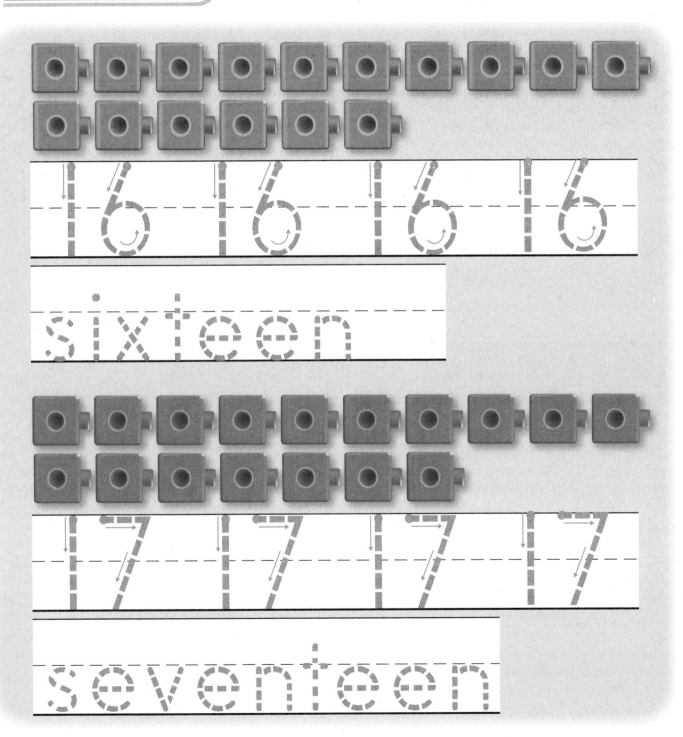

16 16 16 16 16

sixteen

17 17 17 17 17

seventeen

**DIRECTIONS** Count and tell how many. Trace the numbers and the words.

# Share and Show

**1**

## 16
### sixteen

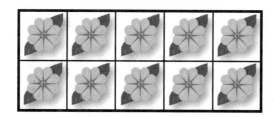 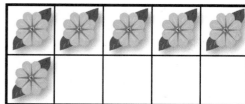

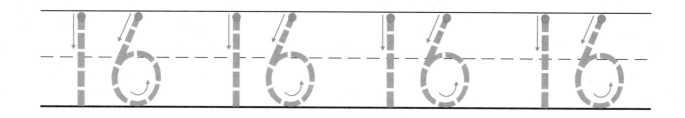

**2** ✓

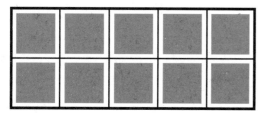 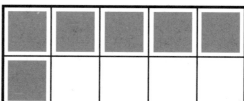

_____

- - - - - - - - -

_____

**3**

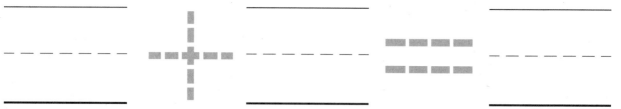

**DIRECTIONS** 1. Count and tell how many. Trace the numbers. **2.** Count and tell how many. Write the number. **3.** Look at the ten frames in Exercise 2. Complete the addition sentence to match.

**404** four hundred four

**4**

# 17
## seventeen

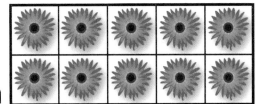

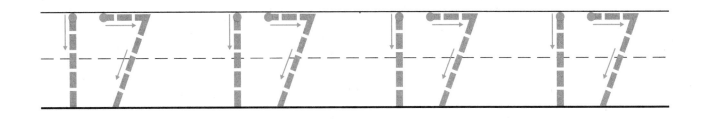

**5**

 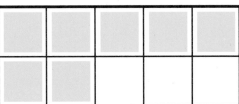

**6**

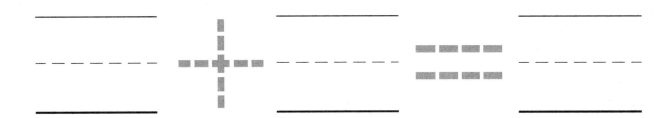

**DIRECTIONS 4.** Count and tell how many. Trace the numbers. **5.** Count and tell how many. Write the number. **6.** Look at the ten frames in Exercise 5. Complete the addition sentence to match.

## Problem Solving • Applications

**7**

17

18

19

**8**

17 = ___ ___ + ___

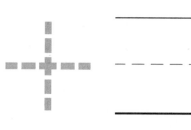

**DIRECTIONS** **7.** Emily picked 10 flowers. Then she picked 7 more flowers. Circle the number of flowers Emily picked. Draw more flowers to show that number. Explain how you know.   **8.** Draw a set of 17 objects. If you circle 10 of the objects, how many more objects are there? Complete the addition sentence to match.

**HOME ACTIVITY** • Ask your child to count and write the number for a set of 16 or 17 objects, such as coins or buttons.

# Count and Write 16 and 17

Common Core **COMMON CORE STANDARD—K.NBT.A.1**
*Work with numbers 11–19 to gain foundations
for place value.*

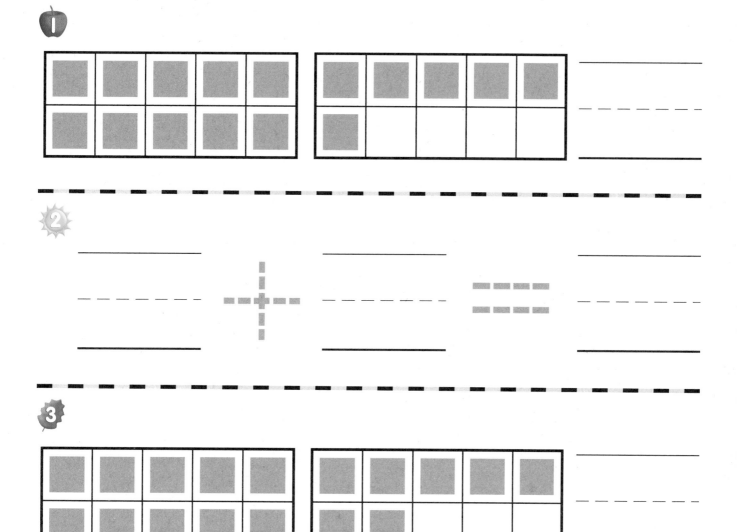

**DIRECTIONS** **1.** Count and tell how many. Write the number. **2.** Look at the ten frames in Exercise 1. Complete the addition sentence to match. **3.** Count and tell how many. Write the number. **4.** Look at the ten frames in Exercise 3. Complete the addition sentence to match.

## Lesson Check (K.NBT.A.1)

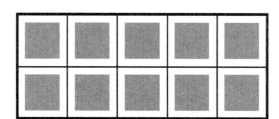 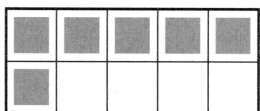

_____ + _____ === _____

## Spiral Review (K.CC.A.3, K.OA.A.3)

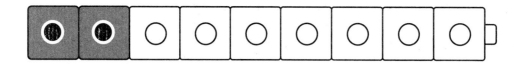

 9 === _____ + _____

_____

_____

**DIRECTIONS** 1. Look at the ten frames. Complete the addition sentence to match. 2. Complete the addition sentence to show the numbers that match the cube train. 3. How many bicycles are there? Write the number.

FOR MORE PRACTICE
GO TO THE
**Personal Math Trainer**

Name _____

# Model and Count 18 and 19

**Essential Question** How can you use objects to show 18 and 19 as ten ones and some more ones?

**Listen and Draw**

Common Core **Number and Operations in Base Ten—K.NBT.A.1**
*Also K.CC.B.4b, K.CC.B.4c, K.CC.B.5*

**MATHEMATICAL PRACTICES**
**MP2, MP3, MP7**

**DIRECTIONS** Use counters to show the number 18. Add more to show the number 19. Draw the counters. Tell a friend what you know about these numbers.

**Chapter 7 • Lesson 9**

four hundred nine **409**

**Share and Show**

**1** 18
eighteen

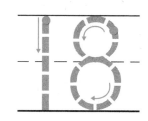

 **2**

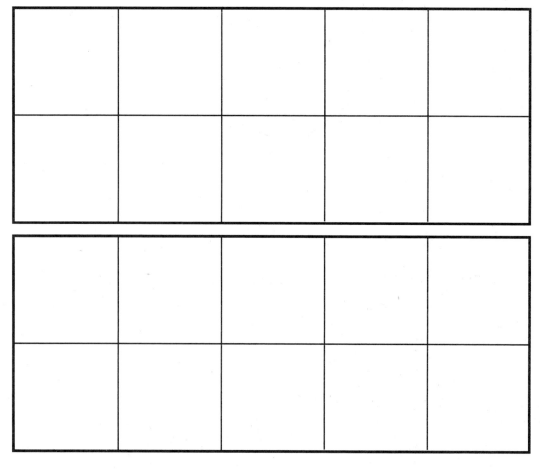

**3**

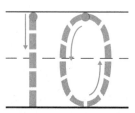

**ones and** _____ **ones**

**DIRECTIONS** 1. Count and tell how many. Trace the number. **2.** Place counters in the ten frames to show the number 18. Draw the counters. **3.** Look at the counters you drew in the ten frames. How many ones are in the top ten frame? Trace the number. How many ones are in the bottom ten frame? Write the number.

**410** four hundred ten

Name _____

**4** **19**
nineteen

**5**

**6**  _____

_ _ _ _ _ _

**ones and** _____ **ones**

**DIRECTIONS** **4.** Count and tell how many. Trace the number. **5.** Place counters in the ten frames to show the number 19. Draw the counters. **6.** Look at the counters you drew in the ten frames. How many ones are in the top ten frame? Trace the number. How many ones are in the bottom ten frame? Write the number.

**Chapter 7 • Lesson 9**

four hundred eleven **411**

## Problem Solving • Applications (Real World)

WRITE Math

❤️ **7**

🐟 **8**

🐚 **9**

18 = === _ _ _ _ _ _ + _ _ _ _ _

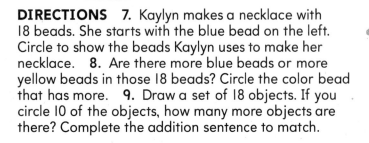

**DIRECTIONS** **7.** Kaylyn makes a necklace with 18 beads. She starts with the blue bead on the left. Circle to show the beads Kaylyn uses to make her necklace.    **8.** Are there more blue beads or more yellow beads in those 18 beads? Circle the color bead that has more.    **9.** Draw a set of 18 objects. If you circle 10 of the objects, how many more objects are there? Complete the addition sentence to match.

**HOME ACTIVITY •** Draw two ten frames on a sheet of paper. Have your child use small objects, such as buttons, pennies, or dried beans, to model the numbers 18 and 19.

Name _____

## Model and Count 18 and 19

Common Core

**COMMON CORE STANDARD—**
**K.NBT.A.1** *Work with numbers 11–19 to gain foundations for place value.*

① 19
nineteen

② 

③ ____ **ones and** ____ **ones**

**DIRECTIONS** **1.** Count and tell how many. Trace the number. **2.** Place counters in the ten frames to show the number 19. Draw the counters. **3.** Look at the counters you drew in the ten frames. How many ones are in the top ten frame? Trace the number. How many ones are in the bottom ten frame? Write the number.

# Lesson Check (K.NBT.A.1)

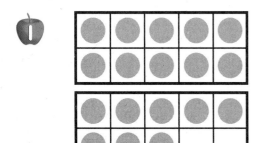

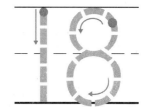

# Spiral Review (K.OA.A.1, K.OA.A.3)

 10 === _____ ___ + ___ _____

## 4 take away 2

_____

- - - - - - -

_____

**DIRECTIONS** 1. Count and tell how many. Trace the number. 2. Complete the addition sentence to show the numbers that match the cube train. 3. Tell a subtraction word problem about the birds. Write the number that shows how many birds are left.

FOR MORE PRACTICE
GO TO THE
**Personal Math Trainer**

Name _____

# Count and Write 18 and 19

**Essential Question** How can you count and write 18 and 19 with words and numbers?

**Common Core** Number and Operations in Base Ten—K.NBT.A.1
*Also K.CC.A.3, K.CC.B.4b*
**MATHEMATICAL PRACTICES**
**MP2, MP7, MP8**

## Listen and Draw

**DIRECTIONS** Count and tell how many. Trace the numbers and the words.

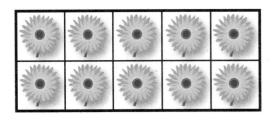

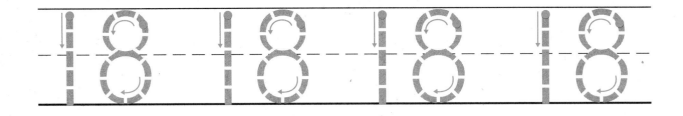

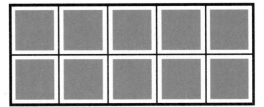

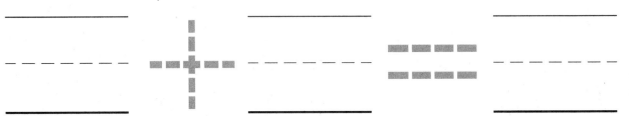

**DIRECTIONS** **1.** Count and tell how many. Trace the numbers. **2.** Count and tell how many. Write the number. **3.** Look at the ten frames in Exercise 2. Complete the addition sentence to match.

Name _____

# 19
## nineteen

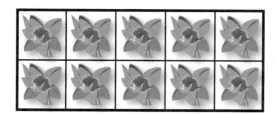 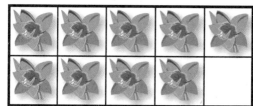

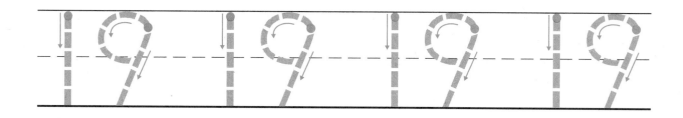

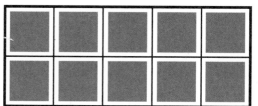 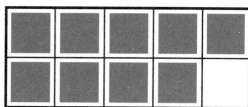

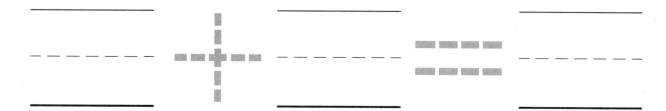

**DIRECTIONS** 4. Count and tell how many. Trace the numbers. 5. Count and tell how many. Write the number. 6. Look at the ten frames in Exercise 5. Complete the addition sentence to match.

**Chapter 7 • Lesson 10**

## Problem Solving • Applications · Real World

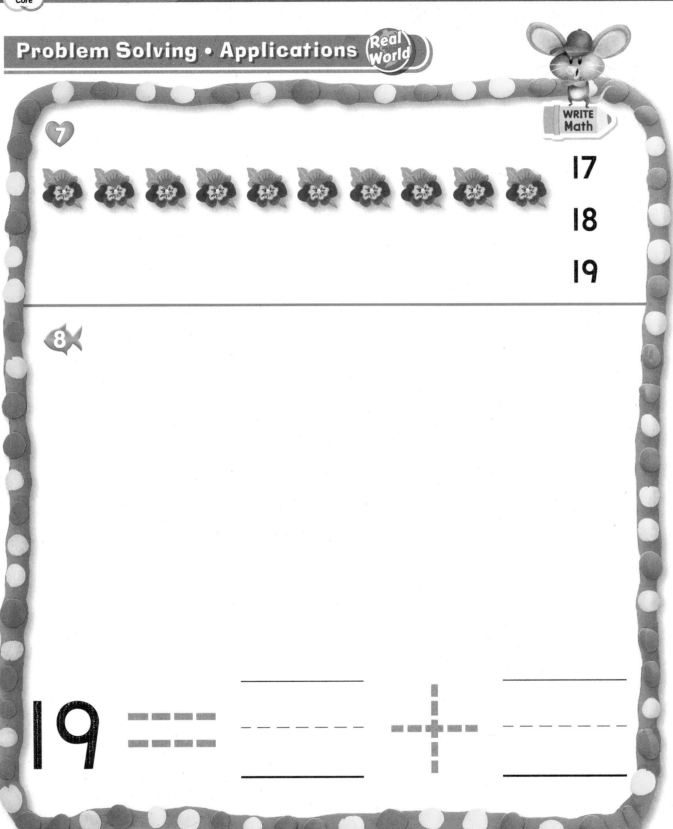

**7**

17

18

19

**8** 🐟

19 ⚌ ___ ___ ___ ✚ ___ ___

---

**DIRECTIONS** **7.** Grace picked a number of flowers 1 more than 17. Circle the number of flowers Grace picked. Draw more flowers to show that number. **8.** Draw a set of 19 objects. If you circle 10 of the objects, how many more objects are there? Complete the addition sentence to match.

**HOME ACTIVITY** • Ask your child to count and write the number for a set of 18 or 19 objects, such as coins or buttons.

**418** four hundred eighteen

© Houghton Mifflin Harcourt Publishing Company

Practice and Homework
## Lesson 7.10

# Count and Write 18 and 19

Common Core

**COMMON CORE STANDARD—K.NBT.A.1**
*Work with numbers 11–19 to gain foundations
for place value.*

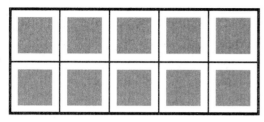 

_____

- - - - - - - - - - - -

_____  _____  _____

_____         _____                _____

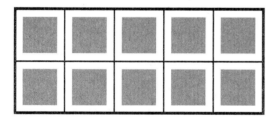 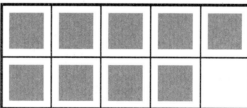

_____

_____

_____  _____ _____

_____                 _____                _____

**DIRECTIONS  I.** Count and tell how many. Write the number.  **2.** Look at the ten frames in Exercise I. Complete the addition sentence to match.  **3.** Count and tell how many. Write the number.  **4.** Look at the ten frames in Exercise 3. Complete the addition sentence to match.

**Chapter 7**

four hundred nineteen **419**

# Lesson Check (K.NBT.A.1)

 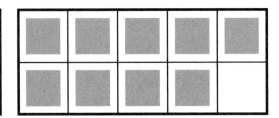

# Spiral Review (K.CC.A.3, K.CC.B.5)

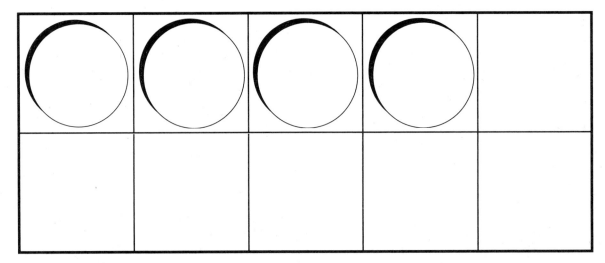

_____

_ _ _ _ _ _ _ _ _

_____

**DIRECTIONS** **1.** Look at the ten frames. Complete the addition sentence to match. **2.** How many more counters would you place to model a way to make 8? Draw the counters. **3.** How many pencils are there? Write the number.

**FOR MORE PRACTICE GO TO THE Personal Math Trainer**

Name _____

 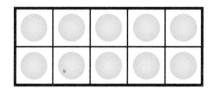

①

_____

— — — — — — —

_____

---

② 

_____

— — — — — — —

_____

---

③

$12$  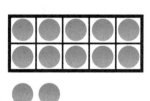 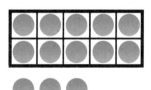  $10 + 2$

---

④

| 13 | ○ Yes | ○ No |
|---|---|---|
| 14 | ○ Yes | ○ No |
| 10 + 3 | ○ Yes | ○ No |

---

**DIRECTIONS** **1–2.** How many counters are there? Write the number.
**3.** Choose all the ways that show 12. **4.** Is this a way to write the number of flowers in the set? Choose Yes or No.

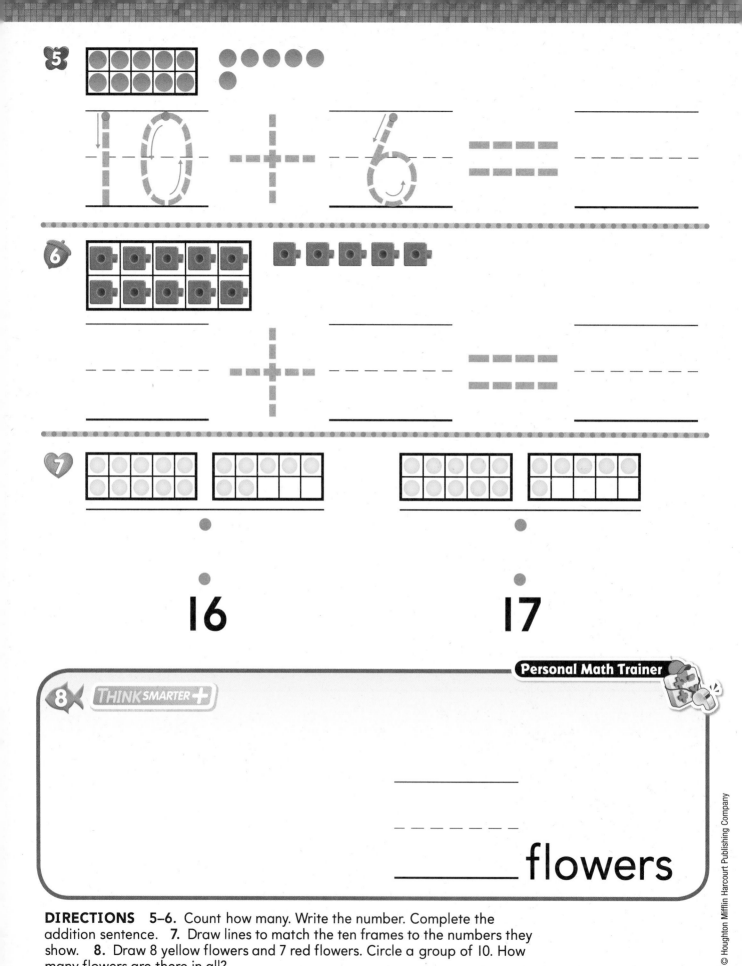

**5** 10 + 6 = ___

**6** ___ + ___ = ___

**7**

16

17

Personal Math Trainer

**8** THINK SMARTER +

_____ flowers

**DIRECTIONS** **5–6.** Count how many. Write the number. Complete the addition sentence. **7.** Draw lines to match the ten frames to the numbers they show. **8.** Draw 8 yellow flowers and 7 red flowers. Circle a group of 10. How many flowers are there in all?

**9**

10 ones and

| 8 |
|---|
| 9 |

ones

**10**

_____ + _____ = _____

_____

**Personal Math Trainer**

**11** THINK SMARTER ➕

10 + _____ = _____

_____          _____

**DIRECTIONS** 9. How many more ones are needed to show the number of peaches? Circle the number. 10. Look at the ten frames. Complete the addition sentence. 11. Ten people are sitting at one table. There are two extra people. How many people are there in all? Draw the table and the people. Complete the addition sentence.

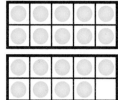

 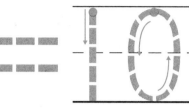 

**DIRECTIONS** **12.** What number do the ten frames show? Complete the addition sentence to show the number. **13.** Draw a set of 11 objects. Circle 10 of the objects. How many more objects are there? Complete the addition sentence to match. **14.** Carrie picked 14 apples. Draw the apples. Circle a group of 10 apples. Count the remaining apples. Complete the addition sentence.

# Represent, Count, and Write 20 and Beyond

**Curious About Math with**

**Curious George**

Watermelon is actually a vegetable and not a fruit.

- How many seeds can you count on this watermelon?

Name _____

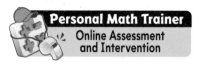
## Explore Numbers to 10

## Compare Numbers to 10

   _____

   _____

## Write Numbers to 10

3  _____  _____   6  _____   8

This page checks understanding of important skills needed for success in Chapter 8.

**DIRECTIONS**  **1.** Circle all of the sets that show 9.  **2.** Circle all of the sets that show 8.  **3.** Count and tell how many. Write the number. Circle the number that is less.  **4.** Write the numbers in order as you count forward.

Name _____

## Vocabulary Builder

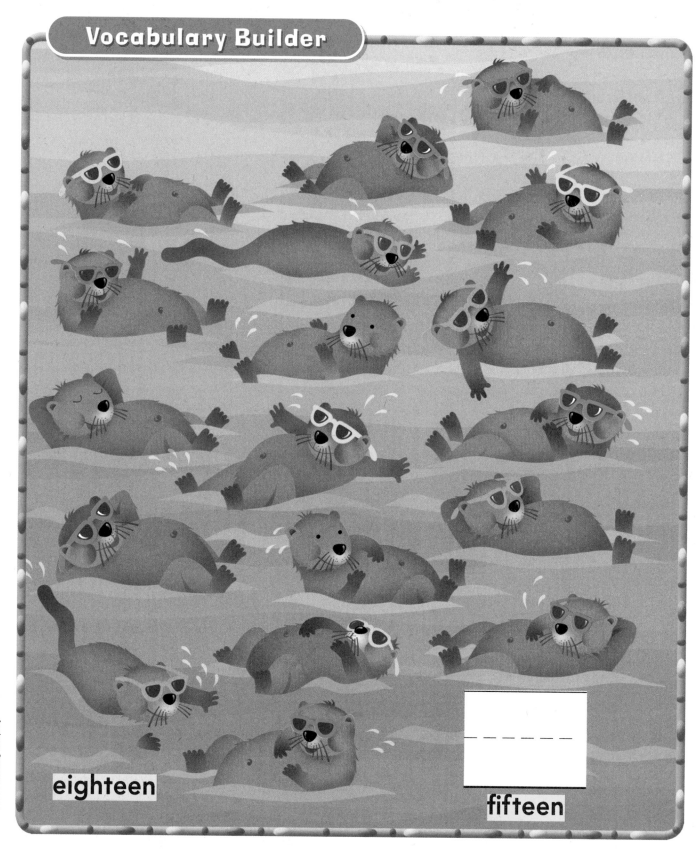

eighteen

fifteen

**DIRECTIONS** Point to each otter as you count. Point to the number word that shows how many otters in all. How many are wearing glasses? Write the number.

**GO DIGITAL**
• **Interactive Student Edition**
• **Multimedia eGlossary**

**Chapter 8**

four hundred twenty-seven **427**

# Who Has More?

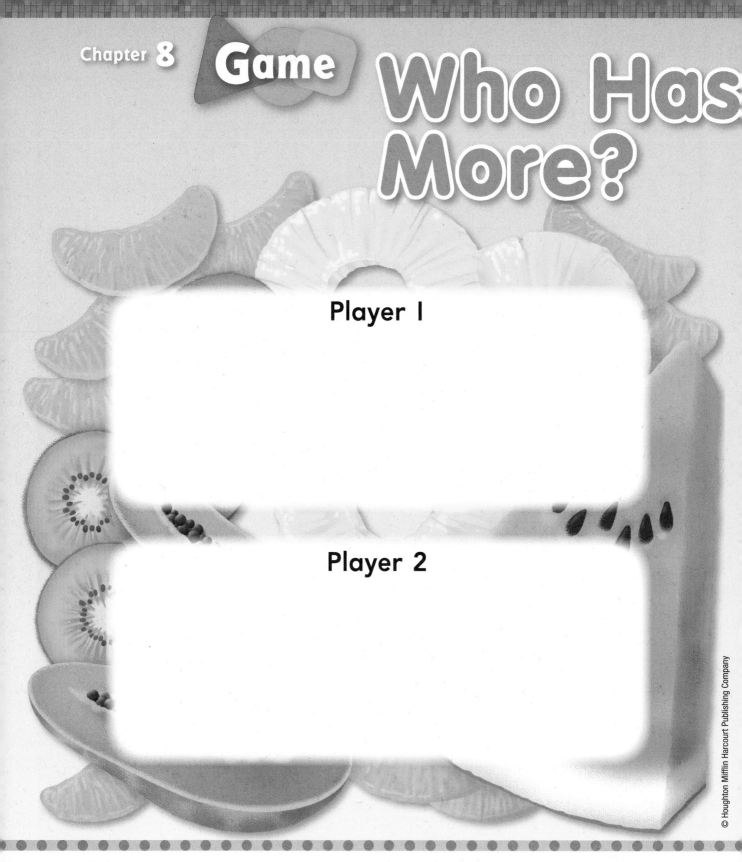

**Player 1**

**Player 2**

**DIRECTIONS** Play with a partner. Each player shuffles a set of numeral cards and places them facedown in a stack. Each player turns over the top card on his or her stack and models that number by placing cube trains on the work space. Partners compare the number of cubes in each cube train. The player with the greater number keeps both of the numeral cards. If both numbers are the same, each player returns the card to the bottom of his or her stack. The player with the most cards at the end of the game wins.

**MATERIALS** 2 sets of numeral cards 11–20, cubes

# Chapter 8 Vocabulary

| | |
|---|---|
| **eighteen**<br>dieciocho<br>21 | **fifteen**<br>quince<br>24 |
| **fifty**<br>cincuenta<br>25 | **one hundred**<br>cien<br>48 |
| **seventeen**<br>diecisiete<br>60 | **sixteen**<br>dieciséis<br>65 |
| **tens**<br>decenas<br>75 | **twenty**<br>veinte<br>81 |

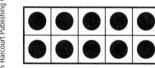

15

18

| 1 | 2 | 3 | 4 | 5 | 6 | 7 | 8 | 9 | 10 |
|---|---|---|---|---|---|---|---|---|---|
| 11 | 12 | 13 | 14 | 15 | 16 | 17 | 18 | 19 | 20 |
| 21 | 22 | 23 | 24 | 25 | 26 | 27 | 28 | 29 | 30 |
| 31 | 32 | 33 | 34 | 35 | 36 | 37 | 38 | 39 | 40 |
| 41 | 42 | 43 | 44 | 45 | 46 | 47 | 48 | 49 | 50 |
| 51 | 52 | 53 | 54 | 55 | 56 | 57 | 58 | 59 | 60 |
| 61 | 62 | 63 | 64 | 65 | 66 | 67 | 68 | 69 | 70 |
| 71 | 72 | 73 | 74 | 75 | 76 | 77 | 78 | 79 | 80 |
| 81 | 82 | 83 | 84 | 85 | 86 | 87 | 88 | 89 | 90 |
| 91 | 92 | 93 | 94 | 95 | 96 | 97 | 98 | 99 | 100 |

↑

| 1 | 2 | 3 | 4 | 5 | 6 | 7 | 8 | 9 | 10 |
|---|---|---|---|---|---|---|---|---|---|
| 11 | 12 | 13 | 14 | 15 | 16 | 17 | 18 | 19 | 20 |
| 21 | 22 | 23 | 24 | 25 | 26 | 27 | 28 | 29 | 30 |
| 31 | 32 | 33 | 34 | 35 | 36 | 37 | 38 | 39 | 40 |
| 41 | 42 | 43 | 44 | 45 | 46 | 47 | 48 | 49 | 50 |

↑

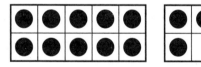 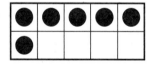

16

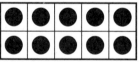 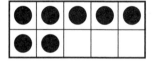

17

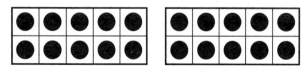 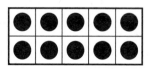

20

| 1 | 2 | 3 | 4 | 5 | 6 | 7 | 8 | 9 | 10 |
|---|---|---|---|---|---|---|---|---|---|
| 11 | 12 | 13 | 14 | 15 | 16 | 17 | 18 | 19 | 20 |
| 21 | 22 | 23 | 24 | 25 | 26 | 27 | 28 | 29 | 30 |
| 31 | 32 | 33 | 34 | 35 | 36 | 37 | 38 | 39 | 40 |
| 41 | 42 | 43 | 44 | 45 | 46 | 47 | 48 | 49 | 50 |
| 51 | 52 | 53 | 54 | 55 | 56 | 57 | 58 | 59 | 60 |
| 61 | 62 | 63 | 64 | 65 | 66 | 67 | 68 | 69 | 70 |
| 71 | 72 | 73 | 74 | 75 | 76 | 77 | 78 | 79 | 80 |
| 81 | 82 | 83 | 84 | 85 | 86 | 87 | 88 | 89 | 90 |
| 91 | 92 | 93 | 94 | 95 | 96 | 97 | 98 | 99 | 100 |

↑
tens

# Memory

**Word Box**
- tens
- twenty
- fifty
- one hundred
- fifteen
- sixteen
- seventeen
- eighteen

**DIRECTIONS** Shuffle the Word Cards. Place each card facedown on a different square above. A player turns over two cards. If they match, the player tells what they know about the word and keeps the cards. If they do not match, the player turns the cards facedown again. Players take turns. The player with more pairs wins.

**MATERIALS** 2 sets of Word Cards

# The Write Way

© Houghton Mifflin Harcourt Publishing Company • Image Credits: (bg) ©Kirsty Pargeter/Alamy

**DIRECTIONS** Draw to show what you know about counting by tens.
**Reflect** Be ready to tell about your drawing.

Name _____

# Model and Count 20

**Essential Question** How can you show and count 20 objects?

**Listen and Draw**

Common Core **Counting and Cardinality—K.CC.B.5**
*Also K.CC.B.4a, K.CC.B.4b, K.CC.B.4c*
**MATHEMATICAL PRACTICES**
**MP2, MP5, MP6**

**DIRECTIONS** Use cubes to model 20. Draw the cubes.

Chapter 8 • Lesson 1

## Share and Show

 **20**
twenty

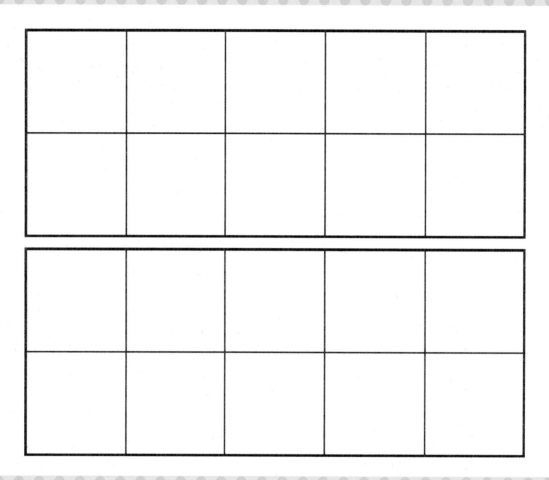

**DIRECTIONS** 1. Count and tell how many. Trace the number.
2. Use cubes to model the number 20. Draw the cubes. 3. Use the
cubes from Exercise 2 to model ten-cube trains. Draw the cube trains.

**430** four hundred thirty

Name _____

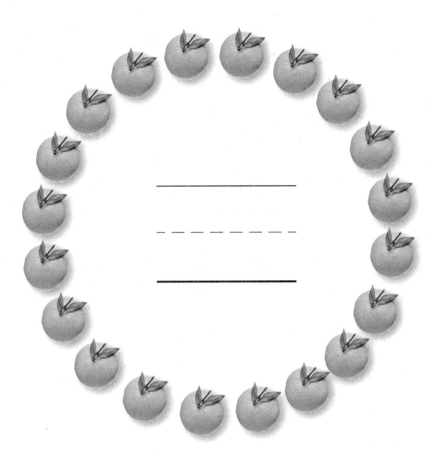

**DIRECTIONS  4–5.** Count and tell how many pieces of fruit.
Write the number. Tell a friend how you counted the oranges.

# Problem Solving • Applications

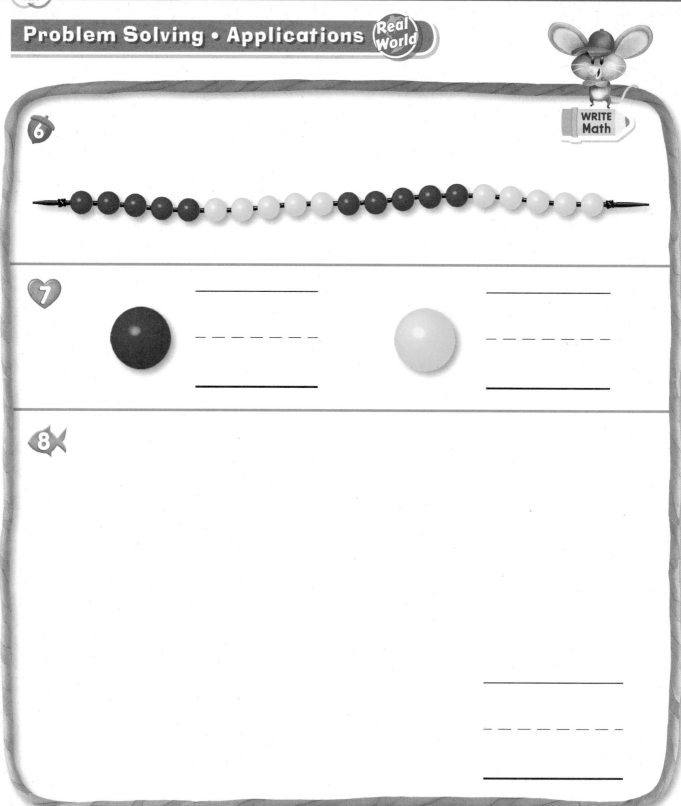

**6**

**7**

**8**

**DIRECTIONS 6.** Lily makes a necklace with 20 beads. Circle to show the beads Lily uses to make her necklace. **7.** How many of each color bead did you circle? Write the numbers. Tell a friend about the number of each color beads. **8.** Draw and write to show what you know about 20. Tell a friend about your drawing.

**HOME ACTIVITY •** Draw two ten frames on a sheet of paper. Have your child show the number 20 by placing small objects, such as buttons or dried beans, in the ten frames.

# Model and Count 20

Common Core

**COMMON CORE STANDARD—K.CC.B.5**
*Count to tell the number of objects.*

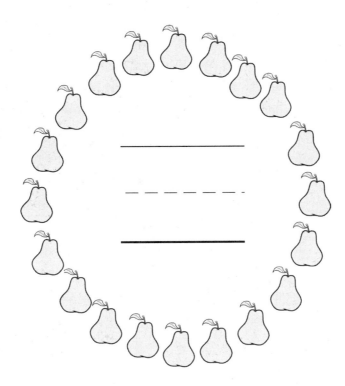

_____

- - - - - - - - - - - -

_____

_____

- - - - - - - -

_____

**DIRECTIONS** **1–2.** Count and tell how many pieces of fruit. Write
the number. Tell a friend how you counted the fruit.

## Lesson Check  (K.CC.B.5)

**1**

_____

- - - - - - - - - - -

_____

## Spiral Review (K.OA.A.5, K.NBT.A.1)

**2**

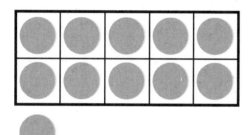

_____

- - - - - - - - - - -

_____

**3**

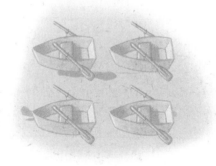

 +  =

**DIRECTIONS** 1–2. Count and tell how many. Write the number. **3.** Tell an addition word problem about the boats. Write and trace to complete the addition sentence.

**434** four hundred thirty-four

FOR MORE PRACTICE
GO TO THE
**Personal Math Trainer**

Name _____

# Count and Write to 20

**Essential Question** How can you count and write up to 20 with words and numbers?

Common Core — **Counting and Cardinality—K.CC.A.3**
*Also K.CC.B.4b, K.CC.B.5*
MATHEMATICAL PRACTICES
MP2

## Listen and Draw

**DIRECTIONS** Count and tell how many cubes. Trace the numbers and the word. Count and tell how many shoes. Trace the numbers.

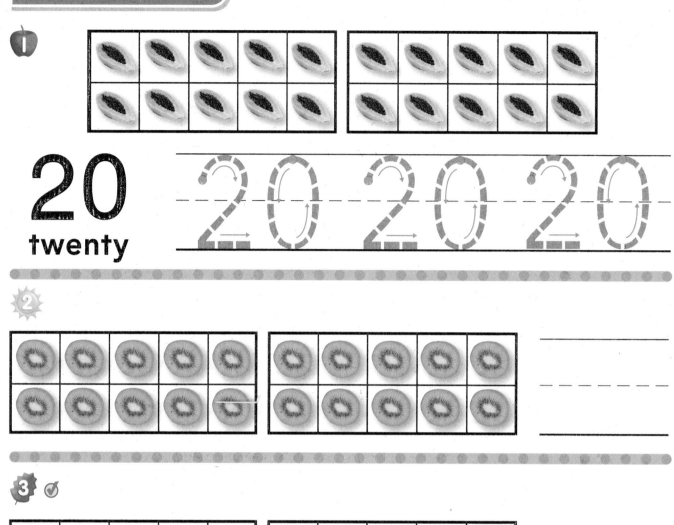

## 20
### twenty

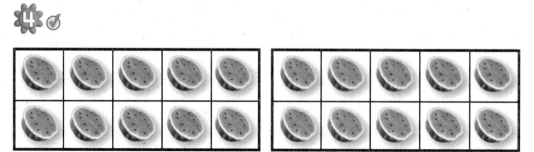

**DIRECTIONS** 1. Count and tell how many pieces of fruit. Trace the numbers as you say them. **2–4.** Count and tell how many pieces of fruit. Write the number.

Name _____

**5**

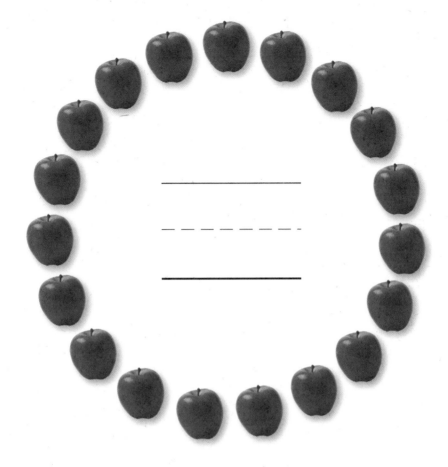

_____

_ _ _ _ _ _ _ _

_____

**6**

_____

_ _ _ _ _ _ _ _

_____

**DIRECTIONS** 5–6. Count and tell how many pieces of fruit. Write the number.

## Problem Solving • Applications  Real World

**WRITE Math**

**7**

18

19

20

**8**

_____

_ _ _ _ _ _ _ _ _

_____

**DIRECTIONS** **7.** David served fruit at his party. Circle a number to show how many pieces of fruit he served. Draw more fruit to show that number. **8.** Draw a set of objects that has a number of objects one greater than 19. Write how many objects are in the set. Tell a friend about your drawing.

**HOME ACTIVITY •** Have your child use small objects, such as pebbles or buttons, to show the number 20. Then have him or her write the number on a piece of paper.

# Count and Write to 20

Common Core **COMMON CORE STANDARD—K.CC.A.3**
*Know number names and the count sequence.*

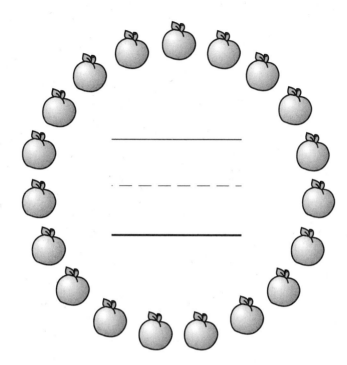

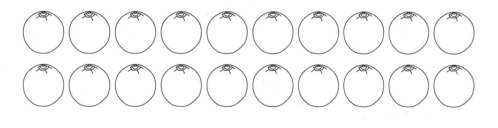

**DIRECTIONS** 1–2. Count and tell how many pieces of fruit. Write the number.

## Lesson Check (K.CC.A.3)

**1**

_____

- - - - - - - - - - - -

_____

## Spiral Review (K.OA.A.5, K.NBT.A.1)

**2**

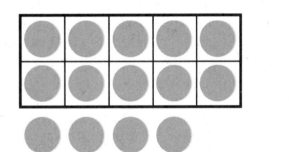

_____

- - - - - - - - - - - -

_____

**3**

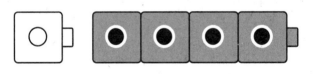

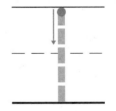  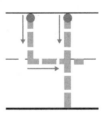

**DIRECTIONS** 1–2. Count and tell how many. Write the number. **3.** Complete the addition sentence to show the numbers that match the cube train.

**440** four hundred forty

FOR MORE PRACTICE
GO TO THE
**Personal Math Trainer**

Name _____

# Count and Order to 20

**Essential Question** How can you count forward to 20 from a given number?

Common Core
**Counting and Cardinality—**
**K.CC.A.2**

**MATHEMATICAL PRACTICES**
**MP2**

**Listen and Draw**

1  2  3  4  5  6  7  8  9  10  11  12  13  14  15  16  17  18  19  20

**DIRECTIONS** Draw a line under a number. Count forward to 20 from that number. Use the terms *greater than* and *less than* to compare and describe the order of numbers. Circle the number that is one greater than the number you underlined. Build cube trains to model the numbers you marked. Draw the cube trains. Circle the larger cube train.

**Chapter 8 • Lesson 3**

four hundred forty-one **441**

© Houghton Mifflin Harcourt Publishing Company • Image Credits: ©Maximilian Stock Ltd./Getty Images

1 2 3 4 5 6 7 8 9 10 11 12 13 14 15 16 17 18 19 20

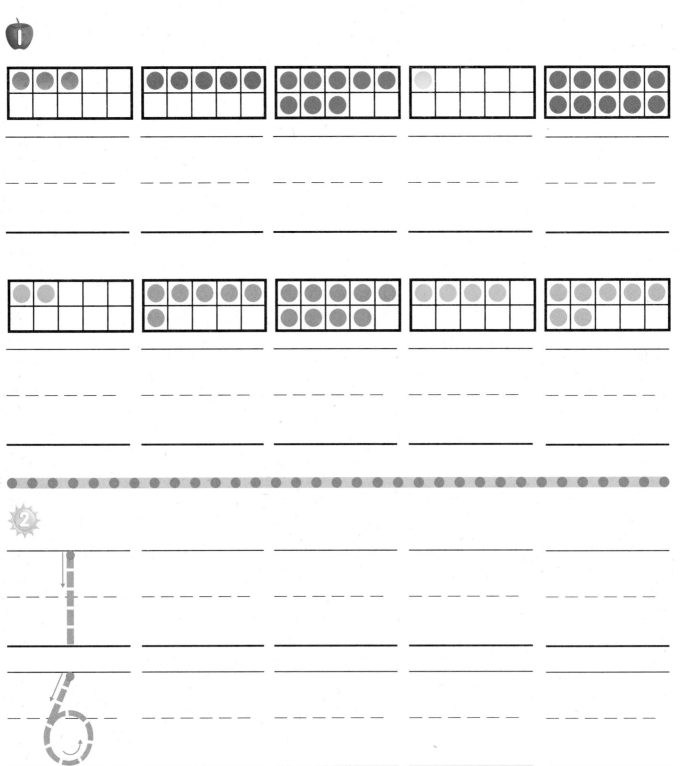

**DIRECTIONS** 1. Count the dots of each color in the ten frames.
Write the numbers. 2. Trace and write those numbers in order.

**3** ✓

---

**DIRECTIONS** 3. Count the dots of each color in the ten frames. Write the numbers. 4. Trace and write those numbers in order.

# Problem Solving • Applications

WRITE Math

⑤

| 1 | 2 | ____ | 4 | 5 |
|---|---|---|---|---|
| 6 | 7 | 8 | 9 | ____ |
| 11 | ____ | 13 | 14 | 15 |
| 16 | 17 | ____ | 19 | 20 |

**DIRECTIONS** **5.** Write to show the numbers in order. Count forward to 20 from one of the numbers you wrote.

**HOME ACTIVITY** • Give your child a set of 11 objects, a set of 12 objects, and a set of 13 objects. Have him or her count the objects in each set and place the sets in order from smallest amount to largest amount.

# Count and Order to 20

Common Core — **COMMON CORE STANDARD—K.CC.A.2**
*Know number names and the count sequence.*

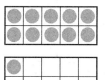   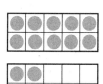 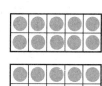

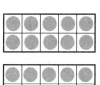 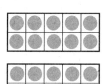 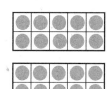  

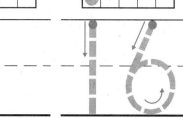

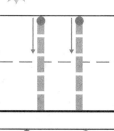

**DIRECTIONS** **I.** Count the dots in each set of ten frames. Trace or write the numbers. **2.** Trace and write those numbers in order.

# Lesson Check

13  14  ____  16  17

---

# Spiral Review (K.CC.A.3, K.OA.A.2)

3 + ____ = ____

---

____

---

**DIRECTIONS** 1. Count forward. Trace and write the numbers in order. 2. Tell an addition word problem about the cats. Circle the cats being added to the group. Trace and write to complete the addition sentence. 3. How many erasers are there? Write the number.

**446** four hundred forty-six

FOR MORE PRACTICE
GO TO THE
**Personal Math Trainer**

Name _____

# Problem Solving • Compare Numbers to 20

**Essential Question** How can you solve problems using the strategy *make a model*?

Common Core  **Counting and Cardinality—K.CC.C.6**
*Also K.CC.C.7*
MATHEMATICAL PRACTICES
**MP2, MP4, MP5**

 Unlock the Problem

**DIRECTIONS**  Alma has a number of yellow cubes one greater than 15. Juan has a number of green cubes one less than 17. Show the cubes. Compare the sets of cubes. Draw the cubes. Tell a friend about your drawing.

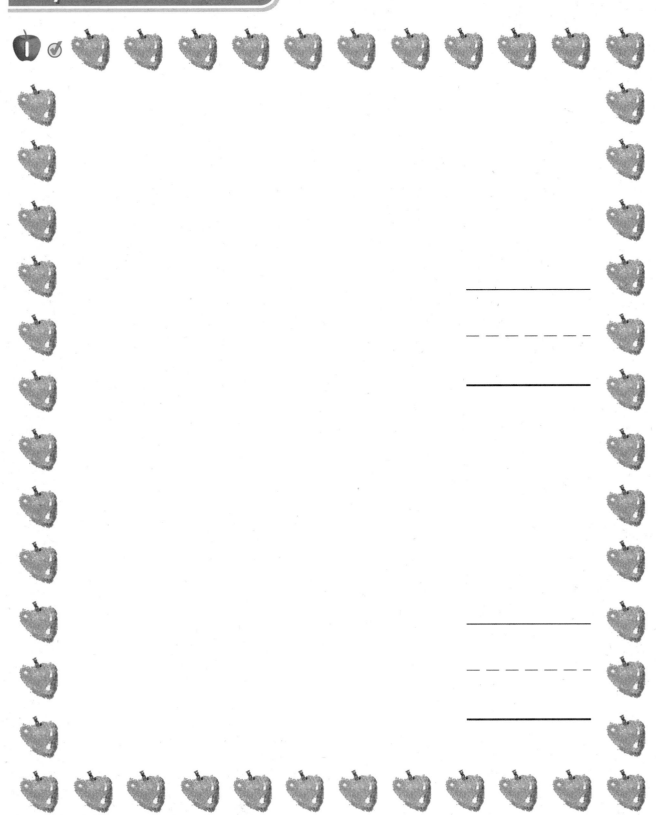

**1.** ✓

_____

- - - - - - - - -

_____

_____

- - - - - - - - -

_____

**DIRECTIONS** **1.** Kiara has 18 apples. She has a number of apples two greater than Cristobal. Use cubes to model the sets of apples. Compare the sets. Which set has a larger amount? Draw the cubes. Write how many in each set. Circle the greater number. Tell a friend how you compared the numbers.

**448** four hundred forty-eight

Name _____

② 

**DIRECTIONS** 2. Salome has 19 oranges. Zion has a number of oranges two less than Salome. Use cubes to model the sets of oranges. Compare the sets. Which set is smaller? Draw the cubes. Write how many in each set. Circle the number that is less. Tell a friend how you compared the numbers.

**HOME ACTIVITY** • Have your child count two sets of objects in your home, and write how many are in each set. Then have him or her circle the greater number. Repeat with sets of different numbers.

**Concepts and Skills**

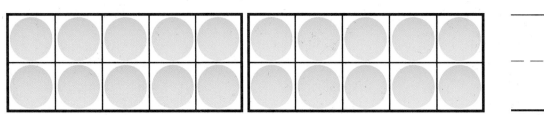

_____

 **2**

_____                    _____

_____                    _____

 **3**

_____                    _____

_____                    _____

**4** THINK SMARTER

15   16   17   18   | 19 |
                    | 20 |

**DIRECTIONS**  **I.** Count and tell how many. Write the number. (K.CC.A.3)
**2.** Write how many pieces of fruit are in each picture. Circle the number
that is less. (K.CC.C.6)  **3.** Write how many pieces of fruit are in each picture.
Circle the number that is greater. (K.CC.C.6)  **4.** What number comes next in
counting order? Circle the number. (K.CC.A.3)

**450** four hundred fifty

Name _____

# Problem Solving • Compare Numbers to 20

Common Core

**COMMON CORE STANDARD—K.CC.C.6**
*Compare numbers.*

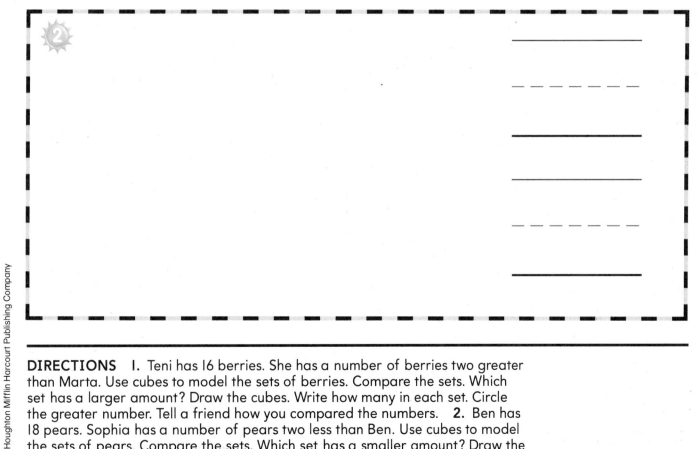

**1** _____

_____

_____

_____

_____

**2** _____

_____

_____

_____

_____

_____

**DIRECTIONS** **1.** Teni has 16 berries. She has a number of berries two greater than Marta. Use cubes to model the sets of berries. Compare the sets. Which set has a larger amount? Draw the cubes. Write how many in each set. Circle the greater number. Tell a friend how you compared the numbers. **2.** Ben has 18 pears. Sophia has a number of pears two less than Ben. Use cubes to model the sets of pears. Compare the sets. Which set has a smaller amount? Draw the cubes. Write how many in each set. Circle the number that is less. Tell a friend how you compared the numbers.

**Chapter 8** four hundred fifty-one **451**

# Lesson Check <sub></sub>(K.CC.C.6)

_____

- - - - - - - - - -

_____

- - - - - - - - - -

_____

# Spiral Review (K.CC.C.6, K.NBT.A.1)

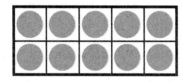
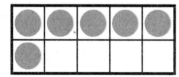

_____

- - - - - - - - - -

_____

**DIRECTIONS** **1.** Jim has 20 grapes. Mia has a number of grapes two less than Jim. Use cubes to model the sets of grapes. Compare the sets. Which set has a smaller amount? Draw the cubes. Write how many are in each set. Circle the number that is less. **2.** Count and tell how many. Write the number. **3.** Count the counters in each set. Circle the set that has a greater number of counters.

**FOR MORE PRACTICE
GO TO THE
Personal Math Trainer**

Name _____

# Count to 50 by Ones

**Essential Question** How does the order of numbers help you count to 50 by ones?

Common Core Counting and Cardinality—K.CC.A.1, K.CC.A.2
MATHEMATICAL PRACTICES
MP7, MP8

**Listen and Draw**

| 1 | 2 | 3 | 4 | 5 | 6 | 7 | 8 | 9 | 10 |
|---|---|---|---|---|---|---|---|---|---|
| 11 | 12 | 13 | 14 | 15 | 16 | 17 | 18 | 19 | 20 |
| 21 | 22 | 23 | 24 | 25 | 26 | 27 | 28 | 29 | 30 |
| 31 | 32 | 33 | 34 | 35 | 36 | 37 | 38 | 39 | 40 |
| 41 | 42 | 43 | 44 | 45 | 46 | 47 | 48 | 49 | 50 |

**DIRECTIONS** Point to each number as you count to 50. Trace the circle around the number 50.

**Chapter 8 • Lesson 5**

four hundred fifty-three **453**

❶

| 1 | 2 | 3 | 4 | 5 | 6 | 7 | 8 | 9 | 10 |
| 11 | 12 | 13 | 14 | 15 | 16 | 17 | 18 | 19 | 20 |
| 21 | 22 | 23 | 24 | 25 | 26 | 27 | 28 | 29 | 30 |
| 31 | 32 | 33 | 34 | 35 | 36 | 37 | 38 | 39 | 40 |
| 41 | 42 | 43 | 44 | 45 | 46 | 47 | 48 | 49 | 50 |

**DIRECTIONS** 1. Point to each number as you count to 50. Circle the number 15. Begin with 15 and count forward to 50. Draw a line under the number 50.

| 1 | 2 | 3 | 4 | 5 | 6 | 7 | 8 | 9 | 10 |
|---|---|---|---|---|---|---|---|---|---|
| 11 | 12 | 13 | 14 | 15 | 16 | 17 | 18 | 19 | 20 |
| 21 | 22 | 23 | 24 | 25 | 26 | 27 | 28 | 29 | 30 |
| 31 | 32 | 33 | 34 | 35 | 36 | 37 | 38 | 39 | 40 |
| 41 | 42 | 43 | 44 | 45 | 46 | 47 | 48 | 49 | 50 |

**DIRECTIONS  2.** Look away and point to any number. Circle that number. Count forward from that number. Draw a line under the number 50.

**Chapter 8 • Lesson 5**

four hundred fifty-five **455**

## Problem Solving • Applications Real World

③

WRITE Math

| 1 | 2 | 3 | 4 | 5 | 6 | 7 | 8 | 9 | 10 |
|---|---|---|---|---|---|---|---|---|----|
| 11 | 12 | 13 | 14 | 15 | 16 | 17 | 18 | 19 | 20 |
| 21 | 22 | 23 | 24 | 25 | 26 | 27 | 28 | 29 | 30 |
| 31 | 32 | 33 | 34 | 35 | 36 | 37 | 38 | 39 | 40 |
| 41 | 42 | 43 | 44 | 45 | 46 | 47 | 48 | 49 | 50 |

**DIRECTIONS** 3. I am greater than 17 and less than 19. What number am I? Use blue to color that number. I am greater than 24 and less than 26. What number am I? Use red to color that number.

**HOME ACTIVITY** • Think of a number between 1 and 50. Say **greater than** and **less than** to describe your number. Have your child say the number.

# Count to 50 by Ones

Common Core    **COMMON CORE STANDARD—K.CC.A.1, K.CC.A.2**
*Know number names and the count sequence.*

1

| 1 | 2 | 3 | 4 | 5 | 6 | 7 | 8 | 9 | 10 |
|---|---|---|---|---|---|---|---|---|----|
| 11 | 12 | 13 | 14 | 15 | 16 | 17 | 18 | 19 | 20 |
| 21 | 22 | 23 | 24 | 25 | 26 | 27 | 28 | 29 | 30 |
| 31 | 32 | 33 | 34 | 35 | 36 | 37 | 38 | 39 | 40 |
| 41 | 42 | 43 | 44 | 45 | 46 | 47 | 48 | 49 | 50 |

**DIRECTIONS   1.** Look away and point to any number. Circle that number. Count forward from that number. Draw a line under the number 50.

# Lesson Check (K.CC.A.1)

| 1 | 2 | 3 | 4 | 5 | 6 | 7 | 8 | 9 | 10 |
|---|---|---|---|---|---|---|---|---|----|
| 11 | 12 | 13 | 14 | 15 | 16 | 17 | 18 | 19 | 20 |
| 21 | 22 | 23 | 24 | 25 | 26 | 27 | 28 | 29 | 30 |

## Spiral Review (K.OA.A.1, K.OA.A.3)

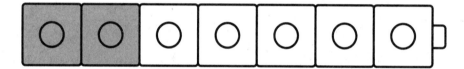

$$7 = \underline{\quad\quad} + \underline{\quad\quad}$$

$$10 - 3 = \underline{\quad\quad}$$

**DIRECTIONS** 1. Begin with 1 and count forward to 20. What is the next number? Draw a line under that number. 2. Complete the addition sentence to show the numbers that match the cube train. 3. Shelley has 10 counters. Three of her counters are white. The rest of her counters are gray. How many are gray? Complete the subtraction sentence to show the answer.

**458** four hundred fifty-eight

FOR MORE PRACTICE
GO TO THE
**Personal Math Trainer**

Name _____

# Count to 100 by Ones

**Essential Question** How does the order of numbers help you count to 100 by ones?

Common Core Counting and Cardinality—K.CC.A.1, K.CC.C.7 Also K.CC.A.2
MATHEMATICAL PRACTICES
MP7, MP8

**Listen and Draw**

| 1 | 2 | 3 | 4 | 5 | 6 | 7 | 8 | 9 | 10 |
|---|---|---|---|---|---|---|---|---|---|
| 11 | 12 | 13 | 14 | 15 | 16 | 17 | 18 | 19 | 20 |
| 21 | 22 | 23 | 24 | 25 | 26 | 27 | 28 | 29 | 30 |
| 31 | 32 | 33 | 34 | 35 | 36 | 37 | 38 | 39 | 40 |
| 41 | 42 | 43 | 44 | 45 | 46 | 47 | 48 | 49 | 50 |
| 51 | 52 | 53 | 54 | 55 | 56 | 57 | 58 | 59 | 60 |
| 61 | 62 | 63 | 64 | 65 | 66 | 67 | 68 | 69 | 70 |
| 71 | 72 | 73 | 74 | 75 | 76 | 77 | 78 | 79 | 80 |
| 81 | 82 | 83 | 84 | 85 | 86 | 87 | 88 | 89 | 90 |
| 91 | 92 | 93 | 94 | 95 | 96 | 97 | 98 | 99 | 100 |

**DIRECTIONS** Point to each number as you count to 100. Trace the circle around the number 100.

| 1 | 2 | 3 | 4 | 5 | 6 | 7 | 8 | 9 | 10 |
|---|---|---|---|---|---|---|---|---|----|
| 11 | 12 | 13 | 14 | 15 | 16 | 17 | 18 | 19 | 20 |
| 21 | 22 | 23 | 24 | 25 | 26 | 27 | 28 | 29 | 30 |
| 31 | 32 | 33 | 34 | 35 | 36 | 37 | 38 | 39 | 40 |
| 41 | 42 | 43 | 44 | 45 | 46 | 47 | 48 | 49 | 50 |
| 51 | 52 | 53 | 54 | 55 | 56 | 57 | 58 | 59 | 60 |
| 61 | 62 | 63 | 64 | 65 | 66 | 67 | 68 | 69 | 70 |
| 71 | 72 | 73 | 74 | 75 | 76 | 77 | 78 | 79 | 80 |
| 81 | 82 | 83 | 84 | 85 | 86 | 87 | 88 | 89 | 90 |
| 91 | 92 | 93 | 94 | 95 | 96 | 97 | 98 | 99 | 100 |

**DIRECTIONS** 1. Point to each number as you count to 100. Circle the number 11. Begin with 11 and count forward to 100. Draw a line under the number 100.

**460** four hundred sixty

Name _____

| 1 | 2 | 3 | 4 | 5 | 6 | 7 | 8 | 9 | 10 |
| 11 | 12 | 13 | 14 | 15 | 16 | 17 | 18 | 19 | 20 |
| 21 | 22 | 23 | 24 | 25 | 26 | 27 | 28 | 29 | 30 |
| 31 | 32 | 33 | 34 | 35 | 36 | 37 | 38 | 39 | 40 |
| 41 | 42 | 43 | 44 | 45 | 46 | 47 | 48 | 49 | 50 |
| 51 | 52 | 53 | 54 | 55 | 56 | 57 | 58 | 59 | 60 |
| 61 | 62 | 63 | 64 | 65 | 66 | 67 | 68 | 69 | 70 |
| 71 | 72 | 73 | 74 | 75 | 76 | 77 | 78 | 79 | 80 |
| 81 | 82 | 83 | 84 | 85 | 86 | 87 | 88 | 89 | 90 |
| 91 | 92 | 93 | 94 | 95 | 96 | 97 | 98 | 99 | 100 |

**DIRECTIONS   2.** Point to each number as you count to 100. Look away and point to any number. Circle that number. Count forward to 100 from that number. Draw a line under the number 100.

## Problem Solving • Applications

WRITE Math

**③**

| 1 | 2 | 3 | 4 | ___ | 6 | 7 | 8 | 9 | 10 |
|---|---|---|---|---|---|---|---|---|---|
| 11 | 12 | 13 | ___ | 15 | ___ | 17 | 18 | 19 | 20 |
| 21 | 22 | 23 | 24 | 25 | 26 | 27 | 28 | 29 | 30 |

**④**

**DIRECTIONS  3.** Place your finger on the number 15. Write or trace to show the numbers that are "neighbors" to the number 15. Say *greater than* and *less than* to describe the numbers.  **4.** Draw to show what you know about some other "neighbor" numbers in the chart.

**HOME ACTIVITY •** Show your child a calendar. Point to a number on the calendar. Have him or her tell you all the numbers that are "neighbors" to that number.

**462** four hundred sixty-two

# Count to 100 by Ones

Common Core

**COMMON CORE STANDARD—K.CC.A.1,**
**K.CC.C.7**
*Know number names and the count sequence.*

| 1 | 2 | 3 | 4 | 5 | 6 | 7 | 8 | 9 | 10 |
|---|---|---|---|---|---|---|---|---|---|
| 11 | 12 | 13 | 14 | 15 | 16 | 17 | 18 | 19 | 20 |
| 21 | 22 | 23 | 24 | 25 | 26 | 27 | 28 | 29 | 30 |
| 31 | 32 | 33 | 34 | 35 | 36 | 37 | 38 | 39 | 40 |
| 41 | 42 | 43 | 44 | 45 | 46 | 47 | 48 | 49 | 50 |
| 51 | 52 | 53 | 54 | 55 | 56 | 57 | 58 | 59 | 60 |
| 61 | 62 | 63 | 64 | 65 | 66 | 67 | 68 | 69 | 70 |
| 71 | 72 | 73 | 74 | 75 | 76 | 77 | 78 | 79 | 80 |
| 81 | 82 | 83 | 84 | 85 | 86 | 87 | 88 | 89 | 90 |
| 91 | 92 | 93 | 94 | 95 | 96 | 97 | 98 | 99 | 100 |

**DIRECTIONS** 1. Point to each number as you count to 100. Look away and point to any number. Circle that number. Count forward to 100 from that number. Draw a line under the number 100.

## Lesson Check (K.CC.A.1)

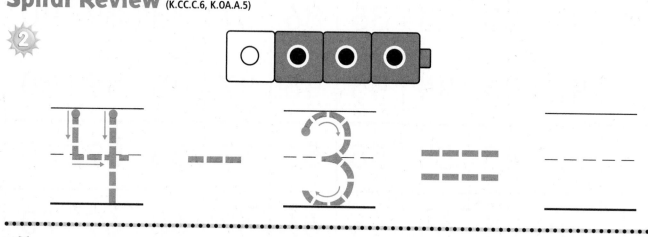

| 71 | 72 | 73 | 74 | 75 | 76 | 77 | 78 | 79 | 80 |
|----|----|----|----|----|----|----|----|----|----|
| 81 | 82 | 83 | 84 | 85 | 86 | 87 | 88 | 89 | 90 |
| 91 | 92 | 93 | 94 | 95 | 96 | 97 | 98 | 99 | 100 |

## Spiral Review (K.CC.C.6, K.OA.A.5)

4 - 3 = _ _ _

**DIRECTIONS** 1. Begin with 71 and count forward to 80. What is the next number? Draw a line under that number. 2. Pete makes the cube train shown. He takes the cube train apart to show how many cubes are gray. Complete the subtraction sentence to show Pete's cube train. 3. Count how many flowers. Write the number. Draw to show a set of counters that has the same number as the set of flowers. Write the number.

**FOR MORE PRACTICE GO TO THE Personal Math Trainer**

Name _____

# Count to 100 by Tens

**Essential Question** How can you count to 100 by tens on a hundred chart?

Common Core · Counting and Cardinality—
K.CC.A.1
MATHEMATICAL PRACTICES
MP6, MP7, MP8

## Listen and Draw

| 1 | 2 | 3 | 4 | 5 | 6 | 7 | 8 | 9 | 10 |
|---|---|---|---|---|---|---|---|---|---|
| 11 | 12 | 13 | 14 | 15 | 16 | 17 | 18 | 19 | 20 |
| 21 | 22 | 23 | 24 | 25 | 26 | 27 | 28 | 29 | 30 |
| 31 | 32 | 33 | 34 | 35 | 36 | 37 | 38 | 39 | 40 |
| 41 | 42 | 43 | 44 | 45 | 46 | 47 | 48 | 49 | 50 |
| 51 | 52 | 53 | 54 | 55 | 56 | 57 | 58 | 59 | 60 |
| 61 | 62 | 63 | 64 | 65 | 66 | 67 | 68 | 69 | 70 |
| 71 | 72 | 73 | 74 | 75 | 76 | 77 | 78 | 79 | 80 |
| 81 | 82 | 83 | 84 | 85 | 86 | 87 | 88 | 89 | 90 |
| 91 | 92 | 93 | 94 | 95 | 96 | 97 | 98 | 99 | 100 |

**DIRECTIONS** Trace the circles around the numbers that end in a 0. Beginning with 10, count those numbers in order. Tell a friend how you are counting.

| | | | | | | | | | |
|---|---|---|---|---|---|---|---|---|---|
| 1 | 2 | 3 | 4 | 5 | 6 | 7 | 8 | 9 | ___ |
| 11 | 12 | 13 | 14 | 15 | 16 | 17 | 18 | 19 | ___ |
| 21 | 22 | 23 | 24 | 25 | 26 | 27 | 28 | 29 | 30 |
| 31 | 32 | 33 | 34 | 35 | 36 | 37 | 38 | 39 | 40 |
| 41 | 42 | 43 | 44 | 45 | 46 | 47 | 48 | 49 | 50 |

**DIRECTIONS** 1. Write the numbers to complete the counting order to 20. Trace the numbers to complete the counting order to 50. Count by tens as you point to the numbers you wrote and traced.

466 four hundred sixty-six

| 51 | 52 | 53 | 54 | 55 | 56 | 57 | 58 | 59 | 60 |
| 61 | 62 | 63 | 64 | 65 | 66 | 67 | 68 | 69 | 70 |
| 71 | 72 | 73 | 74 | 75 | 76 | 77 | 78 | 79 | 80 |
| 81 | 82 | 83 | 84 | 85 | 86 | 87 | 88 | 89 | 90 |
| 91 | 92 | 93 | 94 | 95 | 96 | 97 | 98 | 99 | 100 |

**DIRECTIONS** 2. Trace the numbers to complete the counting order to 100. Count by tens as you point to the numbers you traced.

## Problem Solving • Applications  Real World

3

WRITE Math

| 1 | 2 | 3 | 4 | 5 | 6 | 7 | 8 | 9 | _____ |
| 11 | 12 | 13 | 14 | 15 | 16 | 17 | 18 | 19 | ------ |
| 21 | 22 | 23 | 24 | 25 | 26 | 27 | 28 | 29 | 30 |
| 31 | 32 | 33 | 34 | 35 | 36 | 37 | 38 | 39 | 40 |
| 41 | 42 | 43 | 44 | 45 | 46 | 47 | 48 | 49 | 50 |

**DIRECTIONS  3.** Antonio has 10 marbles. Write the number in order. Jasmine has 10 more marbles than Antonio. Write that number in order. Lin has 10 more marbles than Jasmine. Draw a line under the number that shows how many marbles Lin has. When counting by tens, what number comes right after 40? Circle the number.

**HOME ACTIVITY** • Show your child a calendar. Use pieces of paper to cover the numbers that end in 0. Ask your child to say the numbers that are covered. Then have him or her remove the pieces of paper to check.

© Houghton Mifflin Harcourt Publishing Company

**468** four hundred sixty-eight

## Count to 100 by Tens

COMMON CORE STANDARD—K.CC.A.1
*Know number names and the count sequence.*

| 51 | 52 | 53 | 54 | 55 | 56 | 57 | 58 | 59 | 60 |
| 61 | 62 | 63 | 64 | 65 | 66 | 67 | 68 | 69 | 70 |
| 71 | 72 | 73 | 74 | 75 | 76 | 77 | 78 | 79 | 80 |
| 81 | 82 | 83 | 84 | 85 | 86 | 87 | 88 | 89 | 90 |
| 91 | 92 | 93 | 94 | 95 | 96 | 97 | 98 | 99 | 100 |

**DIRECTIONS  I.** Trace the numbers to complete the counting order to 100. Count by tens as you point to the numbers you traced.

## Lesson Check (K.CC.A.1)

| 1 | 2 | 3 | 4 | 5 | 6 | 7 | 8 | 9 | 10 |
|---|---|---|---|---|---|---|---|---|---|
| 11 | 12 | 13 | 14 | 15 | 16 | 17 | 18 | 19 | 20 |
| 21 | 22 | 23 | 24 | 25 | 26 | 27 | 28 | 29 | 30 |

## Spiral Review (K.CC.A.3, K.OA.A.5)

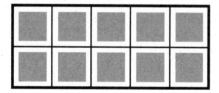  

_____

_ _ _ _ _ _ _ _ _

_____

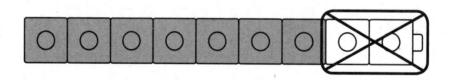

_____  _ _ _ _ _ _ _ _ _

_ _ _ _ _ _    ▪▪▪▪ _ _ _ _

_____    _____

**DIRECTIONS** 1. Count by tens as you point to the numbers in the shaded boxes. Start with the number 10. What number do you end with? Draw a line under that number. 2. How many tiles are there? Write the number. 3. Complete the subtraction sentence that matches the cube train.

**470** four hundred seventy

FOR MORE PRACTICE
GO TO THE
**Personal Math Trainer**

Name _____

# Count by Tens

**Essential Question** How can you use sets of tens to count to 100?

 Common Core · Counting and Cardinality—K.CC.A.1

MATHEMATICAL PRACTICES
MP7, MP8

## Listen and Draw Real World

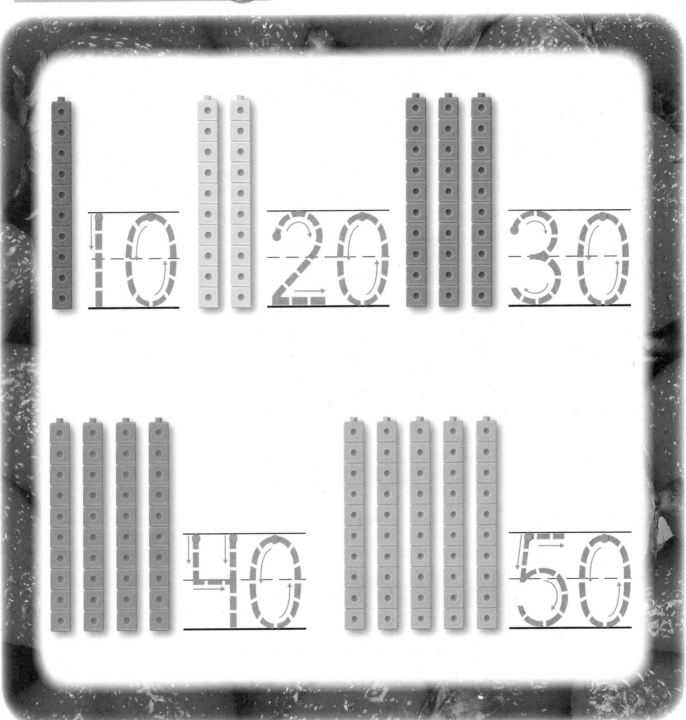

**DIRECTIONS** Point to each set of cube towers as you count by tens. Trace the numbers as you count by tens.

**Chapter 8 • Lesson 8**

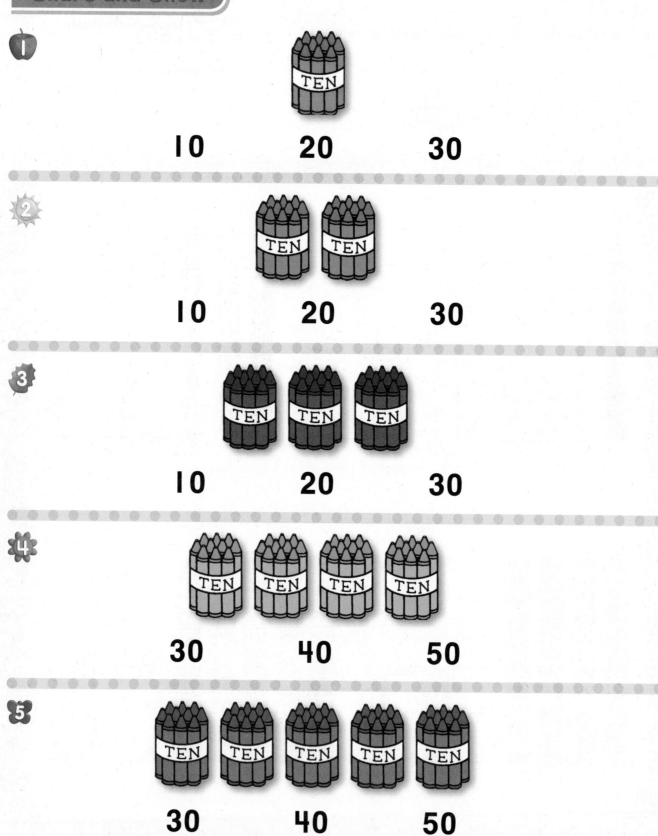

**1**

**10**  **20**  **30**

**2**

**10**  **20**  **30**

**3**

**10**  **20**  **30**

**4**

**30**  **40**  **50**

**5**

**30**  **40**  **50**

**DIRECTIONS** 1–5. Point to each set of 10 as you count by tens. Circle the number that shows how many.

**472** four hundred seventy-two

Name _____

**6** 🌰✓

60          70          80

**7** 💜✓

60          70          80

**8** 🐟

80          90          100

**9** 🐚

80          90          100

**10** 🔟

80          90          100

**DIRECTIONS** 6–10. Point to each set of 10 as you count by tens.
Circle the number that shows how many.

## Problem Solving • Applications (Real World)

**WRITE Math**

**DIRECTIONS** 11. Circle sets of 10 stars. Count the sets of stars by tens.

**HOME ACTIVITY •** Give your child some coins or buttons and ten cups. Ask him or her to place ten coins into each cup. Then have him or her point to each cup as he or she counts by tens to 100.

**474** four hundred seventy-four

Name _____

## Count by Tens

**Common Core** COMMON CORE STANDARD—K.CC.A.1
*Know number names and the count sequence.*

**20**     **30**     **40**

**30**     **40**     **50**

**60**     **70**     **80**

**80**     **90**     **100**

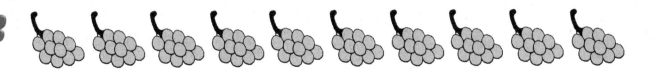

**80**     **90**     **100**

**DIRECTIONS** 1–5. Point to each set of 10 as you count by tens.
Circle the number that shows how many.

## Lesson Check (K.CC.A.1)

60          70          80

---

## Spiral Review (K.OA.A.3, K.NBT.A.1)

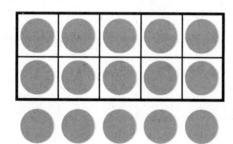

_____

_ _ _ _ _ _ _ _ _

_____

---

4 = = _ _ _ _ + _ _ _ _

---

**DIRECTIONS  1.** Point to each set of 10 as you count by tens. Circle the number that shows how many crayons there are.  **2.** Count and tell how many. Write the number.  **3.** Complete the addition sentence to match the cube train.

**476**  four hundred seventy-six

Name _____

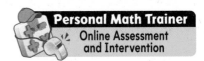

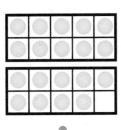  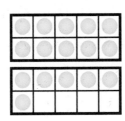  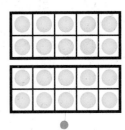

20                    19                    16

_____

- - - - - - - -

_____

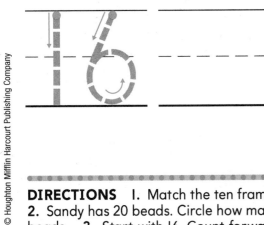

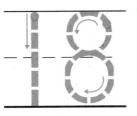        

**DIRECTIONS 1.** Match the ten frames to the numbers that tell how many counters.
**2.** Sandy has 20 beads. Circle how many beads she has. Write the number of
beads. **3.** Start with 16. Count forward. Trace and write the numbers in order.

Chapter 8             **Assessment Options**
                     **Chapter Test**            four hundred seventy-seven **477**

**4**

# 18

○　　　　　○　　　　　○　　　　　○

**5**

| 31 | 32 | 33 | 34 | 35 | 36 | 37 | 38 | 39 | 40 |
|----|----|----|----|----|----|----|----|----|----|
| 41 | 42 | 43 | 44 | 45 | 46 | 47 | 48 | 49 | 50 |

**6**

94　95　96　97　98　99

90
100

**DIRECTIONS** **4.** Choose all the sets with a number of watermelons less than 18. **5.** Begin with 31. Point to each number as you count. Draw a line under the last number counted. **6.** Point to each number as you count. Circle the number that comes next in counting order.

Name _____

| 81 | 82 | 83 | 84 | 85 | 86 | 87 | 88 | 89 | 90 |
| 91 | 92 | 93 | 94 | 95 | 96 | 97 | 98 | 99 | 100 |

50          60          70          80

○          ○          ○          ○

**Personal Math Trainer**

9  THINK **SMARTER** +

_____

_ _ _ _ _ _ _

_____

**DIRECTIONS**  **7.** Circle the numbers that end in a zero.  **8.** Count the crayons by tens. Mark under the number that shows how many.  **9.** Dexter has 20 pencils. He has a number of pencils 1 greater than Jane. Draw the number of pencils Jane has. Write the number.

| 13 | 14 | 15 | Yes | No |
|----|----|----|-----|-----|
| 11 | 15 | 12 | Yes | No |
| 16 | 17 | 18 | Yes | No |

🐢 11

10 ___ 30 ___ 50

▲ 12  THINK SMARTER +

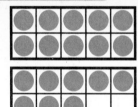

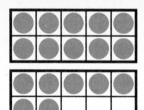

_____   _____   _____

— — — — — — — — —   — — — — — — — — —   — — — — — — — — —

_____   _____   _____

— — — — — — — — —   — — — — — — — — —   — — — — — — — — —

_____   _____   _____

**DIRECTIONS** 10. Are the numbers in counting order? Circle Yes or No. 11. Count by tens. Trace and write to complete the counting order. 12. What number does each set of counters show? Write the numbers. Then write the numbers in counting order.

# Picture Glossary

**above** [arriba, encima]

The kite is **above** the rabbit.

**add** [sumar]

3 + 2 = 5

**alike** [igual]

**and** [y]

 **and**

2 + 2

**behind** [detrás]

The box is **behind** the girl.

**below** [debajo]

The rabbit is **below** the kite.

**beside** [al lado]

The tree is **beside** the bush.

## big [grande]

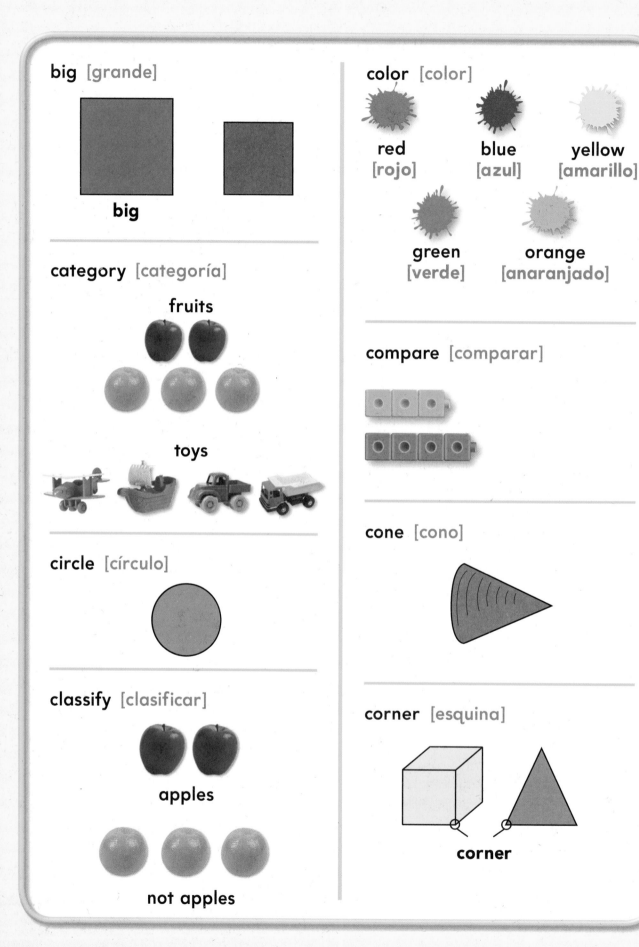

**big**

## category [categoría]

**fruits**

**toys**

## circle [círculo]

## classify [clasificar]

**apples**

**not apples**

## color [color]

**red**
[rojo]

**blue**
[azul]

**yellow**
[amarillo]

**green**
[verde]

**orange**
[anaranjado]

## compare [comparar]

## cone [cono]

## corner [esquina]

**corner**

© Houghton Mifflin Harcourt Publishing Company • Image Credits: (apples) ©Artville/Getty Images; (boat) ©D. Hurst/Alamy; (blue truck) ©C Squared Studios/PhotoDisc/Getty Images

**cube** [cubo]

**curve** [curva]

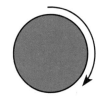

**curved surface**
[superficie curva]

Some solids have
a **curved surface.**

**cylinder** [cilindro]

**different** [diferente]

**eight** [ocho]

**eighteen** [dieciocho]

**eleven** [once]

**fewer** [menos]

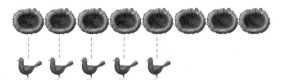

3 **fewer** birds

**fifteen** [quince]

**fifty** [cincuenta]

| 1 | 2 | 3 | 4 | 5 | 6 | 7 | 8 | 9 | 10 |
|---|---|---|---|---|---|---|---|---|----|
| 11 | 12 | 13 | 14 | 15 | 16 | 17 | 18 | 19 | 20 |
| 21 | 22 | 23 | 24 | 25 | 26 | 27 | 28 | 29 | 30 |
| 31 | 32 | 33 | 34 | 35 | 36 | 37 | 38 | 39 | 40 |
| 41 | 42 | 43 | 44 | 45 | 46 | 47 | 48 | 49 | 50 |

**five** [cinco]

**flat** [plano]

A circle is a **flat** shape.

**flat surface** [superficie plana]

Some solids have a
flat **surface**.

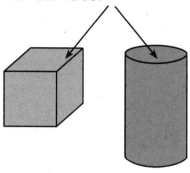

**four** [cuatro]

**fourteen** [catorce]

**graph** [gráfica]

row
[fila]

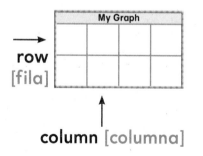

**column** [columna]

**greater** [mayor]

### 9 is greater than 6

**heavier** [más pesado]

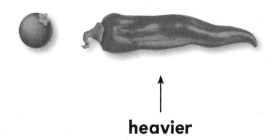

**heavier**

**hexagon** [hexágono]

**in front of** [delante de]

The box is **in front of** the girl.

**is equal to** [es igual a]

$$3 + 2 = 5$$

3 + 2 **is equal to** 5

**larger** [más grande]

2       3

A quantity of 3 is **larger** than a quantity of 2.

**less** [menor/menos]

9 is **less** than 11

**lighter** [más liviano]

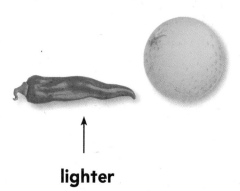

**lighter**

**longer** [más largo]

 **longer**

**match** [emparejar]

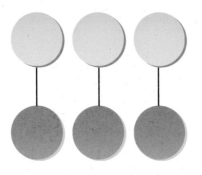

**minus −** [menos]

$$4 - 3 = 1$$

4 **minus** 3 is equal to 1

**more** [más]

2 **more** leaves

**next to** [al lado de]

The bush is **next to** the tree.

**nine** [nueve]

**nineteen** [diecinueve]

**one** [uno]

## one hundred [cien]

| 1 | 2 | 3 | 4 | 5 | 6 | 7 | 8 | 9 | 10 |
|---|---|---|---|---|---|---|---|---|---|
| 11 | 12 | 13 | 14 | 15 | 16 | 17 | 18 | 19 | 20 |
| 21 | 22 | 23 | 24 | 25 | 26 | 27 | 28 | 29 | 30 |
| 31 | 32 | 33 | 34 | 35 | 36 | 37 | 38 | 39 | 40 |
| 41 | 42 | 43 | 44 | 45 | 46 | 47 | 48 | 49 | 50 |
| 51 | 52 | 53 | 54 | 55 | 56 | 57 | 58 | 59 | 60 |
| 61 | 62 | 63 | 64 | 65 | 66 | 67 | 68 | 69 | 70 |
| 71 | 72 | 73 | 74 | 75 | 76 | 77 | 78 | 79 | 80 |
| 81 | 82 | 83 | 84 | 85 | 86 | 87 | 88 | 89 | 90 |
| 91 | 92 | 93 | 94 | 95 | 96 | 97 | 98 | 99 | 100 |

## ones [unidades]

**3 ones**

## pairs [pares]

3

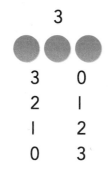

| 3 | 0 |
|---|---|
| 2 | 1 |
| 1 | 2 |
| 0 | 3 |

number **pairs** for 3

## plus + [más]

2 **plus** 1 is equal to 3

2 + 1 = 3

## rectangle [rectángulo]

## roll [rodar]

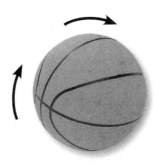

## same height
[de la misma altura]

**same length** [del mismo largo]

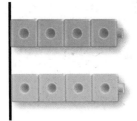

**same number**
[el mismo número]

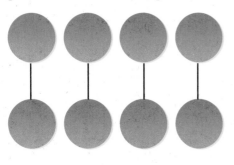

**same weight** [del mismo peso]

**seven** [siete]

**seventeen** [diecisiete]

**shape** [forma]

**shorter** [más corto]

shorter

**side** [lado]

side

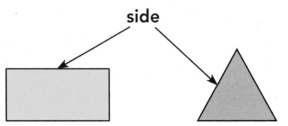

## sides of equal length [lados del mismo largo]

## six [seis]

## sixteen [dieciséis]

## size [tamaño]

**big**          **small**

## slide [deslizar]

## small [pequeño]

**small**

## solid [sólido]

**solid**

A cylinder is a **solid** shape.

**sphere** [esfera]

**square** [cuadrado]

**stack** [apilar]

**subtract** [restar]

**Subtract** to find out how many are left.

**taller** [más alto]

taller

**ten** [diez]

**tens** [decenas]

| 1 | 2 | 3 | 4 | 5 | 6 | 7 | 8 | 9 | 10 |
|---|---|---|---|---|---|---|---|---|----|
| 11 | 12 | 13 | 14 | 15 | 16 | 17 | 18 | 19 | 20 |
| 21 | 22 | 23 | 24 | 25 | 26 | 27 | 28 | 29 | 30 |
| 31 | 32 | 33 | 34 | 35 | 36 | 37 | 38 | 39 | 40 |
| 41 | 42 | 43 | 44 | 45 | 46 | 47 | 48 | 49 | 50 |
| 51 | 52 | 53 | 54 | 55 | 56 | 57 | 58 | 59 | 60 |
| 61 | 62 | 63 | 64 | 65 | 66 | 67 | 68 | 69 | 70 |
| 71 | 72 | 73 | 74 | 75 | 76 | 77 | 78 | 79 | 80 |
| 81 | 82 | 83 | 84 | 85 | 86 | 87 | 88 | 89 | 90 |
| 91 | 92 | 93 | 94 | 95 | 96 | 97 | 98 | 99 | 100 |

↑ tens

**thirteen** [trece]

**three** [tres]

**three-dimensional shapes**
[figuras tridimensionales]

**triangle** [triángulo]

**twelve** [doce]

**twenty** [veinte]

**two** [dos]

**two-dimensional shapes**
[figuras bidimensionales]

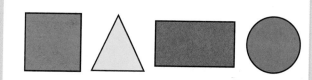

**vertex** [vértice]

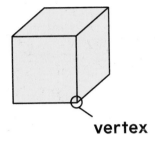

vertex

**vertices** [vértices]

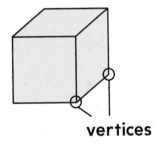

vertices

**zero, none** [cero, ninguno]

**zero** fish

# Correlations

 **COMMON CORE STATE STANDARDS**

## Standards You Will Learn

| Mathematical Practices | | Some examples are: |
|---|---|---|
| **MP1** | Make sense of problems and persevere in solving them. | Lessons 1.3, 1.5, 1.9, 3.9, 5.1, 5.3, 5.4, 5.6, 5.7, 6.1, 6.3, 6.4, 6.5, 6.6, 7.6, 11.3, 11.5 |
| **MP2** | Reason abstractly and quantitatively. | Lessons 1.1, 1.2, 1.3, 1.4, 1.5, 1.6, 1.8, 1.9, 1.10, 2.2, 2.3, 2.5, 3.2, 3.4, 3.6, 3.8, 4.2, 4.4, 5.1, 5.2, 5.3, 5.4, 5.5, 5.6, 5.7, 5.8, 5.9, 5.10, 5.11, 5.12, 6.1, 6.2, 6.3, 6.4, 6.5, 6.6, 6.7, 7.1, 7.2, 7.3, 7.4, 7.5, 7.6, 7.7, 7.8, 7.9, 7.10, 8.1, 8.2, 8.3, 9.4, 9.6, 9.8, 9.10, 10.3, 10.4, 10.5, 12.1, 12.2, 12.3, 12.4, 12.5 |
| **MP3** | Construct viable arguments and critique the reasoning of others. | Lessons 2.1, 2.2, 2.3, 2.4, 2.5, 3.9, 7.1, 7.3, 7.7, 7.9, 10.7, 10.9, 10.10, 11.1, 11.2, 11.3, 11.4, 11.5 |
| **MP4** | Model with mathematics. | Lessons 1.7, 1.9, 2.4, 3.1, 3.9, 4.1, 4.3, 4.5, 5.2, 5.3, 5.4, 6.2, 6.3, 6.4, 7.6, 8.4, 10.6, 10.8, 10.9, 10.10 |
| **MP5** | Use appropriate tools strategically. | Lessons 1.8, 2.1, 2.2, 2.3, 2.4, 3.1, 3.3, 3.5, 3.7, 4.1, 4.5, 5.2, 6.2, 6.7, 7.5, 8.1, 8.4, 9.1, 9.2, 9.3, 9.5, 9.7, 9.9, 9.11, 9.12, 10.1, 10.2, 10.3, 10.4, 10.5, 10.6, 11.1, 11.2, 11.4, 12.1, 12.2, 12.3 |
| **MP6** | Attend to precision. | Lessons 2.5, 4.6, 4.7, 8.1, 8.7, 9.1, 9.3, 9.5, 9.7, 9.9, 10.1, 10.2, 10.3, 10.4, 10.5, 10.9, 10.10, 11.1, 11.2, 11.3, 11.4, 11.5, 12.1, 12.2, 12.3, 12.4, 12.5 |
| **MP7** | Look for and make use of structure. | Lessons 1.7, 1.8, 3.1, 3.3, 3.5, 3.7, 4.3, 5.5, 5.8, 5.9, 5.10, 5.11, 5.12, 7.1, 7.2, 7.3, 7.4, 7.5, 7.7, 7.8, 7.9, 7.10, 8.5, 8.6, 8.7, 8.8, 9.1, 9.2, 9.3, 9.4, 9.5, 9.6, 9.7, 9.8, 9.9, 9.10, 9.11, 9.12, 10.1, 10.2, 10.6 |

## Standards You Will Learn

| Mathematical Practices | | Some examples are: |
|---|---|---|
| MP8 | Look for and express regularity in repeated reasoning. | Lessons 3.3, 3.5, 3.7, 4.5, 4.6, 4.7, 5.5, 6.7, 7.2, 7.4, 7.8, 7.10, 8.5, 8.6, 8.7, 8.8, 9.4, 9.6, 9.8, 9.10, 9.11, 9.12, 10.7, 12.4, 12.5 |
| **Domain: Counting and Cardinality** | | **Student Edition Lessons** |
| **Know number names and the count sequence.** | | |
| K.CC.A.1 | Count to 100 by ones and by tens. | Lessons 8.5, 8.6, 8.7, 8.8 |
| K.CC.A.2 | Count forward beginning from a given number within the known sequence (instead of having to begin at 1). | Lessons 4.4, 8.3, 8.5 |
| K.CC.A.3 | Write numbers from 0 to 20. Represent a number of objects with a written numeral 0–20 (with 0 representing a count of no objects). | Lessons 1.2, 1.4, 1.6, 1.9, 1.10, 3.2, 3.4, 3.6, 3.8, 4.2, 8.2 |
| **Count to tell the number of objects.** | | |
| K.CC.B.4a | Understand the relationship between numbers and quantities; connect counting to cardinality. a. When counting objects, say the number names in the standard order, pairing each object with one and only one number name and each number name with one and only one object. | Lessons 1.1, 1.3, 1.5 |
| K.CC.B.4b | Understand the relationship between numbers and quantities; connect counting to cardinality. b. Understand that the last number name said tells the number of objects counted. The number of objects is the same regardless of their arrangement or the order in which they were counted. | Lesson 1.7 |
| K.CC.B.4c | Understand the relationship between numbers and quantities; connect counting to cardinality. c. Understand that each successive number name refers to a quantity that is one larger. | Lesson 1.8 |

| | | |
|---|---|---|
| **Domain: Counting and Cardinality** | | |
| **Count to tell the number of objects.** | | |
| **K.CC.B.5** | Count to answer "how many?" questions about as many as 20 things arranged in a line, a rectangular array, or a circle, or as many as 10 things in a scattered configuration; given a number from 1–20, count out that many objects. | Lessons 3.1, 3.3, 3.5, 3.7, 4.1, 8.1 |
| **Compare numbers.** | | |
| **K.CC.C.6** | Identify whether the number of objects in one group is greater than, less than, or equal to the number of objects in another group, e.g., by using matching and counting strategies. | Lessons 2.1, 2.2, 2.3, 2.4, 2.5, 3.9, 4.5, 4.6, 8.4 |
| **K.CC.C.7** | Compare two numbers between 1 and 10 presented as written numerals. | Lessons 3.9, 4.7, 8.6 |
| **Domain: Operations and Algebraic Thinking** | | |
| **Understand addition as putting together and adding to, and understand subtraction as taking apart and taking from.** | | |
| **K.OA.A.1** | Represent addition and subtraction with objects, fingers, mental images, drawings, sounds (e.g., claps), acting out situations, verbal explanations, expressions, or equations. | Lessons 5.1, 5.2, 5.3, 6.1, 6.2, 6.3 |
| **K.OA.A.2** | Solve addition and subtraction word problems, and add and subtract within 10, e.g., by using objects or drawings to represent the problem. | Lessons 5.7, 6.6, 6.7 |
| **K.OA.A.3** | Decompose numbers less than or equal to 10 into pairs in more than one way, e.g., by using objects or drawings, and record each decomposition by a drawing or equation (e.g., $5 = 2 + 3$ and $5 = 4 + 1$). | Lessons 1.7, 4.1, 5.8, 5.9, 5.10, 5.11, 5.12 |

H15

## Standards You Will Learn

| Domain: Operations and Algebraic Thinking | | |
|---|---|---|
| **Understand addition as putting together and adding to, and understand subtraction as taking apart and taking from.** | | |
| **K.OA.A.4** | For any number from 1 to 9, find the number that makes 10 when added to the given number, e.g., by using objects or drawings, and record the answer with a drawing or equation. | Lessons 4.3, 5.5 |
| **K.OA.A.5** | Fluently add and subtract within 5. | Lessons 5.4, 5.6, 6.4, 6.5 |
| **Domain: Number and Operations in Base Ten** | | |
| **Work with numbers 11–19 to gain foundations for place value.** | | |
| **K.NBT.A.1** | Compose and decompose numbers from 11 to 19 into ten ones and some further ones, e.g., by using objects or drawings, and record each composition or decomposition by a drawing or equation (e.g., 18 = 10 + 8); understand that these numbers are composed of ten ones and one, two, three, four, five, six, seven, eight, or nine ones. | Lessons 7.1, 7.2, 7.3, 7.4, 7.5, 7.7, 7.8, 7.9, 7.10 |
| **Domain: Measurement and Data** | | |
| **Describe and compare measurable attributes.** | | |
| **K.MD.A.1** | Describe measurable attributes of objects, such as length or weight. Describe several measurable attributes of a single object. | Lesson 11.5 |
| **K.MD.A.2** | Directly compare two objects with a measurable attribute in common, to see which object has "more of"/ "less of" the attribute, and describe the difference. | Lessons 11.1, 11.2, 11.3, 11.4 |

| Domain: Measurement and Data | | |
| --- | --- | --- |
| **Classify objects and count the number of objects in each category.** | | |
| **K.MD.B.3** | Classify objects into given categories; count the numbers of objects in each category and sort the categories by count. | Lessons 12.1, 12.2, 12.3, 12.4, 12.5 |
| **Domain: Geometry** | | |
| **Identify and describe shapes (squares, circles, triangles, rectangles, hexagons, cubes, cones, cylinders, and spheres).** | | |
| **K.G.A.1** | Describe objects in the environment using names of shapes, and describe the relative positions of these objects using terms such as *above, below, beside, in front of, behind,* and *next to.* | Lessons 10.8, 10.9, 10.10 |
| **K.G.A.2** | Correctly name shapes regardless of their orientations or overall size. | Lessons 9.1, 9.3, 9.5, 9.7, 9.9, 10.2, 10.3, 10.4, 10.5 |
| **K.G.A.3** | Identify shapes as two-dimensional (lying in a plane, "flat") or three-dimensional ("solid"). | Lesson 10.6 |
| **Analyze, compare, create, and compose shapes.** | | |
| **K.G.B.4** | Analyze and compare two- and three-dimensional shapes, in different sizes and orientations, using informal language to describe their similarities, differences, parts (e.g., number of sides and vertices / "corners") and other attributes (e.g., having sides of equal length). | Lessons 9.2, 9.4, 9.6, 9.8, 9.10, 9.11, 10.1 |
| **K.G.B.5** | Model shapes in the world by building shapes from components (e.g., sticks and clay balls) and drawing shapes. | Lesson 10.7 |
| **K.G.B.6** | Compose simple shapes to form larger shapes. | Lesson 9.12 |

# Index

**Eighteen**
    count, 409–412, 415–418
    model, 409–412
    write, 415–418

**Eleven**
    count, 361–364, 367–370
    model, 361–364
    write, 367–370

**Equations**
    addition, 243–246, 249–251, 255–258,
        261–264, 267–270, 273, 276,
        279–282, 285–288, 291–294,
        297–300
    subtraction, 323–326, 329–331,
        335–338, 341–344

**Essential Question.** In every Student
    Edition lesson. Some examples are: 13,
    43, 311, 329, 687, 705

**Expressions**
    addition, 231–234, 237–240
    subtraction, 311–314, 317–320

**F**

**Family Involvement**
    Family Note. *See* Family Note
    Home Activity. *See* Home Activity

**Fifteen**
    count, 385–388
    draw a picture, 391–393
    model, 385–388
    use numbers to, 391–393
    write, 385–388

**Fifty,** 453–456

**Five**
    compare
        numbers to, 81–84, 87–90, 93–95,
            99–102, 105–108
        by counting sets to, 105–108
        by matching sets to, 99–102
    count, 37–40, 43–46
    draw, 37–40, 46
    fluently add within, 231–234,
        243–246, 249–251, 273–276
    fluently subtract within, 311–314,
        323–326, 329–331, 335–338
    model, 37–40
    ways to make, 49–52
    write, 43–46

**Five frames,** 13–15, 25–27, 37–39, 81–82,
    87–88, 93–94

**Flat,** 603–606, 609–612. *See also*
    Two-Dimensional Shapes.

**Flat surface,** 586, 592, 598

**Four**
    count, 25–28, 31–33
    draw, 25–28
    model, 25–28
    write, 31–33

**Fourteen**
    count, 373–376, 379–382
    model, 373–376
    write, 379–382

**G**

**Games**
    At the Farm, 686
    Bus Stop, 12
    Connecting Cube Challenge, 648
    Counting to Blastoff, 80
    Follow the Shapes, 572
    Number Line Up, 118
    Number Picture, 492
    Pairs That Make 7, 230
    Spin and Count!, 180
    Spin for More, 310
    Sweet and Sour Path, 360
    Who Has More?, 428

**Geometry,** 481–488 *See* Shapes;
    Three-dimensional shapes;
    Two-dimensional shapes

**Glossary,** H1–H12

**Graph,** concrete, 705–708, 711–714

**Greater,** 87–90

**Guided Practice.** *See* Share and Show

**H**

**Hands On,** 13–19, 25–28, 37–40, 49–52,
    55–58, 81–84, 87–90, 93–95, 119–122,
    131–134, 143–146, 155–158, 181–184,

© Houghton Mifflin Harcourt Publishing Company